SHAKESPEARE
STUDIES

SHAKESPEARE STUDIES
Volume XXXVIII

EDITED BY

SUSAN ZIMMERMAN
Queens College
The City University of New York

and

GARRETT SULLIVAN
Pennsylvania State University

ASSISTANT TO THE EDITORS
LINDA NEIBERG
The Graduate Center, CUNY

Madison • Teaneck
Fairleigh Dickinson University Press

Associated University Presses
2010 Eastpark Boulevard
Cranbury, NJ 08512

The paper used in this publication meets the requirements of the American National Standard for Permanence of Paper for Printed Library Materials Z39.48-1984.

International Standard Book Number 978-0-8386-4270-2
International Standard Serial Number: 0-0582-9399

All editorial correspondence concerning *Shakespeare Studies* should be addressed to the Editorial Office, *Shakespeare Studies,* English Dept., Queens College, CUNY, Flushing, NY 11367. Orders and subscriptions should be directed to Associated University Presses, 2010 Eastpark Boulevard, Cranbury, New Jersey 08512.

Shakespeare Studies disclaims responsibility for statements,
either of fact or opinion, made by contributors.

PRINTED IN THE UNITED STATES OF AMERICA

Contents

Articles

Review Article

Reviews

Contents

Contributors

HARRIETTE ANDREADIS is Professor of English at Texas A&M University. She is currently at work on an extended study of the century-long publication history of the Dyden/Tonson edition of Ovid's *Heroides.*

CATHERINE BELSEY is Research Professor in English at Swansea University. Her most recent books are *Why Shakespeare?* (2007) and *Shakespeare in Theory and Practice* (2008).

PETER BROWN is Professor of Medieval English Literature at the University of Kent at Canterbury. He has recently completed a book for Oxford University Press of Chaucer's cultural contexts.

MARK THORNTON BURNETT is Professor of Renaissance Studies at Queen's University, Belfast.

RICHARD BURT is Professor of English and Film Media Studies at the University of Florida. He is the author of *Licensed by Authority: Ben Jonson and the Discourses of Censorship* (1993), *Unspeakable ShaXXXspeares: Queer Theory and American Kiddie Culture* (1998), and *Medieval and Early Modern Film and Media* (2008). Dr. Burtt has co-edited a special issue of *Exemplaria* on "Movie Medievalism" (2007) and is editor, most recently, of *Shakespeare after Shakespeare: An Encyclopedia of the Bard in Mass Culture and Popular Culture* (2006) and *Shakespeare After Mass Media* (2001). He held a Fulbright scholarship in Berlin, Germany, 1995–96, and taught there at the Free University and the Humboldt University.

THOMAS CARTELLI is Professor of English and Film Studies at Muhlenberg College. He is author of *Repositioning Shakespeare: National Formations, Postcolonial Appropriations,* and co-author, with Katherine Rowe, of *New Wave Shakespeare on Screen.* His most recent publication is a Norton Critical Edition of *Shakespeare's Richard III.*

LINDA CHARNES is Professor of English and West European Studies at Indiana University, Bloomington, and is the author of several books and many essays on Shakespeare and early modern culture. Her most recent book is *Hamlet's Heirs: Shakespeare and the Politics of a New Millennium.* She is currently working on a book-length study of Shakespeare, interactive theater and the cultural logic of the "fourth wall."

BRINDA CHARRY teaches at Keene State College, New Hampshire. Her areas of research include early modern Orientalism, early modern Anglo-Ottoman relations and representations, and Shakespeare in India.

DONALD HEDRICK is Professor of English at Kansas State University, where he teaches courses on film, popular culture, and gender. His most recent book is *Shakespeare Without Class: Misappropriations of Cultural Capital,* co-authored with Bryan Reynolds.

ROBERT HORNBACK, Associate Professor of English at Oglethorpe University, has authored several articles focused on the early modern comic in journals such as *Shakespeare International Yearbook, Medieval and Renaissance Drama in England* (FDUP), *English Literary Renaissance, Early Theatre, Studies in English Literature, Exemplaria,* and *Comparative Drama,* as well as in collections such as *The Blackwell Companion to Tudor Literature* and *Thunder at a Playhouse: Essaying Shakespeare and the Early Modern Stage* (SUP). Having published *The English Clown Tradition from the Middle Ages to Shakespeare* (2009), he is currently completing *Early Blackface Fools and Their Legacy: Essays in the Emergence of Proto-Racism,* with the support of fellowships from the Folger Shakespeare Library and the Newberry Library.

ALEXANDER C. Y. HUANG is Assistant Professor of Comparative literature at Pennsylvania State University, University Park, and Research Affiliate in Literature at the Massachusetts Institute of Technology. He is the author of *Chinese Shakespeares: Two Centuries of Cultural Exchange* (2009), editor of a special issue of *Borrowers and Lenders: The Journal of Shakespeare and Appropriation* (2009), and coeditor of *Shakespeare in Hollywood, Asia and Cyberspace* (2009), *Class, Boundary and Social Discourse in the Renaissance* (2007), and *Shakespeare Performance in Asia.*

NORA JOHNSON is Professor of English at Swarthmore College and author of *The Actor as Playwright in Early Modern Drama* (2003). She is currently at work on a study of high and low cultural uses of Shakespeare in nineteenth-century America.

DOUGLAS LANIER is Professor of English and Director of the UNH London Program. He has published widely on Shakespearean adaptation in various genres and media, including *Shakespeare and Modern Popular Culture* (2002). His most recent article, "Retail'd to Posterity: Shakespeare and Marketing," concerns Shakespeare and the history of advertisement. He is currently at work on two projects: a consideration of film adaptations of *Othello* faithful and free and a survey of intellectual disaffection in early Modern England.

COURTNEY LEHMAN is Professor of English and Film Studies and Director of the Humanities Center at the University of the Pacific. She is the author of *Shakespeare Remains: Theater to Film, Early Modern to Postmodern* (2002) and has recently completed a book on *Romeo and Juliet* adaptations.

ANIA LOOMBA is Catherine Bryson Professor at the University of Pennsylvania where she teaches English, Comparative Literature, and South Asian Studies. Her publications include *Colonialism/ Postcolonialism* (1998), *Shakespeare, Race and Colonialism* (2002), and, with Jonathan Burton, *Race in Early Modern Europe: A Documentary Companion (2007)*.

DAVID MIKICS, Professor of English at the University of Houston, is the author, most recently, of *A New Handbook of Literary terms* (2007) and *Who Was Jacques Derrida?* (2009), as well as essays on Shakespeare, Milton, and other subjects. His next book, *The Art of the Sonnet,* co-written with Stephen Burt, will be published in 2010.

SCOTT L. NEWSTOK teaches at Rhodes College. He is author of *Quoting Death in Early Modern England* (2009), editor of *Kenneth Burke on Shakespeare* (2007), and co-editor, with Ayanna Thompson, of *Weyward Macbeth: Intercessions of Race and Performance* (2010).

MARCY L. NORTH is Associate Professor of English at Pennsylvania State University. She is currently completing a book on scribal labor and fashionable verse in post-print manuscript culture.

LAURIE OSBORNE is the N.E.H./Class of 1940 Distinguished Professor of the Humanities at Colby College. She is currently working on several projects on televised Shakespeare and Shakespeare in popular culture.

KATHERINE ROWE, Professor of English at Bryn Mawr, writes about reading, writing, and performance from the Renaissance to the digital age. Trained as a scholar of Renaissance drama, she turned her attention to questions of media history and adaptation, most recently in the co-authored monograph *New Wave Shakespeare on Screen* (2007). A recipient of grants from the NEH, the Mellon Foundation, and the PA Department of Education that support her work in media history, Dr. Rowe is a member of the editorial board of *Shakespeare Quarterly* and Associate Editor of *The Cambridge World Shakespeare Encyclopedia*.

GREG COLÓN SEMENZA is Associate Professor of English at University of Connecticut. He is the author of *Sport, Politics, and Literature in the English Renaissance* (2004), *Graduate Study for the 21st Century: How to Build an Academic Career in the Humanities* (2005), and, with Laura L. Knoppers, *Milton in Popular Culture* (2006), and the editor of *The English Renaissance in Popular Culture* (2010). He is currently at work on a novel and a monograph entitled *Fictional Milton*.

WILLIAM H. SHERMAN is Professor of English at the University of York and author of *Used Books: Making Readers in Renaissance England*.

LAUREN SHOHET teaches English at Villanova University. She is the author of *Reading Masques: The English Masque and Public Culture* (2010) and is currently working on a book about genre and Renaissance adaptations.

HENRY S. TURNER is Associate Professor of English at Rutgers University, New Brunswick. He is the author of *The English Renais-*

sance Stage: Geometry, Poetics, and Practical Spatial Arts (2006) and *Shakespeare's Double Helix* (2008).

VIRGINIA MASON VAUGHAN is Professor of English at Clark University in Worcester, Massachusetts. She is the co-editor of *The Tempest* for the Third Arden Series and is currently completing *The Tempest: Shakespeare in Performance.*

WILLIAM N. WEST is Associate Professor of English, Classics, and Comparative Literary Studies at Northwestern University. He is working on a project about understanding and confusion in the Elizabeth theaters.

SHAKESPEARE
STUDIES

FORUM

After Shakespeare
on Film

Introduction

Greg Colón Semenza

Our forum, "after shakespeare on film," invites leading Shakespeare on film scholars to share some exploratory musings on four basic but hopefully provocative questions: First, what is the future of Shakespeare on celluloid now that the cinema boom provoked by Kenneth Branagh's *Henry V* (1989) appears to have run its course? Second, what is the future of Shakespeare and film studies now that a formerly ghettoized subfield has been assimilated—at least halfheartedly—by the scholarly Shakespeare industry? Next, what current and future technologies, if any, are likely to supplant film as the primary vehicle for disseminating Shakespeare within mass culture markets? Finally, how will the alternative technologies discussed in these pages—YouTube, Kindle, Web 2.0, digital cinematography, and so on—impact the scholarly teaching and theorization of Shakespeare's work and cultural legacy?

As such questions would imply—oscillating as they do between interest in imaginative engagements of Shakespeare on one hand, and critical approaches to them on the other—the respective fates of cinematic Shakespeare and Shakespeare studies depend in many ways on one another. Especially after the so-called Great Recession, levels of support for the humanities in higher education will have much to do with questions about the practicality or real-world applicability of the subjects we study; and let's face it, no other subfield of Shakespeare studies has done more to locate and theorize the functions of Shakespeare in our world—the world outside of the ivory tower—than Shakespeare on film (and Shakespeare and popular culture) studies. If we are indeed "after" Shakespeare on film, we may also be after Shakespeare, precisely because the popularity, diversity, and marketability of Shakespeare films have advertised for several generations of nonscholars the continuing relevance of the playwright we study and teach. Multi-million-dol-

lar film productions of Shakespeare's plays authorize—for mainstream audiences, for a large percentage of our students, and for
bean-counting administrators—the continuing relevance of a 450-
year-old playwright; the success of these films hinges largely on
their educational usefulness, and their educational usefulness
hinges on the approval or, at least, the interest of a few Shakespeare
scholars. There is great, often unrecognized practicality in what we
do, and yet practicality is not typically a major criterion for respect-
ability in a Western educational tradition that has historically
boasted of the "intrinsic value" of the liberal arts and sciences.

This practicality is one reason why the subfield of Shakespeare
on film studies is important. It's the reason why it has become more
acceptable in academe, leading in recent years, for example, to the
running of regular workshops and an occasional plenary session at
the Shakespeare Association of America (SAA) annual convention.
Conversely and contradictorily, it's the reason why it continues to
be snubbed by the scholarly Shakespeare industry; for example,
how many essays on the subject have appeared in the pages of
Shakespeare Quarterly (especially outside of the single issue devoted to the subject almost ten years ago)? Finally, I'm guessing that
it's also the reason why some of us may be so eager to designate the
end of Shakespeare on film, the precise moment when we are
"after" it, because if history is any guide, only the death of the medium will validate the medium as an unequivocally worthy subject
of academic study.

For the record, I don't think we are after Shakespeare on film, at
least not any more than we are after Shakespeare and theater or,
for that matter, Shakespeare and the written word. While it seems
inevitable that film technology per se will gradually be replaced by
digital and other yet-to-be-invented technologies of various kinds,
and while we will continue to see an ever-proliferating number of
small-screen Shakespeares presented through various media, it
seems unlikely that big-screen Shakespeares will simply cease to
be in the immediate future, or that our basic film experience will
be transformed beyond recognition by these new technologies.
Film's role as the primary disseminator of Shakespeare in mass culture is rapidly changing as it faces more and more competition from
other media, but this is likely, paradoxically, to result in the greater
acceptability of film in Shakespeare studies for the simple reason
that it can no longer be regarded as the field's ugly stepchild.

What we probably *are* after—and this has much to do with the new technologies—is a central interest in the Shakespeare film as a mere adaptation of either a Shakespeare play or printed text. Barbara Hodgdon has argued that traditional scholarly emphases on Shakespeare's text as the "primal scene of theatrical and cinematic reproduction" hinder our ability to clearly read performances (and, I would add, the very concept of performance), especially those performances that put "Shakespeare's text to work in ways not licensed or valued by a community of (literary) readers or [those] which offer . . . a political or ideological agenda which calls into question other critical (and theatrical) constructions of 'the text itself.' "[1] If film's value for Shakespeare studies was originally felt to reside in its apparent closeness to theater, such value was measurable in large part according to how successful certain cinematic "reproductions" were at upholding the shifting political and ideological agendas of the Shakespeare scholarly establishment. Film has been increasingly exposed, however, as a relatively limited medium in comparison with more "real," experiential, and interactive media of the sort described herein by several contributors. What seems promising about this fact is that the burden of fidelity—which has plagued performance and performance studies from the beginning—seems no longer to be much of an issue, allowing artists greater freedom to generate new Shakespeares without even thinking about trying to get it "right" (see Cartelli's essay). The increasing dominance of such "slant" Shakespeares also allows us greater freedom to analyze performances on their own terms—allows us, that is, to explore the "intrinsic value" of specific performances and engagements of Shakespeare's work.

I am arguing, somewhat contradictorily, for the benefits of greater freedom to leave the Shakespeare text behind and, at the same time, for the practicality of our ability to demonstrate the continuing relevance of the Shakespeare text. How do we reconcile these two ideas? In part by recognizing that escape from the tyranny of the "original" results in new cultural artifacts that will permanently alter both the constitution and the concept of what we designate the "Shakespeare text." As several contributors to this forum note, even when film becomes truly extinct, the archive remains, and film—more than scholarly essays or theatrical performances—will serve as our memory of Shakespeare in the twentieth and early twenty-first centuries; as Richard Burt and Scott Newstok suggest here, "history since the twentieth century cannot be understood apart from the history of film." Further, no matter how slant Shakespeare performances are and how accepting of them we become, appreciation of slant will inevitably—though not entirely—depend on its relation to the straight line, and the straight line, I argue, will always be drawn in the undergraduate classroom. I can remember years ago, while teaching a Shakespeare course in London, my surprise and irritation at discovering that every one of my students tended to prefer relatively conservative, period-dress productions of the plays we were studying to modernizations, offshoots, or otherwise more inventive productions such as single-gender performances. In the film section of the course, students requested that we watch Olivier's 1955 *Richard III* rather than Richard Loncraine's provocative 1996 film of the same play (as much as I admire the former, I insisted on screening the latter). Years later, some of these very students, now in or just out of graduate school, would confess to some degree of embarrassment about their former taste in performances, which served only to remind me what my own preferences were when I was an undergraduate. I scorned slant Shakespeare. I was threatened by it, in fact, because I was struggling hard to understand these difficult plays, and the easiest way I could cope with my own failures was to dismiss what appeared to be so obviously wrong about others' interpretations. I suspect that as long as Shakespeare's plays continue to be taught, straight Shakespeare will have his place. It is exciting to speculate about how much more radical even straight Shakespeare will appear to be in the wake of technologies with which, in comparison, most films—indeed, film itself—will wind up looking almost as old-fashioned as books. Still, film—or something like film—is likely to remain for some time the medium most capable of establishing the straight line against which more experimental or slant Shakespeares will be evaluated. As Kathy Rowe suggests in her essay, "film texts could emerge as objects fitted to the structures of authority, oversight, and cultural value that organize academic practice."

Regardless of how Shakespeare films are used, the future of Shakespeare on film does seem secure enough for the time being, then. But what about the future of Shakespeare on film studies? Even for scholars, it isn't so much film that's dead as it is the "film" typically conceived of by literature professors who've tended to ignore how film works as its own medium.[2] Are scholars changing their views of what Shakespeare on film actually is and can do because the films are really changing so drastically? Or is our growing willingness to look at film as film—through a greater familiarity with film theory than an earlier generation of literary scholars possessed—helping us to see more clearly what certain Shakespeare films (Welles's, for example) were doing all this time? Certainly, such new eyes would help us to deepen our understanding of films that have already been written about fairly extensively. The first two answers to our question, then, are that we can expect a considerable expansion of Shakespeare on film scholarship and a noticeable shift toward criticism that is more theoretically informed by film studies (as the essays that follow make clear). Next, as Mark Thornton Burnett suggests, we can anticipate that world cinema is likely to be the next, if not the final, frontier for Shakespeare on film scholarship. If media and technology are causing us to rethink traditional structures of knowledge and authority, then certainly a greater consideration of alternative structures of knowledge and authority—as in non-Western ones—should impact how we understand art in media and technology. Finally, Shakespeare on film scholarship will be impacted by how willing we are to study emergent media and technological engagements of Shakespeare's work. While we are more likely to see Shakespeare on film essays in the pages of our top journals than we have in the past, and this is a good thing, I hope that at least a few brave scholars will be willing to eschew the type of security such acceptance will bring, eagerly embrace the fascinating questions raised by the Shakespeares that emerge after film, and manage to convince others of their value, which, after all, speaks directly to our value as well.

*   *   *

I would like to thank the ten contributors to this forum, individuals whose work I greatly admire, who have been brave enough to anticipate *in print* where the future may lead us.[3] Since their essays are relatively short (approximately three thousand words), I will let the work speak for itself, though I want to close by mentioning briefly a few of the overlapping ideas that unify our discussion. First, as the opening essay by Tom Cartelli will make abundantly clear, slant Shakespeare will quite possibly emerge as the new straight line, relegating "faithful" adaptations—especially original-language productions—to academic venues likely to seem nostalgic in but a few years. Like Cartelli, Don Hedrick, Laurie Osborne, and Kathy Rowe consider traditional film against cutting-edge Shakespeare engagements that "*present* the multi-storied past, variegated present, and networks of association of individual plays, using

every digital resource available" (Cartelli; his emphasis). Examining such interactive and intermedial Shakespeare phenomena as the CalArts *King Lear,* digital art, and Web 2.0, they ask how Shakespeare's cultural value—and the cultural value of the Shakespeare film—is impacted for better or worse by emergent, user-generated environments or experiential productions. Generally speaking, Lauren Shohet, Courtney Lehmann and, in a collaborative essay, Richard Burt and Scott Newstok, all think about ways in which traditional conceptions of the "archive" are being transformed by new technologies and/or cinematic developments. Shohet demonstrates the ways in which YouTube locates Shakespeare performance in "re-use"—that is, in "practices of cross-referencing, fast-forwarding, and replaying that allow students to work with performances in ways that scholars habitually work with texts"; Lehmann and Burt and Newstok argue that the value of filmic engagements of Shakespeare lies largely in what they reveal about the non-Shakespearean histories they write, record, and even theorize. Our conversation ends with two essays exploring the appropriation of the Shakespeare film legacy by two proliferating but relatively underexplored forms of adaptation: the graphic novel and the non-Anglophone Shakespeare film. Theorizing the current boom in graphic novelizations of Shakespeare, Doug Lanier notes the texts' fascinating "conversion of Shakespeare to visual form" and simultaneous "retextualization"—their production, that is, of a modern Shakespeare defined as much by the visual (i.e., filmic) heritage as the critical/textual one. Mark Thornton Burnett gets the final word, not only because his essay reminds us there are places where Shakespeare on film is thriving but also because, in his call for "alternative paradigms that acknowledge exchange . . . expose current inequities of space and place, [and] stand as testimony to the ethical valences of a global Shakespearean citizenship," he suggests a course not just for Shakespeare on film studies, but for Shakespeare studies in general.

Notes

1. Barbara Hodgdon, *The Shakespeare Trade: Performances and Appropriations* (Philadelphia: University of Pennsylvania Press, 1998), xii–xiii.
2. For further thoughts about the problems of this tendency, see my essay,

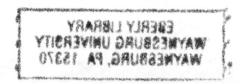

"Teens, Shakespeare, and the Dumbing Down Cliché: The Case of *The Animated Tales*," *Shakespeare Bulletin* 26 (2008): 37–68.

3. In addition, I wish to thank Garrett Sullivan and Susan Zimmerman, editors at Shakespeare Studies, who've been actively promoting more work in the field of Shakespeare on film and mass culture studies. I would also like to thank Bambi Mroz for her editorial assistance.

Doing It Slant: Reconceiving Shakespeare in the Shakespeare Aftermath

Thomas Cartelli

> What we take to be Shakespeare on film has no future, or it has only a future past perhaps already being mourned in the ashes of the archive. Have you checked the listings at your movie theaters recently? Know what I mean?
>
> —Richard Burt (e-mail exchange)

OUR SHARED PROMPT "After Shakespeare on Film" encourages us to survey the latest breaking frontiers opened up by new media—Shakespeare gaming, virtual Shakespeare, digital archiving, and so on—and decide which ones promise the most in the way of returns for our scholarly investment. Like most of us, I find the Internet a game-changing resource, and consider the possibilities endless for media-oriented Shakespeare scholars to feed off what its constantly unfolding frontiers make available, as my closing comments will indicate. But given my negligible interest in most Shakespeare riffings on YouTube—today's top ten on Bardbox gives us, along with part 1 of Stephen Cavanagh's estimable Derry *Hamlet* (2005), a schoolyard of six-year-olds reciting "To be or not to be," a clip of the initially amusing Cat Head Theatre that grows tedious in its second minute, and a mash-up called *My Dinner with Andre the Giant* that doesn't take that long to annoy—I can't imagine doing much critically with such resources other than pedestrian sociologizing on the democratic populism of the Internet.[1] And even as some of the best minds of my generation virtualize themselves on Second Life, I find the prospect of generating avatars within a Shakespearean framework—much less writing about it—about as appealing as participating in the human chess game at the New Jersey Renaissance Fair.

While I'm lolling on my Procrustean bed, I might add that I also find the phrase and the prospect opened up by "after film" a tad preemptive. I don't really think the cinema, which has already died as often as Shakespeare's Cleopatra, will be truly dead anytime soon, at least as we now know it. Quality films may no longer be available outside the precincts of festivals, museums, or Netflix, and screens will continue to get smaller. But car chases and meeting cute will no doubt remain box-office manna for some time to come, while stubbornly eccentric artists like Pedro Costa, Bela Tarr, and Guy Maddin persist in making the most audience-unfriendly feature films on record. *Shakespeare* on film is more of a muddle because of the comparative lack of product at the moment. There are, of course, more Shakespeare-related films being generated than meets the unroving eye, especially when we widen ours to take in what's being circulated out in the world at large, from India's *Maqbool* (2003) and *Omkara* (2006), to Singapore's *Chicken Rice War* (2000), to Italy's *Sud Side Stori* (2000) to Northern Ireland's *Mickey B* (2007).[2] Though all of these films merit discussion, none of them—among which we should include Alexander Fodor's low-budget glam-*Hamlet* (2007) and the four updatings that comprise *ShakespeaRe-Told* (2005)—arguably operates at the sophisticated level of address as Julie Taymor's *Titus* (1999) or Michael Almereyda's *Hamlet* (2000). And that, as I'll discuss below, is a large part of the problem for those of us for whom pop culture and prose Shakespeare often comprise two unappealing sides of the same coin. But I have a related concern here that has less to do with the death of film, or the death of Shakespeare on film, than it does with the rapidly diminishing legibility of "original-language Shakespeare," which to some parties implies the death of Shakespeare itself. And this prompts me to wonder aloud what *about* or pertaining to Shakespeare we think we will be spinning (and spinning off) in film and new media in the not-too-distant future.

In a chapter of her new book, *Shakespeare and the Problem of Adaptation,* where she surveys the positions of several of *ShakespeaRe-Told*'s critics and dissenters, M. J. Kidnie quotes Trevor Nunn to the effect that "Ultimately for me, it's the language that matters—no language, no Shakespeare."[3] As I note in my review of that book, Kidnie finesses Nunn's objection by demonstrating how the series' *Macbeth,* scripted by Peter Moffat, compensates for the loss of Shakespeare's language by "writing what at times registers as strange television dialogue." She claims that in authoring Shakespeare "for a new medium and a new millennium," Moffat projects "a distinctive authorial *effect* that is consistent with modern perceptions of the canon as high art," and that "[p]aradoxically, it is this slanting proximity to the work, one's ability to hear the 'Shakespeare' in Moffat's *Macbeth,*" that makes the film a legitimate "instance" of Shakespeare's work.[4] Kidnie is entirely right here, but her being right undercuts some of what she tries to claim for other productions in the series. If it's the "slanting proximity" of hearing the "Shakespeare" in Moffat's *Macbeth* that makes *Macbeth* Moffat's, then what's the effect of *not* hearing the Shakespeare, but instead *seeing* a Shakespeare-derived plot flattened and deformed by the romantic and comedic genre conventions of British commercial television in the series' versions of *A Midsummer Night's Dream* and *Much Ado About Nothing?*[5]

As a quondam champion of Geoffrey Sax's recent televised updating of *Othello,* I do not mean to reject out of hand every example of what I am calling "prose Shakespeare." Indeed, as scripted by Andrew Davies, the 2001 ITV *Othello* offers brilliantly apt readings of and substitutions for Shakespeare's language, as does, in a more minor key, *Mickey B,* an Educational Shakespeare Company (ESC) updating of *Macbeth,* set in Maghaberry Prison in Northern Ireland, directed by Tom Magill and cowritten by Magill and two of his convict-actors Sam McLean and Jason Thompson. Both screenplays are not only differently literate but literary, their updating apparently having been generated by reasons other than the need for mass legibility. But such films stand as proverbial exceptions that prove a related rule, that being that Shakespeare is seldom now identified with the language of his plays as much as with their major characters and plots. Even in recent original-language film adaptations, ranging from Luhrmann's *Romeo + Juliet* (1996) to Almereyda's and Fodor's *Hamlet* films, speakers variably accelerate, flatten, or slur their lines as if to imply that taking verse-speaking seriously would be inconsistent with filmic realism, and that, in the end, the word is *not* the thing. One does not need, in the end, to endorse Nunn's traditionalist stand to wonder what is so singularly Shakespearean about plots—which Shakespeare himself appropriated and adapted from one medium to another—to have them be the one thing Shakespeare's adapters have decided to remain faithful to in updatings as far afield as the *ShakespeaRe-Told* (SRT) *Much Ado* and *Dream* and Vishal Bhardwaj's *Maqbool* and *Omkara.*[6]

Not to belabor the chicken-and-egg question, but what accounts for this situation? Is it merely the conventional privileging of plot in mainstream cinema and television alike that is responsible for both the supersession of original-language Shakespeare and the avoidance of substitute dialogue that might itself be construed as too literary or inventive? Is this supersession rather the predictable by-product of the accelerated displacement of language by image in contemporary visual media in general, a process that began more than one hundred years ago with the advent of silent film? Or is it generated by the perception that both original-language Shake-speare and other avowedly literary forms of contemporary address have become too challenging for mainstream audiences? (This very question makes me wonder whether such a concern motivated Kenneth Branagh's notorious cutting of so many of Rosalind's lines in his recent televised version of *As You Like It* [2007]). I would assume that any answer would have to include parts of all three explanations, the first two classifiable in terms of medium specific-ity, with the third tied more to corporate marketing projections than to conclusions based on sustained study or analysis of literacy change (though observations of our own students' growing inabil-ity, or reluctance even to try, to grapple with Shakespeare's lan-guage could no doubt confirm them).

If Shakespeare cannot continue to exist in language that either is becoming incomprehensible to most audiences, or held to be so by those who control the media of production, can his plots alone—firmly yoked as they are to no more than a few well-known characters—both signify and authorize what is construed to be rec-ognizably Shakespearean? My answer would be yes, certainly, and especially for those who get or prefer to take their Shakespeare sec-ondhand, that is, through the media of updatings and spin-offs. In the first place, since the plots serve as structural frameworks for the most famous plays ever written, some half dozen of which continue to make the rounds of most every secondary school in the English-speaking world, they have become deeply embedded in that world's cultural imaginary, some even achieving the status of myths of universal application. (This is especially the case for plays like *Romeo and Juliet* and *King Lear,* whose plot has been ef-fectively naturalized in films as far afield as the postwar American films *House of Strangers* [dir., Frank Mankiewicz, 1949] and *Bro-ken Lance* [dir., Edward Dmytryk, 1954] on the one hand, and Akira Kurosawa's *Ran* [1985] on the other, in most cases without audiences perceiving the lineal connection.) And, since the plots are nonetheless malleable and freely available to anyone to revise or flesh out, they may, in their new permutations, prove appealing to audiences new to, or completely innocent of, Shakespeare (a group growing larger by the minute).

This is not to say that I anticipate the tyranny of plot to prompt either original-language Shakespeare or Shakespeare's centrality in intertextual transactions to disappear anytime soon. And this is because of three practices I would like to elaborate on in the space remaining. The first of these is the continued use of original language in feature film productions that take far more manifest liberties with setting, dramatic structure, and chronology, and that are particularly venturesome in their use of interpolated visual material and editing practices. The most memorable recent examples of this kind would be the aforementioned films by Luhrmann, Taymor, and Almereyda, whose repurposed style and mode of address convey the same "slanting proximity" to their originals as does the language Moffat deploys in his SRT version of *Macbeth*. However inferior it may seem by comparison, Alexander Fodor's variably ghoulish and mannered *Hamlet*—which deploys sounds, settings, and a phenomenology derived from *The Matrix* films as systematically as *Forbidden Planet* (1956) mixed 1950s science fiction stylings with popular (mis)understandings of Freud to generate a *Tempest* for its time—also provides a promising example of doing original-language Shakespeare slant on-screen. In choosing for no obvious reasons to transform Polonius into the sadistic young vixen, Polonia, to turn Horatio into Hamlet's fetching female friend, and to make the even more fetching Ophelia a dependent junkie, Fodor clearly aims to lay a youth-oriented soft-porn—and variably misogynistic and homophobic—gloss on what is often a palpably self-indulgent experiment.[7] Fodor's *Hamlet* is maddeningly erratic throughout, due no doubt to his lack of experience in the role of master director and script doctor extraordinaire (the "Who is Fodor?" section of the Web site glibly answers, "The son of a Hungarian porn film director, making films out of Berlin and Amsterdam, up to the age of ten he thought all women walked around in the nude," and confesses, "An essential ethos though carries forward from his childhood—there's no point making something if no one watches it"). But the film is also venturesome in ways that most original-language Shakespeare films are not, particularly in its deployment of temporal discontinuity, textual reorganization, presentational acting, and, especially, its use of a virtual space Fodor appropriates from *The Matrix* (1999) and names the "ghost room"—which becomes the staging ground for Hamlet's meeting with the ghost of his father, for Ophelia's suicide, and, more intriguingly, for several out-of-time sequences when (where?) Hamlet as a child interacts with his still-ghostly father. This device in particular demonstrates how new media can effect not only technical, but phenomenological changes in cinematic conventions, in this instance the conventional flashback, which is here dislocated from a fixed place in a single thinking subject's past to the status of floating recurrence in a stream of seemingly unauthored images and sounds. If other aspects of the film's editing and cinematography seem too much under the influence of Mike Figgis's decidedly slant take on *The Duchess of Malfi,* in his 2001 film *Hotel,* that is not, in my view, an unwelcome direction for Shakespeare on-screen to go.[8] It will, in any event, be interesting to compare Fodor's gender-bendings with Julie Taymor's decision to cast Helen Mirren in the role of the female magus, Prospera, in her forthcoming version of *The Tempest.*[9]

A second, somewhat less-established practice involves the return of heretofore repressed Shakespearean verse in modern-language adaptations, something that happens to particularly memorable effect in *My Own Private Idaho,* Gus Van Sant's 1992 spin on Shakespeare's *Henriad* and Welles's *Chimes at Midnight* (1966). The Shakespearean repressed also returns in other places where we would least expect to find it, such as, for example, in SRT's versions of *Much Ado About Nothing* and *The Taming of the Shrew,* but also in *Mickey B,* which, as we proceed, may emerge as the unsung hero of this piece. In three instances in *Much Ado,* we find the play's adapters taking the kinds of risk that most updatings seldom venture by invoking the name and words of Shakespeare in ways that suggest that they and their characters are living both in the play's and the playwright's aftermath. The first time this occurs is when Benedick playfully quotes the phrase "Is this a dagger?" as he brandishes a kitchen knife. The second, more sustained moment occurs in Beatrice and Benedick's recitation of and commentary on Shakespeare's sonnet 116, which ironically concludes with their affirming the poem's claims about marriages of true minds on the basis of the "fact" that Shakespeare really did live and love. The third is when the scriptwriter, David Nicholls, evidently decided that even a contemporary audience could comprehend something as straightforward as Shakespeare's "There's nothing in this world I love so well as you. Isn't that strange?" a close enough approximation of the lines Benedick speaks in *Much Ado* (the play) 4.1.267–68 to count as quotation more than paraphrase.

Though it may seem as if I have heretofore lamented the loss of original language in contemporary screen versions of Shakespeare, what I've rather meant to do is critique the loss of pleasure occasioned by their writers' submission (willing or compelled) to the lowest (and laziest) common linguistic denominators (a tendency traceable from William Reilly's willfully inarticulate *Men of Respect* [1990] to SRT's *Midsummer Night's Dream*). By contrast, when the two otherwise remote languages of Shakespearean verse and contemporary prose cross as they do here, a considerably richer product results that mixes and matches elevated and elevating discourse with seemingly unstudied and naturalistic dialogue. As the line or lines from the original are uttered—as they are also in the SRT *Taming* when Petruchio says, "How brightly shines the moon," and Katherine responds, "That's the sun, you bollocks"— both residual and emergent forms of the play engage in productive collaboration with one another even as they compete for dominance.

The impulse to allow what has been repressed to reemerge and reestablish itself is unusually pronounced in *Mickey B,* where the odds are arguably greater for such disparate discourses to clash or collide. Yet no doubt owing to the fact that the three scriptwriters have devised an often-impenetrable form of thieves' cant to substitute for Shakespeare's language, when that language reemerges—as it does, for example, in an only slightly abbreviated version of Macbeth's "sound and fury" speech—it may well sound, at least to the ears of Anglo-American viewers, less strange than the updated Anglo-Irish dialogue, which contains such initially impenetrable localisms as "craic," "dozer," "mucker," "swolley," "lost your marleys," and "throw a warbler," among many others. This naturalization of Shakespearean dialogue through the back door, as it were, complements a concomitant naturalization of the action of the play itself, which effects the transition from Scottish court to Northern Irish prison more smoothly than one might imagine possible.[10] The Maghaberry *Macbeth* is modestly filmed, and its acting is often as wooden as one might expect, especially in its title role. But the film's ability to remain site-specific—going so far as to substitute Emiliano Zapata's revolutionary vaunt, "Better to die standing than to live on your knees," for Macbeth's more rivalrous "Why should I play the Roman fool and die / On mine own sword?"— while reverting to Shakespearean forms when it cannot claim to do better, in much the way that Benedick, in the SRT *Much Ado,* is compelled to say "There's nothing in this world I love as well as you," bodes well for future collaborations of this kind in the Shakespeare aftermath.

A third practice that I would like to see developed further involves artists and scholars alike, either separately or in collaboration, employing digital resources to mount reproductions of plays that directly draw on their filmic, theatrical, cultural, and critical histories in the traces of Julie Taymor's *Titus* and, especially, Peter Greenaway's 1992 *Prospero's Books,* which is certainly recognizable now, as it was not then, as a trailblazing experiment in database cinema.[11] Such a thought no doubt smacks of that "future past perhaps already being mourned in the ashes of the archive" that the ever-prescient Richard Burt summons up in words I've deployed as this essay's epigraph. But in the Shakespeare aftermath I envision, where the practice of doing original-language productions may largely be relegated to college, university, and summer festival stages, the possibility of making films that no longer seek to perform a version of a play so much as to *present* the multistoried past, variegated present, and networks of association of individual plays, using every digital resource available, not only seems a consummation devoutly to be wished but a prospect already in our grasp. Indeed, should Shakespeare have even less of a future in the feature-film marketplace than I anticipate, opportunities may well be afforded for a postnarrative screen Shakespeare to develop, geared to the multimediated strengths of the Internet, where the artful assembly, display, and delivery of a rich database of information, sounds, and bodies in motion could trump the desire to have successive iterations of Shakespeare's plays reduced to a single narrative and interpretive line. This may sound as if I am advocating a form of encyclopedic documentary, better delegated to the domain of an interactive Web site than to feature film. But both the time and technology seem ripe for the development of films that bring plays or pieces of plays into vibrant—sometimes collusive, sometimes colliding—engagement with what's been made of those plays over time, even as they are in the act of being remade in the present, reimagined and repurposed.[12]

Notes

1. Christy Desmet finds more at work in YouTube videos than I do. Distinguishing her approach to the subject from Richard Burt's "suggestion that much of Shakespop is 'post-hermeneutic,'" Desmet argues "that what gives the amateur productions that I discuss their particular character is their focused *attention* on specific moments of action and, more important, specific speech acts from the parent text. The engagement between Shakespeare and appropriator is thoroughly rhetorical, a matter of textual give-and-take rather than a wholesale usurpation of the Bard's words and authority," in "Paying Attention in Shakespeare Parody: From Tom Stoppard to YouTube," *Shakespeare Survey* 61 (2008): 227. As in the days of silent film—when about five hundred Shakespeare-oriented films were made—it is likely the plays' familiarity and status as common property that makes them so often serve as subject matter for parody or imitation. I find YouTube material that challenges the Bard's authority in more provocative ways more interesting. See, for example, the contributions of Akala, the self-styled black British Shakespeare, at http://www.youtube.com/watch?v = KCcqS6AP8uI&NR = 1 and http://www.youtube.com/watch?v = CqZYaFd9YCY&feature = related.

2. Compelling new scholarship is being devoted to such developments. See, for example, Alexander C. Y. Huang, *Chinese Shakespeares: Two Centuries of Cultural Exchange* (New York: Columbia University Press, 2009), and Mariacristina Cavecchi, "Shakespeare in Vucciria: Fair Verona in Roberta Torre's *Sud Side Stori*," in C. Dente and S. Soncini, eds., *Across Time and Space: Shakespeare translations in present-day Europe* (Pisa: Plus/Pisa University Press, 2008), 89–106.

3. *Shakespeare and the Problem of Adaptation* (New York: Routledge, 2009), 114.

4. Ibid., 119.

5. I am clearly treading on subjective ground here, one person's absolute aberration being another's signal triumph. Given spatial constraints, I neglect commenting here on SRT's version of *The Taming of a Shrew* and Billy Morrissette's *Scotland, PA*, both of which I admire, though for reasons that have less to do with their writing than with their "slant" approach to the process and problem of adaptation.

6. Despite being set at an upscale three-star London restaurant, even the more venturous Moffat *Macbeth* reproduces plot-turns in Shakespeare's play that have no reason to be retained in its updated urban scenario (e.g., the murder of its surrogates for Lady Macduff and her children).

7. In a gesture that links his project to Second Life role-playing, Fodor devised a stylish promotional Web site for his film in which major characters—each of whom is designated either a pawn, knight, or king in a chess game apparently designed and executed by Hamlet's father's ghost—have their private thoughts expressed in parodic soap-opera formats. See, for example, the entry for Ophelia (subtitled "A Rabbit Caught in the Headlights"): "It's because I'm a woman isn't it? People think that just because you're a woman you can't think then how come people always say how nice my room is. I picked all the colors. It was me. You can't be thick and do that sort of thing" (http://www.hamletmovie.co.uk). Fodor also generously supplies three attributed but incompletely referenced reviews,

one of which slams the film for failures and excesses that the other two recuperate and celebrate. For example, what "Donald Richmond" laments—"The acting's appalling, lines mumbled, even stuttered, the beautiful cadences totally ruined"—"John Solamans" considers "very clever stuff . . . that has all the hypnotic grip of watching an open fire" (http://www.hamletmovie.co.uk/Reviews/Reviews1.html).

8. It's worth noting here that in addition to *Hotel,* two other films that have done it slant to considerable success are Derek Jarman's *Edward II* (1991) and Alex Cox's *Revengers Tragedy* (2002), and that the "it" in question has not been Shakespeare, an indication, perhaps, of filmmakers' reluctance to tamper too much with the Bard.

9. For a glimpse of Taymor's plans, see the following synopsis on the film's imdb.com Web page: "In Julie Taymor's version of 'The Tempest,' the gender of Prospero has been switched to Prospera. Going back to the 16th or 17th century, women practicing the magical arts of alchemy were often convicted of witchcraft. In Taymor's version, Prospera is usurped by her brother and sent off with her four-year daughter on a ship. She ends up on an island; it's a tabula rasa: no society, so the mother figure becomes a father figure to Miranda. This leads to the power struggle and balance between Caliban and Prospera; a struggle not about brawn, but about intellect" (*Written by Anonymous,* http://www.imdb.com/title/tt 1274300/plotsummary).

10. As Jason Thompson, the convict-actor who plays the role of Ladyboy, the film's transvestite surrogate for Lady Macbeth, states, "There's plenty of boys in here" that can stand comparison with Macbeth, whose "greatest motivating factor is his ambition," adding that "if they weren't ambitious, they wouldn't be in jail because they wouldn't try to get something that they didn't already have." Of the updating of the play itself, Tom Magill, the film's director states, "I know that Shakespeare is important enough to keep and how we keep Shakespeare and make him relevant to an audience today is by updating or translating him and making him accessible to a new generation and a new group of people. And I think that's exactly what we're doing with the Macbeth project at Maghaberry." Both comments are made in the documentary section of the film's DVD.

11. See Peter Donaldson, "Shakespeare in the Age of Post-Mechanical Production: Sexual and Electronic Magic in *Prospero's Books,*" in Richard Burt and Lynda Boose, eds., *Shakespeare the Movie II: Popularizing the Plays on Film, TV, Video, and DVD* (New York: Routledge), 105–19. Also see Lev Manovich, *The Language of New Media* (Cambridge: MIT Press, 2001), 212–43, for a sustained discussion of database cinema. In a Deleuzian reading of *Prospero's Books,* Timothy Murray writes that "Through digital imagery, Deleuze believes, the panoramic organization of space loses the vertical privilege of direction, the screen becomes a data bank through which information replaces nature, and the 'brain city' is subject to the perpetual reorganization of world-memory." In "You Are How You Read: Baroque Chao-Errancy in Greenaway and Deleuze," in Murray's *Digital Baroque: New Media Art and Cinematic Folds* (Minneapolis: University of Minnesota Press, 2008), 132. This is presumably not an exchange that Deleuze favors.

12. The case I'm making here is directly inspired by the brilliantly slant reproduction of Monteverdi's *Orfeo* I recently witnessed, which matched a synopsis of Ovid's story with the fragmentary musical theme of *Black Orpheus* (1959) with pitch-perfect renditions of early parts of the opera, followed by the company's reluctance to continue in that mode, followed by a percussive attack that accommo-

dated the ruptures of *The Rite of Spring* to the rhythms of Bahia, followed by bitter recitatives of contemporary relationships gone bad that spoke on behalf of Eurydice, followed by a concluding return to Monteverdi, but this time far more expressively pitched and idiosyncratically rendered than at the start of the proceedings: newly charged, as it were, or recharged. If such productions can be fabricated by a few skilled artists and technicians for performance on a narrow stage in a tent, surely intertextual experiments in kind can be generated on a grander scale for viewing on our shrinking but ever-proliferating screens. *Orfeo* was performed and produced by the Dutch music-theater ensemble, Veenfabriek, under the artistic direction of Paul Koek. The performance in question took place on Governors Island, New York City, September 13, 2009, as part of the New Island Festival.

King Lear or *Bolt:* The Entertainment Unconscious from CalArts to Disney

Donald Hedrick

I WAS WRONG ABOUT AL-QAEDA. After their 9/11 attack on New York and Washington, I watched as usually sensible rural Kansans suddenly imagined immanent attacks on their football stadiums and recreational reservoirs. Apparently since "they" hated all Americans and our "freedom," "they" were out to kill any of us, anywhere, anytime. "Homeland security" dominated self-serving political discourse, bolstering police and surveillance coffers. I believed, on the other hand, that the targets were more deliberately elective, that the terrorists were indifferent to our entertainment venues but were targeting *symbols* of economic, military, and political power.[1]

This week, however, a captured Al-Qaeda training manual called for "blasting and destroying the places of amusement, immorality and sin." Local Kansas officials were taking secret "steps to keep fans safe at sporting events," at the same time reassuring fans that they "should not be fearful of attending Saturday's sellout football game . . ."[2] Such tactically mixed messages—"it's a secret how secure you are," and "we are afraid but unafraid"—also reveal a certain anxiety about those entertainment locations, which is important for understanding Shakespeare's relation to the popular, determined in what I call the "entertainment unconscious." In this essay, I will explore its form as an unstable Shakespearean link between an avant-garde production of *King Lear* and an animated Disney picture as each negotiates a complex nostalgia for film and an anxiety about film's rivals.

In a forthcoming essay entitled "Forget Film," I propose sullying film's contemporary hegemony over "late Shakespeareanism" in scholarly Shakespeare on film professionalization.[3] Such professionalization nevertheless provides distinct theoretical power when film serves as a master paradigm for approaching Shakespeare historically, its techniques identifiable even *within* Shakespeare.

Following Walter Benjamin's designation of Paris as "capital of the nineteenth century,"[4] I suggested that Hollywood's decaying sovereignty over the twentieth century might well be followed by another symbolic site: Las Vegas, capital of the twenty-first century. That always degraded site, featuring participatory entertainments threatening the image machine, could recapture the reviled designation of "mere entertainment" that earlier slandered and promoted film. More important, it represents the commercial logic Theodor Adorno terms "sportification"—the tendency of entertainment to function like a sport, as we see it doing, for example, in "reality shows."[5] Vegas's simulations and amplifications might even teach Shakespeareans more about image production, were we to replay Robert Venturi's sixties guide to postmodernism, *Learning from Las Vegas.*[6] We may, in turn, learn more about "entertainment value's" origins in Elizabethan theater by paying more rigorous theoretical attention to Vegas.

To further theorize "entertainment value," I propose an instance of a shared "entertainment unconscious," using a Shakespearean template, in the contrary directions of elite and antielite works. While Walter Benjamin notes how the "highest and lowest mimesis [can] shake hands" dependent on each other,[7] here I propose a more violent feat, namely, to send these two engines onto a collision course to expose their deep cultural similarity and to gauge the seismic significance of that crash.

Some description is required for these works, whose niche audiences might appear mutually exclusive, either everyday children accompanied by parents or friends, or progressive aficionados of Shakespeare. For the latter, the CalArts production of *King Lear* was an especially "live" "experience," taking place throughout the thirty-thousand-square foot former Edison Company warehouse, now the Brewery Arts Complex, in Los Angeles in 2003. Directed by leading avant-garde director Travis Preston, the performance used an all-female cast with an imposing African American actress, Fran Bennett, as lead. A distinctive feature was that throughout its five "movements," the audience walked throughout the theater space, promenade-style, through monumental landscapes exemplifying the bleak aspects of the play as a contemporary wasteland. As one performance theorist described it: "The CalArts *Lear* story is not exclusively a journey of personal discovery. It is also a deeply disturbing expedition for the audience, who move more literally— and hence more memorably than ever in my theater experience— across a nightmarish postindustrial landscape, with Lear as their unwitting and witless guide."[8] The audience moved from place to place, to a theater in the round, on elevated walkways, and into rows of chairs.

But its most memorable and inventive technological feat was the movement employing sloped chairs that formed a set of thirty-by-thirty-feet gym-style bleachers, befitting entertainment's "sportification." The chairs were enclosed on all sides by black curtains, with a rectangular opening at the front through which the audience observed the actors, as in a cinema frame. Most remarkable, this entire seating section rested on a motorized platform, so that it could be "panned" from place to place, giving the seated audience the impression that the live actors inhabited a movie screen, moving in and out of this framo ac tho "oamora" of tho audionoo aloo moved. Competitive with its "other" entertainment, namely, film, the theater maintains a critical approach to its rival, even as it draws on *relative entertainment value* for aesthetic purposes. And yet its other competitor, and part of the deeper entertainment unconscious to which it owes allegiance, as we will see, is the very sense of participation and "sportification" that Vegas and other "rides," rather than Hollywood, amply afford.

Bolt, an animated film requiring more explication here, is also a journey narrative, literally about finding one's way back "home." In it the dog Bolt tries to return to his "person" Penny after accidentally getting himself shipped from the West to the East Coast. In a remarkably violent opening sequence in which Bolt must rescue Penny from black-clad, powerfully armed enemies in air and on land, we are given Bolt's bionic backstory of implanted superpowers, such as his famed "superbark," which rips up highways to thwart hoards of onrushing villains.

We soon discover, however, that this impossible-looking chase *was* impossible: it was being filmed for a movie. We thus encounter *Bolt*'s chief conceit: neither the action-hero dog of the opening scene, nor even the action-hero actor of the reveal, Bolt is rather a dupe in entertainment culture's *Wonder-Lassie*-meets-*The Truman Show.* Only *thinking* he has real powers, he is being secretly filmed, an unknowingly exploited creature of the studio's comically profit-obsessed directors and executives. Cynically, they know that to be believable to his child fans, the dog-actor must imagine himself a superhero, as he is to hamster-fanboy Rhino, his childlike companion whose dream-come-true is accompanying Bolt on his transcontinental odyssey.

The setup anticipates cynically punctured fantasies, with their eventual patching up. Winningly combining puppy and little girl, the film must provide complementary self-critique, thus mimicking a film like *Shakespeare in Love*—as a machine for Hollywood to manufacture self-forgiveness. Its harder edge gets folded into sentimental foam, as Bolt's journey teaches what it means to be a *dog*. He learns animal humanism, that is, that *nothing canine is alien to me,* just as Lear learns he is a member of his own species—if not lower, as the little dogs bark at him.

Bolt's sentimental education occurs under blue midwestern skies midway upon his return home. Coterminous with this geographic heart, the film's narrative teaches Bolt how to be a "regular dog," to sport puppylike with other dogs, and even *to fetch.* In Hollywood's version of performativity, these lessons don't come *naturally*: his mentor for reidentification, no Fool or rustic Kent, is a savvy, tough-talking New York City stray cat, Mittens, who has to explain how Bolt's tongue should hang out when sticking his head out a car window. Accordingly, *Bolt*'s nostalgia-infused background songs include "I Thought I Lost You," sung by John Travolta and Miley Cyrus, and "Barking at the Moon," whose refrain is, "There is no home like the one you've got / 'Cause that home belongs to you, / Woo hoo, here I come / Woo hoo, back to you." Despite its folksiness, the "home you've got" is Hollywood.

One need not read *Bolt* as Shakespearean "adaptation" to see its narrative morphology of *Lear,* as it records a journey simultaneously physical, geographic, and spiritual. Each protagonist must become physically weaker for insight to happen: a storm weakens the already aged king, and Bolt believes that foam packing peanuts destroy his superpowers. Each is geographically displaced from his kingdom: Lear meanders on the heath, and Bolt is immersed into the counter-Hollywood locales of New York and the Midwest. At crucial moments, each experiences moral crisis: Lear, no longer "flattered like a dog," learns about universal injustice; Bolt, flattered like a human, learns of his role in universal deception. Broad themes are easy enough to provide parallels: the perils of stardom as action hero or king; the fictional nature of cultural or political power; and most profound, authority failing to recognize its own fictionality.[9]

As Bolt travels west of the Midwest, the film anticipates its return home to filmland. There the travelers find themselves beneath the Hollywood Hills sign, overlooking a vast plain of welcoming points of light. Yet in the quest for location, location, location, the entertainment unconscious of the film has already found a prior site, where the journey has stalled and even threatened to end—Las Vegas. Entranced by the Strip's neon and the dancing fountains before the Bellagio hotel, the travelers overnight, but not on the Strip. Instead, they go a few blocks east, where the film exposes what often shocks and surprises new visitors to Las Vegas: behind the Strip, now revealed as just another stage set, extends a vast wasteland of empty, trash-laden, undeveloped, starved scrubland and broken-down equipment. All is dismal by day.

This striking and unusual visual underlines the thematic moment, for here we observe Bolt's deepest identity crisis. Here Mittens desperately pitches a plan for them to move permanently into two adjacent cardboard boxes she has proudly arranged. This image of borderline homelessness foregrounds a crumbling backdrop of ruined buildings, including a symbolically fallen neon star from a demolished hotel sign—an anxious epiphany anticipating the state of entertainment to come. Now Hollywood seems home, to Vegas' motel, and seems true, to Vegas' false. Bolt, of course, dramatically rejects the temptation, pushing on to Hollywood, now by contrast a redeemed location of *traditional, permanent entertainment* rather than one of transient sensations and sign decay.

Bolt's brief, broken-down Vegas landscape characterizes the apocalyptic West Coast look of the CalArts *Lear,* whose director was inspired by combined personal experiences—Karbala in 1999 Iraq and car accidents along the infamous Interstate 5 to San Diego—which led him to stage actual wrecked automobiles over Lear's blasted heath. Like the species-othered characters of *Bolt,* the production defamiliarized Shakespeare's tragedy through its all-female cast and African American lead. The reviewer found the CalArts *Lear* politically successful and provocative, going beyond typical "self-knowledge" interpretations seeking sympathy for Lear—a mode of interpretation that is here undercut by the *movement* of the audience in changing perspectives. Critical of absolutist political power then and now, the production had been enormously successful in France, driven as it was by its arch topicality during the Bush administration.

The reviewer and the director, however, reveal a constitutive ambivalence about entertainment value, amplified when Shakespeare is at stake and marking its complex structural position between Hollywood and Las Vegas.[10] She commends the production's "risk" factor in allowing an association with performance modes of "frivolous entertainment and mindless sensation."[11] At the same time she fears that its "techno-gimmickry" might overwhelm its political content. What seems clear from my experience of this performance, however, is that this *Lear*'s cumulative effect was to create a Las Vegas–like city space, a deliberately scaled-down monumentality suitable for walking about from site to site, like the five-eighths-scale version of the Eiffel Tower at the Paris casino. As in Las Vegas, the theatrical wandering is managed and controlled by also scaling down the "democratic" *choice* of pleasures redefining our pursuit of happiness. Yet its "ways," replacing city streets since there is really only one left, are administered and tactical distractions: to walk from the check-in desk to one's room requires a patron to negotiate an immense field of slot machines in between. The lovely dancing Bellagio fountains appear to be a "free" spectacle along the Strip, but benches are conspicuously absent along its sidewalk. Nonproductive lingering—what Benjamin describes as the prehistory of *amusement*—is thus discouraged or disallowed. The fountain show lasts just long enough for a pause before moving on, unless one buys dinner, as I did, at the open-air, partly faux-French steakhouse just across the Strip. As Adorno explains, the culture industry's "free time" allows no real leisure, unless bound to profitable time.[12] Vegas' entertainment unconscious transforms language itself, as casinos now hire "dealertainers" who must mimic some celebrity in order to entertain their customers while dealing cards, thus ratcheting up job skill requirements for the same pay. All of these instances constitute a distinct *coerciveness* at the very heart of the entertainment culture.[13]

Travis Preston intended his show to be "a *Lear* for LA,"[14] but that entailed some regard for the distinctly non-LA. The production suggested some resistance to Las Vegas, but in its unconscious there is anxiety even about that desire. We detect this in the rather strained and cautious interview of Fran Bennett, where barely coded language describes the production as "a different approach to theater" (Bennett) and as "a fascinating experience to play with" (interviewer).[15] Evident of Las Vegasization, the latter phrase—to play with experience—suggests the movie narrative afterlives of the archetypal Vegas weekend, and therefore *relative entertainment value,* whether comic (*The Hangover*), tragic (*Leaving Las Vegas*), or even tragicomic (*Showgirls*). "Buzz" is thus generated about the "experience," just as the CalArts *Lear* seems itself designed to produce. The interview skirts around how overwhelming such a set and concept would be for actors; ambiguous descriptions of the "isolation" and "alienation" of characters seem to imply that of the actors as well. When asked if the technology "enhanced the text," Bennett claimed to be "unaware" of all the technology or of the audience in their "camera box," because unable to see what *they* saw: "As an actor I cannot let that affect me. I can't even be affected by the fact that you are moving or by whatever you're feeling in the box as it and you move."[16] Isolation within a manufactured barrage of fun clinically describes the typical Vegas experience, reversed-image a mirror to this deliberately unamusement ride. Following entertainment value's logic, Bennett notes, albeit not especially convincingly, that the experimental *Lear* always gave the audience a choice of what it was doing, such as whether or not to accept earphones handed out one time.[17]

Since we know how *Lear* ends, we can return to *Bolt*'s post-Vegas ending to see what happens to our canine, now redeemed after warding off the threat of Vegas and, knowing himself, purified for rescuing and restoring film to its rightful throne. Arriving in movietown, Bolt meets three locals—comic chorus pigeons who match the Brooklynese pigeons we saw in New York. Shallow and on the make, they take Bolt for a film producer, pitching him their loopy proposal for a film: Bolt meets space aliens (a movie we see screened at *Bolt*'s end). Playing along in order to get their help, Bolt in his newly achieved identity reenters the inauthentic world *willingly.* As entertainment is transformed, Bolt is no longer the duped but rather the one doing the duping, a "natural" evolution of actor into producer.

Entering the busy film studio, as Rhino ecstatically celebrates entering "the belly of the beast," Bolt is suddenly crushed to see his mistress giving affection to a new dog. He doesn't realize that, just as in the film's opening scene, what he sees is "just a movie," a filming of Jenny and the actor-dog replacing Bolt. Like Lear's too late learning, Bolt leaves dejectedly, just as a fire accidentally starts on the sound stage and quickly gains destructive force, much like the fantasy destructions of LA. As the now really endangered Penny is left stranded in mid-air by the crew, Bolt realizes his error, rushes into the fire, and attempts to rescue her, now for real, with brave but realistically fearful doggy heroism.

With sublime daring for a children's film, what follows is devastating in reproducing emotionally Shakespeare's most grim plot turn. Winding through smoke and flames, Bolt reaches a final impasse—an air vent to the outside, but one too small for *her* to go through. What happens next should drive a real child-fan into hysterical despair, a moment as bleak as the failed final rescue of Shakespeare's play, or as the death of Bambi's mother: giving up when there is no way out, not saving himself, Bolt quietly lies down beside her unconscious body—even more resigned than Lear, who laments how he might have saved his daughter. And so, Bolt resigns to their end together, a canine king who has finally learned true love and how to be a nonaction hero, at last, at home, on the set.

No children's film could ever end like *Lear,* of course, though few would dare to lie down so closely beside it as it expires. Yet as the flames and smoke surround them, Bolt's pause gives him time to notice a little pipe leading up along the wall. Into it, he manages to "speak" a few final barks. By the amplifying power of the tube, his barks are carried upward and outside, as if an emergency broadcast to the helpless firemen, who then proceed to rescue the couple. This amplification of voice—comically fooling Rhino into thinking it Bolt's "superbark"—invokes nostalgia for film at its own entertainment origins, before talkies but after theater: the magic of make-believe with limited, not ever-expanding technical means. A traditional apparatus, like the tradition of Shakespeare, returns to save film, no longer suffering under the cruel criteria of Vegas' standards.[18]

Both CalArts and *Bolt* fear and dally with the threatening future of Vegasization, registered on the one hand in the imagination of a future apocalyptic wasteland and on the other as a longing for film as home, which, in contrast to that desert, allows a quasi-genuine identity. The avant-garde theater's entertainment unconscious is deeper than that of the Disney film. It shares the children's film's logic, however, in acknowledging a more immediate and experiential place as entertainment competitor-collaborator, like the early modern rivalry of the classic arts, now commercialized. In Disney, Vegas' role is the cultural purgatory through which Bolt must pass to redeem cinema. In CalArts, Vegas' role is confined to the participatory role of the spectator's problematic agency, "choosing" the proffered and preselected entertainment modes, whether *walking* through the warehouse "city" or else *riding* in its cinematic black box. Directly represented in Disney and indirectly in CalArts is the twenty-first century's location par excellence, inviting us also to consider its original formation in the early modern entertainment laboratory of Shakespeare's own location.

Within a broader political and economic framework, Las Vegas identifies with today's aptly named "casino capitalism," which has collided with ours and the world's economies.[19] The "entertainment" form thus stands for a financial capital model helping to produce current excesses, global misery, and near catastrophe while furthering a decline of U.S. international authority replaying the Shakespearean and historical loss of monarchical authority.

I was right about Al-Qaeda after all. What their recent statements about destroying "amusement" reveal is not a practical motive to attack entertainment venues, or even merely a hyperbolically religious fundamentalism, but rather a real identification of entertainment value as a key symbolic location of Western multiple and decentered influence and administration. Political, economic, and even military domination are all thoroughly infused at some level with entertainment's hegemonic value, in reciprocal relation with spectacles of invasion, torture, corruption, complicity, speed, and risk. Contradictions within the Western entertainment unconscious may be comparable to those of terrorists. The force of this unconscious explains the submerged or revealed anxiety about Las Vegas that becomes a crucial sign for both popular and antipopular art.

The assault on places of economic, military, and political power then congeals further within a complex entertainment imaginary as a dominant force of culture, so that imagined assaults on localized entertainment venues count as politically equivalent to actual terrorist attacks on any social, economic, or military infrastructure, where in any case they would be more likely to occur in reality. It is not that Al-Qaeda would never attack a place of entertainment, usually off their radar, but rather that the ideological structure of entertainment is built into the very vengeful consciousness of any attack, as entertainment through casino capitalism crystallizes what is profoundly always an other. Such an unconscious can even form a core of rage, becoming a sign threatening to others, but also to us.

Notes

The position of the present essay regarding "entertainment" terrorist targeting may require further complication or revision, since the essay was composed prior to the May 1, 2010, bomb threat at Times Square.

1. For a strong semiotic-political reading of the architectural objectives of terrorism, see Terry Smith, *The Architecture of Aftermath* (Chicago: University of Chicago Press, 2006).

2. Jesse Fray, "KU officials mum on any changes they're making after feds issue terror alert for sports stadiums," *Lawrence Journal World,* Sept. 22, 2009, http://www2.ljworld.com/news/2009/sep/22/ku-officials-mum-any-changes-theyre-making-after-f/.

3. Donald Hedrick, "Forget Film: Speculations on Shakespearean Entertainment Value," in *The English Renaissance in Popular Culture: An Age for All Time,* ed. Greg Semenza (New York: Palgrave Macmillan, 2010).

4. Walter Benjamin, "Paris, Capital of the Nineteenth-Century," in *The Arcades Project* (Cambridge, MA: Harvard University Press, 1999), 3–13.

5. Theodor W. Adorno, "The Schema of Mass Culture," in *The Culture Industry* (New York: Routledge, 1991), 89. For further examination of "entertainment value" and "sportification" in Shakespeare's London, see Donald Hedrick, "Real Entertainment: Sportification, Coercion, and Carceral Theater," in *Thunder at a Playhouse,* ed. Matt Kozusko (Selinsgrove: Susquehanna University Press, forthcoming).

6. Robert Venturi, Denise Scott Brown, and Steven Izenour, *Learning from Las Vegas* (Cambridge: MIT Press, 1972). As a recent exhibition now reveals, Venturi uncannily linked Las Vegas to a more disturbing version of the Disney animation empire, in 1988 sketches for Euro Disney, showing "cutout billboards of menacing-looking cartoon characters lined up on both sides of a seemingly endless roadway." Nicholas Ouroussoff, "The Lessons of Las Vegas Still Hold Surprises," *The New York Times,* December 23, 2009, C–1, C–5.

7. Benjamin, *Arcades,* 531.

8. Una Chauduri, "Regime Change: *King Lear* in Los Angeles, George Bush in Iraq, Americans in France," *Drama Review* 48, no. 1 (Spring 2004): 88.

9. The present conjunction of Shakespeare and popular children's animation is strengthened by Judith Halberstam's argument for progressive understanding of current animated children's films and game culture. As she writes, "We should be learning how to wander through a video game without ever winning or how to take pleasure in a film without a happy ending (48)," "Animation," *Profession 2009* (New York: Modern Language Association, 2009): 44–49.

10. A provisional set of oppositions between Hollywood and Las Vegas would include the following: passive/participatory, body as seen/body as experienced, scopic control/distraction, niche audience/democratized audience; educational/noneducational, taste/sportification. For a further listing, see Hedrick's "Forget Film."

11. Chaudhuri, "Regime Change," 89.

12. Theodor Adorno, "Free Time," in *The Culture Industry* (New York: Routledge, 1991; repr., 2001), 187–97.

13. For the early modern instantiation and origin of this, see Donald Hedrick's discussion of early modern coerciveness, and even occasional incarceration, on the Elizabethan stage in "Real Entertainment."

14. Chauduri, "Regime Change," 91.

15. "Fran Bennett," in *North American Players of Shakespeare,* ed. Michael W. Shurgot (Newark: University of Delaware Press, 2007), 312. Bennett admits that if she did the play for her LA Women's Shakespeare Company, "it would never be like this" (311).

16. Ibid.

17. Ibid., 312.

18. Compare the displacement of film here to Benjamin's observation about the "profound displacement painting must submit to being measured by the standards of photography . . ." *Arcades,* 685.

19. For gambling's relation to the early modern theater, by way of "actor wagers," see Hedrick, "Forget Film."

iShakespeare: Digital Art/Games, Intermediality, and the Future of Shakespearean Film

Laurie Osborne

IN THE FALL OF 1996, I was lucky enough to be in New York City when Kenneth Branagh's *Hamlet* opened in all its 70 mm glory at the Paris Theatre. During the summer of 2009, I watched the same film on the two-inch screen of an iPod. Although this variation of screen size is admittedly extreme, these two experiences underscore key features in twenty-first-century digitized performance: multiple screens, multiple technologies, and proliferating mechanisms of audience control. Shakespearean film faces a digital world.

The year after Branagh's *Hamlet* was released, Janet H. Murray analyzed digital narrative and predicted "a continued loosening of the traditional boundaries between games and stories, between films and rides, between broadcast media (like television and radio) and archival media (like books and videotape), between narrative forms (like books) and dramatic forms (like theater or film), and even between the audience and the author."[1] However, Murray could not have anticipated how many different kinds of screens would become sites for twenty-first-century literary and cinematic boundary-loosening. Beyond television and movie theaters, our computer screens now host streaming video of Shakespearean performances, including Peter Donaldson's Shakespeare Performance in Asia Web site (http://web.mit.edu/shakespeare/asia/) and Ian McKellan's *King Lear,* which currently airs on demand on the PBS Web site (http://video.pbs.org/video/1075274407/program/9793 59658).[2] Several Shakespearean films are now available through digital pay-per-view from iTunes. In addition, Shakespeare's texts appear on WebTV, our computer screens, and Amazon's Kindle screens as e-books.

What has followed "Shakespeare on film" is Shakespeare on screens. Because we now find Shakespeare's works on a range of these performance/textual surfaces, the technologies that enable these encounters, enrich them, and render them all-too-swiftly obsolete will continually influence Shakespearean film in the twenty-first century. At the least, Shakespearean film will become a crucial archive for creative work; at the most, Shakespeare's works may fully enter digital existence, living up to and beyond W. B. Worthen's exploration in "Shakespeare 3.0."[3] The future of Shakespeare on film depends on the qualities that digital worlds require: interactivity through participation and procedures, and audience immersion through spatial and encyclopedic environments.[4]

To put it another way, which screens Shakespeare will inhabit after his lengthy stint on the big one may rely on whether his plays prove suitable for manipulation and immersive exploration. Does Shakespeare invite the creative interactivity of digital play, and, if so, in what ways? The explosion of YouTube Shakespeare videos suggests that his plays provide a useful starting place for do-it-yourself video production. From stop-action Claymation (http://www.youtube.com/watch?v = q5OKUBVb4sI) to musical performances of *Macbeth* (http://www.youtube.com/watch?v = YVOEoW R44ug), Shakespearean YouTube hosts more than rare performance recordings like the summary film of the Wooster Group *Hamlet* (http://www.youtube.com/watch?v = wAO2XOOsbK8). "Canonical" films prove useful, even recyclable, for example, in the mini-boom of YouTube Ophelia music videos—such as *Ophelia's Immortal* (http://www.youtube.com/watch?v = qs0m9dGI5zQ) and *Hamlet's Immortal* (http://www.youtube.com/watch?v = AZm4g RBzY20), which set clips of Kate Winslet's performance in Branagh's *Hamlet* to an array of pop songs. Many of these films exploit the plays' susceptibility to adaptation, already made plain in the flurry of Shakespearean teen adaptations (*10 Things I Hate About You, Get Over It, O,* and *She's the Man*). So far, however, enthusiasm for small-screen Shakespearean productions has not translated into sustained presence in games or digital performance works, even at a time when gaming and digital environments have begun to influence film production.

Not only has the recent dynamic interplay between games and films been accelerating, but the newest media format, Blu-ray, also derives from developments in gaming. Blu-ray technology initially drove the Sony PlayStation, enabling a game platform to run films

that fit its format and enhancing interactivity with film.[5] As far as
Blu-ray Shakespearean films go, the transfer has been comparatively slow. While readily generating Web sites, DVD commentaries, and sometimes Web-based or freestanding educational materials,
Shakespearean movies do not typically inspire the kinds of games
that have driven this latest technological shift and benefit most
from it. At this point, we can reasonably ask whether Shakespeare
will advance or wither in cinematic production if that production
becomes more normatively a multilevel commercial enterprise in
consumer immersion or even deeply tied to the new interactive access and image detail promised by Blu-ray. The corollary issue is
whether Shakespeare's works will inspire wholly new productions
within these performance platforms. Questions remain about
whether the immersive, interactive, spatial, and temporal possibilities enabled by digital media suit Shakespeare's works and what
role Shakespearean film might serve in new intermedial forms.

    At the moment, Shakespeare participates in the emergent world
of digital and Web-based performance in ways that have provocative implications, particularly for Shakespeare on film. Here I draw
on a range of examples: two computer games, *Hamlet: A Murder
Mystery* (1997) and *Macbeth Interactive* (2005); two relatively simple interactive online "games/performances," *Hamlet: The Text
Adventure* (http://versificator.co.uk/hamlet/) and *The HyperMacbeth,* by Kid Koma (http://digilander.libero.it/dlsan/splash/mac_
gallery.htm); and two more sophisticated digital projects, Indiana
University's synthetic world *Arden I* (http://mypage.iu.edu/~castro/
arden.html) and Herbert Fritsch's *hamlet_X* (http://www.hamlet-
x.de/).[6] This small sample of digital Shakespeare suggests a couple
of intriguing prospects for Shakespeare in popular culture: potential empowerment of Shakespearean film as an intermedial form
and growing focus on Shakespearean characters, whose after- and
alter-lives are currently also burgeoning in popular fiction.

    The signals about Shakespeare's role in digital art are mixed. Al-
though Shakespeare is a common referent in Janet Murray's study
of digital narrative potential in *Hamlet on the Holodeck* (1997) and
a frequent touchstone in Timothy Murray's recent study of digital
art in *Digital Baroque* (2008), Shakespearean plays and films have
been all but invisible in the gaming world since 1997 when Branagh's *Hamlet: A Murder Mystery* promised gamers the opportunity
to interact with the cinematic/theatrical experience.[7] The player's
alternative goal for Hamlet—to revenge the father and win the

throne—represents a reworking of the plot that apparently offers both agency and immersion in the world of *Hamlet,* but, as Mike Bernstein and Diane Greco point out, "[i]llusions that place the reader on stage necessarily founder when promised freedom of action is contradicted by the limitations of the simulated environment."[8] For example, the third level of *Hamlet: A Murder Mystery* challenges the player with editing film:

> the player (as Hamlet) [must] edit three filmstrips in order to proceed. Just as Hamlet stages his "play within the play," we created a "stage" on which the player must come up with his own play to "catch the conscience of the King." He is provided frames from filmstrips in order to edit the three parallel versions of the deaths of Kings included by Shakespeare . . . Priam's slaughter by Pyrrhus, the Murder of Gonzago (the Player King), and the killing of Hamlet senior by Claudius. The player must edit these filmstrips in order to continue the game. There's a lot of cutting and splicing (it's not easy), and the exercise amounts to the player's creation of his own film.[9]

Project producer Arlene Steibel implies that the player has a high degree of control in exploring the environment and arranging the narrative, but she overstates the case since the gamer must reproduce the sequence already present in Branagh's production. If you array the different images in proper (though not always intuitive) order, a bell rings, notifying you of your success, and the film clip plays across the various "frames" of the game board. Moreover, the gamer's other successes are rewarded only by variations on Branagh's film: Ophelia survives by "undrowning" as the clip runs backward, and the gamer/Hamlet takes his seat on the throne upon winning with a clip from the film's second scene. Shakespearean film both enables and disables the interactive potential of the game.

Interestingly, Bernstein and Greco identify both choice and the discovery of limits as key features in current interactive digital environments with reference to Shakespeare: "If you make *Hamlet* a game, it has to be rigged so that actions taken by a reasonable and sane reader-protagonist—not to mention a wildly inventive one—do not derail the train of events that must ensue if this is to be *Hamlet* and not, say, *Timon of Athens* or *A Midsummer Night's Dream.*"[10] To put it another way, the narrative tragedy of Shakespeare's play requires a certain sequence of events to be *Hamlet,* but interactive games and digital performance ostensibly give the player/audience the choice of action. Bernstein and Greco's argument assumes that *Hamlet* has a stable identity and represents established narrative form in contrast to the structured unpredictability of reader-driven digital art. However, the variability shown in both textual studies and popular adaptations of the play qualifies this view of *Hamlet*. Moreover, *Hamlet: A Murder Mystery* shows film's potential as a key middle ground for digital works: film offers both reiterable narrative form and the varying choices created by film editing. Shakespearean film, in particular, draws on his canonical status and therefore even more vividly emphasizes the creative power of directorial choices, now effected through digital editing.

Even though *Macbeth Interactive* is more obviously educational, the game was created in conjunction with three film versions of *Macbeth—Hollywood, Hollywood/Short & Sweet,* and *Elizabethan.* Sold from the promisingly named Web site gamingshakespeare.com, the game uses clips from its own films as clues and posits filmmaking as the game's goal. The money that the player collects through accurate Shakespearean puzzle-solving only allows him/her to buy a predetermined array of performance necessities, including several that are specific to film. The game ends when the player has completed the script work and acquired all the necessary materials and resources. His/her film is then hailed as a big hit; however, the Globe theater audience seems to applaud, and no actual film work or creative interaction with cinematic fragments occurs.

By incorporating Shakespearean film, these games suggest its comparative durability while showing both its utility and its limitations for enabling audience immersion and creative interactions. Despite the shifting map and changing areas that are available for player interaction, *Macbeth Interactive* lacks the immersive quality of the most effective computer or online games. The animation and settings are largely static, as are many of the recurring puzzles: "Will" Shakespeare jumps for words or phrases against a static backdrop, images of the Globe or dialogue text appear as puzzle pieces to be sorted out, or players must move speech bubbles to the appropriate speakers. The game lacks a clear point-of-view movement through the virtual world, and the only sounds outside the film clips are the harp trill signaling success and an occasional speech. This limited mobility and near-silence inadvertently proves how necessary cinematic motion and sound track are for creating a sense of immersion. By default, the film clips provide the only realistic movement and sound in the environment.

Online Shakespeare games/performances raise the level of interactivity, and, in doing so, they demonstrate the value digital environments derive from Shakespearean character. For example, *Hamlet: The Text Adventure* asks the gamer to type in text so he/she can move around Elsinore, pick up items, and talk to the characters in the play, albeit in colloquial rather than Shakespearean language. However, the player soon encounters Othello, Juliet, Mistress Quickly, Richard III, and Macbeth. Shakespearean characters, more than the plot of the play, enable or block the player/Hamlet. Without either sound or image, *Hamlet: The Text Adventure* represents a digital environment where Shakespearean language could rule; in fact, the game creators specifically invoke the powers of language: "Unlike most modern computer games, which rely on insanely complex graphics hardware to show you what's going on, the text adventure uses a technology of unsurpassed advancement—the English language—to project the images directly into your imagination."[11] However, character dominates the interactions, originating with the player who inhabits the role of Hamlet.

Kid Koma's *HyperMacbeth: Lyrics by William Shakespeare* allows its audience to link to the underlined terms in a single line: "The <u>queen</u>, <u>my lord</u>, is <u>dead</u>." These words lead to hyperlinked textual fragments from Lady Macbeth's famous soliloquy, from Macbeth's musings on the poisoned chalice of ambition, and from his oft-quoted response to Lady Macbeth's death, respectively. The player's further choices among links generate an array of musical motifs aligned at times with horizontal layers of largely abstract visuals. While using and linking fragments of these speeches draws Koma's *HyperMacbeth* surprisingly close to the educational games in *Macbeth Interactive,* Koma's digital environment neither rewards correct language order nor punishes variations. In fact, the player/performer often has a choice of two or more links for the same word on-screen. The person who chooses the links creates the performance, but characters anchor the speeches. The comparative stability of "the queen" and "my lord" on the Web page, like the player's assumption of the role of Hamlet in the text adventure, suggests that Shakespeare's characters are an attractive resource for digital art. These relatively simple examples of digital Shakespeare imply a centrality of character that more sophisticated online Shakespearean environments bear out.

Now only accessible as freestanding games, *Arden I* and *II* once enabled interactive online game play in Shakespeare-inflected worlds, both superimposed on the popular multiplayer game base, *Neverwinter Nights.* The project ran from 2006 to 2008, but Edward Castronova notes that "*Arden I* is our 'Shakespeare Game,' the complex version that most people did not want to play," so that game was quickly superseded by *Arden II,* set in medieval England.[12] At the 2008 Shakespeare Association meeting, Peter Holland and Linda Charnes explored the implications of *Arden I* in detail and speculated about the potential of the multiplayer universe for Shakespearean performance and study.[13]

Here I address only the remains of *Arden I,* which, even in reduced format, establishes its Shakespearean dimension by incorporating characters from the plays. Although the game's bank of ready-made player identities derives from *Neverwinter Nights* rather than the Shakespearean canon, the player, as "Merom Rescher, true neutral druid gnome," can talk to Peter Quince, Falstaff, or Perdita; observe (but not read) a glowing folio; or seek information about the guilds from Holofernes and Nathaniel. As in *Hamlet: The Text Adventure,* the range of Shakespearean characters reaches beyond the narrowing canon registered in Shakespearean film. Moreover, even though I was unable to corner Dull and talk to him before the school's globe in order to see the promised performance from *Love's Labor's Lost,* a film clearly appeared, however briefly, in *Arden I.* While including film in both its animation and reward, *Arden I* displays an investment in character as the mechanism for enabling the player to choose quests, accomplish tasks, or pursue guild membership.

Herbert Fritsch's *hamlet-X* takes on directly my question about Shakespeare's suitability for the particular traits of digital storytelling. Fritsch considers Shakespeare, or at least *Hamlet,* as eminently appropriate for interactive digital innovations in theater. As Birgit Wiens puts it, "according to Fritsch's reading of the Shakespearean tragedy, the prince lived in a fundamental dilemma that perfectly reflects the digital condition: 'To be or not to be' (*Hamlet III.*1.56) which Fritsch relates to the basic *digital code,* 0 and 1" (author's emphasis).[14] In addition to brilliantly tracking the forms that Fritsch's installation has taken, Wiens analyzes his intermedial emphasis on "the variety of ways in which cultural heritage is *channeled* and *changed through different media*" (author's emphasis).[15] For Fritsch, the story of Hamlet "was presented by Shakespeare as a civilized myth, and, after centuries of stiffening and fossilization. . . . He wants once again to be ripped apart, chopped into separate parts and spoken by many voices."[16] The "viele Munder," also translated as "numerous mouths," that speak Hamlet are *both* characters and films.

My admittedly limited assessment of the Web site and the DVDs for *hamlet_X* bears out Wiens's observations about the artistic consequences of the project's appearance on German television, where the venue undermined the interactivity Fritsch desired in favor of the 111 short films he made.[17] On DVD, Fritsch's Shakespearean films endure beyond the interaction and immersion of the digital installation or the temporary exposure of the television special.[18] Among the interactive games still remaining on the Web site, virtual karaoke enables the visitor, given appropriate software, to participate in a fixed dialogue as either Hamlet or Ophelia—a limited choice that nonetheless accentuates the importance of character position for the player.[19] Moreover, the brevity and frequent tight focus of these films, well suited for Internet screening, emphasize "Portraits, or interviews" with characters that include "the gynecologist of Gertrude, the gatekeeper of the castle, the investment advisor of Claudius, or the fencing coach of Hamlet." Fritsch identifies these particular films as a "further level" where "one can take oneself unrestrained through the different eras and . . . where the story can be completely differently and totally freely spun."[20] Please note, however, that the total freedom envisioned here is grounded in the 111 film fragments that form the narrative frame.

These examples raise the prospect that Shakespeare's characters provide an appealing entry into immersive and interactive art and that Shakespearean film supplies a valuable mechanism for combining interactivity with narrative parameters. The lure of reimagining Shakespeare's characters and their lives, exemplified in Jasper Fforde's *Something Rotten* (2004), Susan Fraser King's *Lady Macbeth* (2008), and L. Jagi Lamplighter's *Prospero Lost* (2009),[21] authorizes the player/performer's agency in digital performance. Beyond the aptness of Shakespearean film's implication in both stability and creative revision, the variable past access and uncertain futures of these digital projects also help explain their tendency to invoke or rely on film. *Arden I* now underscores the pressures of the steady and swift press of obsolescence in both games and film since the base game, *Neverwinter Nights,* is out of date, and the Arden multiverse is gone. This transience and platform vulnerability, also evident in the now nonfunctional *Hamlet: A Murder Mystery,* indirectly points to the greater stability of

Shakespearean film. The persistence of Shakespearean films across formats from celluloid, to VHS/BETA, to DVD, and now, potentially, to Blu-ray suggests that these artworks have become canonical and thus pave the way for similar durability of Shakespearean films in the future. In the context of increasing intermedial flow and technological change, such persistence should encourage digital artists to extend their explorations of Shakespeare's plays and characters and future filmmakers to invest in Shakespeare.

Notes

1. Janet Murray, *Hamlet on the Holodeck* (Cambridge: MIT University Press, 1997), 64.

2. Peter S. Donaldson, "The Shakespeare Electronic Archive: Collections and Multimedia Tools for Teaching and Research, 1992–2008," *Shakespeare: Journal of the British Shakespeare Association* 4 (2008): 234–44.

3. W. B. Worthen, "Shakespeare 3.0," in *Alternative Shakespeares 3*, ed. Diana Henderson et al., 54–77 (New York: Routledge, 2008).

4. Murray, *Hamlet on the Holodeck*, 71.

5. Greg Tarr, "Blu-ray Players Come of Age at International Ces," *TWICE: This Week in Consumer Electronics* 24, no. 1 (2009): 82.

6. *Hamlet: A Murder Mystery*, EEME Interactive/CastleRock Entertainment, 1997; *Macbeth Interactive*, A Shakespeare's World Production, 2005; *Hamlet: The Text Adventure*, http://versificator.co.uk/howtoplay.html; Kid Koma, *HyperMacbeth: Lyrics by William Shakespeare*, http://digilander.libero.it/dlsan/splash/mac_gallery.htm; Edward Castronova, "Arden—The World of William Shakespeare," http://mypage.iu.edu/~castro/arden.html; and Herbert Fritsch, *hamlet-X*, http://www.hamlet-x.de/.

7. Murray, *Hamlet on the Holodeck*, and Timothy Murray, *Digital Baroque: New Media Art and Cinematic Folds* (Minneapolis: University of Minnesota Press, 2008).

8. Mark Bernstein and Diane Greco, *"Card Shark* and *Thespis:* Exotic Tools for Hypertext Narrative," in *First Person: New Media as Story, Performance, and Game*, ed. Noah Wardrip-Fruin and Pat Harrigan, 178 (Cambridge: MIT Press, 2004).

9. Arlene Stiebel, e-mail to author, November 3, 1997.

10. Bernstein and Greco, *"Card Shark* and *Thespis*," 178.

11. *Hamlet: The Text Adventure*, http://versificator.co.uk/howtoplay.html.

12. Castronova, "Arden—The World of William Shakespeare."

13. Peter Holland, "Luncheon Address" (paper presented at the annual meeting of the Shakespeare Association of America, March 12–15, 2008) and Linda Charnes, "Shakespeare and the Meaning of Second Life" (paper presented at the annual meeting of the Shakespeare Association of America, March 12–15, 2008).

14. Birgit Wiens, "Hamlet and the Virtual Stage: Herbert Fritsch's Project *hamlet_X*," in *Intermediality in Theatre and Performance*, ed. Freda Chapple and Chiel Kattenbelt, 223 (New York: Rodopi, 2006).

15. Ibid., author's emphasis 225.

16. Fritsch, *Projekt,* trans. Wiens, 225.

17. Wiens, "Hamlet and the Virtual Stage," 226.

18. *hamlet_X,* vols. 1–3 (Film Galerie, 2003).

19. Fritsch, *Animationen,* "3 User."

20. Fritsch, *Projekt,* trans. Susannah Hufstader.

21. Jasper Fforde, *Something Rotten* (New York: Viking, 2004), Susan Fraser King, *Lady Macbeth* (New York: Crown, 2008), and L. Jagi Lamplighter, *Prospero Lost* (New York: Tom Doherty Associates, 2009).

Crowd-Sourcing Shakespeare: Screen Work and Screen Play in Second Life

Katherine Rowe

ACADEMIC FILM STUDIES has dedicated many decades to establishing the principle that films are, in a deep intellectual sense, basically like books: richly historically situated, formally complex, inviting critical analysis and theoretical formulations. Understood in these ways, film texts could emerge as objects fitted to the structures of authority, oversight, and cultural value that organize academic practice. This process is contested and continuing, and reflection on its unevenness provokes speculation about the future. What opportunities and challenges to such institutional assimilation do new media offer academics—Shakespeareans in particular? To my mind the most compelling and urgent are those posed by the transformations colloquially known as "Web 2.0," less a term of technological change than of behavioral change. Web 2.0 denotes the collaborative, creative, socially networked behaviors of humans interacting with each other through shareable, dynamic content online. The labor and play that take place in this mode in virtual environments constitute an increasingly important kind of public engagement with Shakespeare. For literary scholars, closer attention to such engagements can expand our understanding of the public perceptions of value invested in Shakespeare specifically and the Renaissance generally. As important, Shakespeare environments online offer direct encounters with the core conflicts new modes of knowledge-making on the Web generate for scholars.*

This essay explores those conflicts by focusing on the fictions of ownership governing three Shakespearean locations in Second Life®, an online world that combines social networking, gaming,

---

Editor's note: *To read a version of this essay with illustrations and hyperlinks, go to Katherine Rowe's home page. http://www.brynmawr.edu/english/Faculty_andStaff/rowe/research.html

and 3-D design. The platform welcomes a growing number of academics as visitors and residents. Since it was launched, it has hosted five virtual Globe theaters, one with a regular acting company. In Second Life you may explore historical re-creations of sixteenth-century Europe inhabited by intentional communities, and you can enter simulations ("sims") of numerous literary works, including some remarkable multimedia installations. The client software's 3-D surround creates a powerful sense of proprioception and architectural space, making it attractive as a teaching space for theater studies.[1]

Second Life provides a useful exemplum of the opportunities for creative, public engagement with Shakespeare online because its business model is rapidly becoming a dominant one: the drive to leverage user-generated content. Linden Lab created the platform in response to a growing recognition in the gaming industry that a player's ability to modify game environments is a key index of her enjoyment. Two technical features distinguish such virtual worlds. They are *persistent:* what you build here lasts when you log off. And they are *extensible:* designed for open-ended collaborative world building. Players interact through avatars in environments they build themselves. Imagine your avatar as a cross between a car, a telephone, a doll, and a puppet, and you will have a good sense of the interface Second Life provides for movement, communication, and self-performance.[2]

A year or so into operation, Linden Lab added what was then a revolutionary feature to their terms of service, granting players intellectual property rights in their virtual creations. Yet ownership in Second Life remains a fiction in two important ways. In legal and commercial terms, the Lockean discourse of builder-ownership invoked in company slogans obscures far more complex intellectual property relations. Not only is the "extension of the body" in this platform predicated on a technical "interface of extensibility from which the company profits," but "the 'medium' with which game players mix or join their labor . . . is neither undifferentiated nor common; Linden 'land' is always already code that is owned by the corporation."[3] What's more, within the socially immersive communities of Second Life, a virtual Globe theater can only exist in a real way by consent and participation of other residents.

A fly through three Renaissance sims in Second Life illustrates the different permutations this conundrum of property takes and the challenges they pose for scholars. Read together, these sims

foreground the ideological divisions between our academic practices and what Michael Warner has labeled "uncritical reading,"
nonscholarly modes of textual encounter that lack the analytic distance and independent agency we prize. Broaching his critique of
critical reading, Warner traces its roots in immersive and affective
textual practices that academics usually figure as the opposite of
independent thought. The experience of a modern Western literature classroom, as Warner observes, all too often sounds like ad-
monishment—"don't read like vacation readers on the beach, like
escapists, like fundamentalists, like nationalists, like antiquarians,
like consumers, like ideologues, like sexists, like tourists, like your-
selves."[4] Noting that critical reading has always been one among
many competing frameworks, Warner historicizes these counterdistinctions, suggesting we use them to forget our disciplinary origins in just such amateur practices. A parallel, more difficult
critique might be pursued by challenging the counterdistinctions
themselves. How might we approach immersive, affective, and
practical modes of interpretation as equal, perhaps competing
frameworks *for thinking,* not as the opposites of thinking? My pursuit of this question in Second Life began as fieldwork with students and colleagues. I owe a special debt to Alice Dailey, whose
voice may be heard several times in the discussion that follows.

I. Renaissance Island: The Parish of Reading Primley Group

We begin in Renaissance Island, an elaborate sixteenth-century
build created "by a group of dedicated historians" who make up
the Parish of Reading Primley group. The modes of property in the
historical Renaissance that operate here are vexed and various:
property imagined in terms of estate and labor (as rights to specific
social roles), as propriety (community standards of decorum), and
property in expertise.

Teleporting in, you resolve at a beautiful Tudor library, with elab-
orately carved wood panels and a book collection. A scan of the
shelves shows the latest biographies of Renaissance celebrities, a
First Folio facsimile of *Love's Labor's Lost,* and various how-tos.[5]
The bibliophilic historicism performed here turns out to be in some
tension with a competing dedication to fantasy role-playing in Renaissance Island—a blend of Renaissance Faire with Plimoth Plantation. Residents (those who pay to join the group) play the landed

class, of course; tourists are offered free clothing and invited to join in as "peasant lass" or "peasant lad." Social encounters involve faux Tudor English and titles—"Milady," "Milord." If you don't join in, you are likely to be politely ignored.

For all their play at Tudor rank, members of the group make what is essentially a populist claim on the sixteenth century—one that is in some tension with book learning as Shakespeareans claim it. An exchange between a colleague known as "Barbary" in Second Life, and the resident tour guide illustrates this tension. When they first meet, Barbary's guide asks her about her name and she explains its source: a character in *Othello* mentions a "maid called Barbary" (3.3.393). As they tour the parish—jousting ring, gallows and rack, Globe theater, thatch cottages with perennial borders, crenellated castle—her guide observes that he hasn't read Shakespeare and reels off a number of inaccurate claims about life in the period. Barbary is cautious with her own expertise. Any new relationship in Second Life can easily fizzle, constructed as it is through the narrow bandwidth of text chat. Becoming "the one who knows more" can flip the polarities of authority and disintegrate social relationship with remarkable speed. Aside from building things, social relationship is *the* main reason to be in Second Life, so Barbary is thinking "how do I hold this together so the other person doesn't flee, so I can find things out and get oriented?" Meanwhile, Sixteenth-Century Guy is still puzzled by her name. So she explains again: " 'Barbary' is a name *from* a Shakespeare play, not a character *in* the play; that leaves me room to invent myself." He writes back, "You're in the play *now*."

His reply assumes (and affirms) a shared desire for unscripted access to the Renaissance. In this sim, that access unfolds in a dramatic *now* that, while deeply preoccupied with the sixteenth century, is expressly unlike the knowledge represented by a play text in that it is emergent and dynamic. Sixteenth-Century Guy invokes a governing metaphor for play in Second Life, that of populist theater. In the words of Linden Lab's vice president of product development, "People want to be *perceived as creative* by customizing their surroundings, to have their moments on the stage."[6] The subject of performance is the build, and the authority that matters in Second Life is the authority of those who build—who have, in Lockean terms, made the Renaissance their property by mixing their labor with it.[7] As Barbary observes, in Renaissance Island, this mode of propriety makes her academic training "not only superfluous, but potentially threatening to him; at the least it's socially disabling to me." And yet such fan relationships with the Renaissance legitimate (and, as Warner would remind us, animate) every aspect of our field.

II. The SLiterary Virtual Globe Theater

The SLiterary Shakespeare Company (SLSC) sponsors a more traditional invitation to "be in the play," but one that shows similar tensions between a populist ideal of a Shakespeare available to all and the propriety that results when you build what's felt to be an authentic Shakespearean space. This Globe hosts noninterpretive, nonconceptually complex Shakespeare similar to what one would find at the London Globe. At first glance, performances so conventional seem to miss the point of Second Life as an unscripted medium. Yet, as in Renaissance Island, the subject of performance here is the build, as much as the players. The theater is based on C. Walter Hodge's conjectural diagrams, scaled to fit avatars onstage and in the stalls.

Actors working in this Globe agree the architecture has a "special" feel. The conceits that gloss this specialness echo Linden Lab's claims for Second Life as a populist performance medium. Like the promotional clips for the Globe at Renaissance Island, the default position for the director's camera at the SLiterary Globe quotes the opening shots of Olivier's *Henry V:* with a "thatch zoom" that pulls the viewer from a panoramic long shot down into the center of the circling roof, to the stage.[8] Audience experience is similarly characterized by rotating pans of the stalls that stress our interaction and collectivity in this space. Notably, the same "stall pan" motif predominates in tourist footage of the New Globe in London: typically, the camera (video or cell phone) is positioned above the groundlings and pans across them, past the stage, circling around the bustling stalls.[9] As Peter Donaldson has observed, this rotational pan is a signature of first-person gaming, where it conveys autonomous player agency and choice.[10] For both actual and virtual Globe theaters, the motif embeds first-person agency in collective audition. As in the eighteenth century, one chooses to go to the theater here to see oneself and be seen with everyone else.

Despite this insistence on popular access and audience agency, a dominant feature of any sim is that it is owned—in the case of the

SLiterary Globe, owned by the designer, by virtue of the Lockean fictions that govern property relations here. This became clear in late 2008 when, like many brick-and-mortar playing companies, the SLiterary Shakespeare Company fell into conflict over resources. The cost of renting the four sims on which the Globe is built is not inconsiderable, and financial pressures triggered a debate over ownership, described by the designer as a "coup." Her sense of propriety in the build was so strong at the time that she preferred that the Globe be broken down to constitutive bits rather than sold to the company.

III. Foul Whisperings

In both Renaissance Island and the SLiterary Globe, a perspective that sees Shakespearean texts and environments in terms of a history of debates over authority and propriety—as our field has learned to do over the last several decades—puts one in direct conflict with their governing fictions. Worse, to enter these locales in the subject position of "the one who knows the history better" and who reads these claims critically is merely to introduce variations in the contest over what counts as authentically Renaissance or Shakespearean. This may be why both Barbary and I feel such relief and excitement when we discover "Foul Whisperings," a *Macbeth* installation that successfully breaks down oppositions between critical distance and immersive enthusiasm, fan and scholar, player and designer.[11] This sim was built collaboratively by a professor of digital media and education, a director, and a multimedia artist and producer, and funded by the New Media Consortium. Allusively rich, its associations range from Kurosawa's *Throne of Blood* to Janet Adelman. The sim is "dedicated to the exploration, adaptation and performance" of the play in ways that feel free of propriety and authorial presence.[12] No one resides here; all are invited to teach and learn. In other words, this is fandom for an academic Shakespearean. In "Foul Whisperings," one moves through a half dozen linked theatrical spaces, anchored in the play text and structured thematically: different scenes explore the uncanny agency of language, the play of light and dark, deception, human violence, horror. As with any good multimedia installation, meaning in these scenes is constituted immersively, by the person passing through them. That person is addressed variously as student, scholar, fan, historian, player, tourist, museum-goer, director, designer.

In several scenes, the sim uses the technical possibilities of Second Life to challenge our sense of control over meaning. Fragments of play text float unfixed through the landscape and audioscape, the lines unsexed—delivered in both male and female voices. Scale, distance, and direction dilate and contract in ways that are genuinely disorienting and spooky. In a series of tour puzzles, one walks down a telescoping pathway into entrapping darkness, or loses one's head. Or one wanders into a concrete Cobweb Forest, marked by the ghosts of Hiroshima, only to discover that returning were as tedious as going oe'r. In a chamber surrounded by scenes of modern torture and holocaust, reminiscent of Taymor's *Titus,* one finds oneself locked in a phantom battle. Follow a rose arbor, and the avenue gradually reveals itself to be governed by Lady Macbeth's command to "look like the innocent flower, yet be the serpent under it." As the roses resolve into ghostly hands, her words double and redouble, hissing around one's virtual feet.

In each scene, objects that look like the codex of *Macbeth* contain notecards, offering teacherly "provocations" to close-read passages of text, investigate historical contexts, and generate new material through writing or performance. The cards array multiple opportunities for engagement—formalist, aesthetic, historicist, theatrical, analytic, immersive—in ways that mutually reinforce rather than contest each other. In this symbolically rich environment, what is between the covers of a codex is revealed as dynamic, emergent, and constituted anew in each engagement by a reader/performer. There is even a place for iconic authorship here, represented as such and tucked away at the edge of the surf, so it will not affect your encounter with *Macbeth* before you approach the text in other ways.

Over a semester, a good course could do this work: arraying different ways of using, consuming, and re-creating Shakespeare's works, helping students explore and compare the different frameworks for thinking invested in each approach. With its distributed, user-generated builds, Second Life accelerates such a comparatist view and formalizes it—making this one of the better media we have now for surveying different modes of engagement with Shakespeare. In the process, it offers new opportunities for reading more expansively, finding ourselves in an array of subject positions from fan to expert.

IV. Small-node Shakespeare

Whether or not Shakespeareans embrace such virtual environments, we should internalize two cautions from them. The first is that what makes "Foul Whisperings" compelling to *me,* as a Shakespeare scholar, may be precisely that it offers what I already know and care about. When it unbalances me or reveals something new about *Macbeth,* it does so in ways that are consistent with modes of authority (historiography, performance, close reading, appropriation) that I already embrace. "Foul Whisperings" exists on the same platform as the other two sims explored here, but as of this writing no structures link them or bridge their disparate modes of knowing Shakespeare. Indeed, my relative comfort in this spooky sim invokes a concern at the heart of debates in new media studies about the trade-offs between extensibility, on the one hand, and audience fragmentation on the other. The phenomenon of building and inviting others into an elaborate literary simulation is a subset of a larger culture of participatory fandom and interactive audiences emerging online.[13] Does this proliferation of small-node formats enable "a range of social actors that would once have been excluded" from mass media, and offer "an opportunity for previously silenced voices to be heard"?[14] Or, as Dana Polan has worried, does the proliferation of multiple channels and platforms mean that "such voices simply disappear into their niche and resonate only lightly beyond their increasingly fragmented target audience"?[15] In this context, "Foul Whisperings" parses as a very small content niche (Shakespeare scholar-fans), the comfort of which is in direct proportion to its emptiness. For Polan, the proliferation of niches catering to individual desires and experiences threatens to destroy any possibility of a Gramscian "national-popular—a folk culture that would speak to citizens in a common or shared fashion." He concludes with the speculation that, "This might be the function of ideology today: not so much to offer a collective imaginary that everyone can be sutured into so much as to provide no sharing of positions and thereby push potential social actors back toward private passions that serve as little more than hobbies."

The second caution is that the excellence of this sim depends, finally, on scholarly expertise, not on crowd-sourcing or open collaboration. It is a teaching sim, after all, as well as an appreciation and a new media installation. In this respect its structures of authority are no different than those animating a good critical essay.

By contrast, Renaissance Island is a far more collaborative build and at the same time a far less rich experience, though it is closer to a Web 2.0 vision of crowd-sourced content. Rich in collaborators and yet impoverished in the intellectual payoffs and aesthetic insights their engagement offers, the sim reads, in Polan's context, like the work of private hobbyists. It may be more populated than "Foul Whisperings"; it may also be as closed to new ideas and growth.

The news that Shakespearean materials activate questions of ownership in an emerging media platform may be unsurprising, since appropriation and cultural property are long-standing concerns for Shakespeareans. Most of us are all too familiar with the weird, often antagonistic relationship between Shakespeare as the property of mass culture and academic Shakespeare. Yet Polan reminds us that for better and worse, niche cultures will not function as mass culture does. The deep but fragmented engagements offered by platforms like Second Life put keen pressure on the subject position familiar to our field: enemy of cultural capital, positioned to critique its invidious structures, yet professionally secured by their mass distribution of cultural values. Some of our works make it onto the virtual shelves in Second Life. Yet we still have to learn how Shakespeare scholarship can compete in the distributed arenas of cultural value fostered by user-generated environments. To plant deep roots in these content fields, we must grapple with multiple tasks: recognizing critical thinking in unfamiliar modes and locations, internalizing Polan's cautions and developing practices that engage crowd-sourcing, investing expertise in each user who builds the collaborative resources he or she will want to keep returning to. What those practices should look like is the conversation we now need to be pursuing as a field.

Notes

1. A good example is the King's College Visualisation Lab project, *Theatron 3*, discussed in Joff Chafer and Mark Childs, "The Impact of the Characteristics of a Virtual Environment on Performance: Concepts, Constraints and Complications." Paper delivered at ReLIVE08: Researching Learning in Virtual Environments, Open University, November 19–20, 2008.

2. Tom Boellstorff surveys these different social modes in *Coming of Age in Second Life* (Princeton: Princeton University Press, 2008).

3. Andrew Herman, Rosemary J. Coombe, and Lewis Kaye, "Your Second Life?" *Cultural Studies* 20 (2006): 201–2.

4. Michael Warner, "Uncritical Reading," in *Polemic: Critical or Uncritical,* ed. Jane Gallop (New York: Routledge, 2004), 15.

5. At latest visit, these included Stanley Wells, *Shakespeare & Co.* (2007), a host of biographies of monarchs and nobles, David Crystal's *Glossary* (2002), Duffin's songbook collection, and a homegrown manual on fencing.

6. C. R. Ondrejka, "Escaping the Gilded Cage: User Created Content and Building the Metaverse," *New York Law School Law Review* 49 (2005): 86. My emphasis.

7. John Locke, *Second Treatise of Government,* 11.5.27.

8. Compare the credit sequence in Laurence Olivier, dir., *Henry V* (1944) with the thatch zoom in "Renaissance Island Globe Grand Opening" (2007) USA. Machinima movie created by Bernadette Swanson (HVX Silverstar, at the Machinima Institute in Second Life).

9. Compare the presentation of audience and stalls in Olivier's credit sequence with the following: "Shakespeare's Globe Theater, London," the "pan-around" posted on YouTube by Joey Leake (aelfwine14), February 11, 2007, http://www.youtube.com/watch?v = Bv5uN-dzizI; Remi Kiranov, "The Globe" (2008) USA, screen shot posted December 19, Flickr.com, and Kirk Rutter, "The Globe Theater," video posted on YouTube July 30, 2007, http://www.youtube.com/watch?v = YWdTyIRemcE.

10. Peter Donaldson, "Game Space/Tragic Space: Julie Taymor's *Titus,*" in *A Companion to Shakespeare and Performance,* ed. Barbara Hodgdon and W.D. Worthen, (Cambridge: Blackwell, 2005).

11. See http://slurl.com/secondlife/Macbeth/44/54/54.

12. *Virtual Macbeth,* home page.

13. Henry Jenkins, "Quentin Tarantino's Star Wars? Digital Cinema, Media Convergence, and Participatory Culture," in *Rethinking Media Change: The Aesthetics of Transition,* ed. D. Thorburn and H. Jenkins (Cambridge: MIT University Press, 2003), 211–30.

14. John Sinclair, *Contemporary World Television* (London: British Film Institute, 2004), 5.

15. Dana Polan, " 'I Got Plenty of Nothing (and Nothing's Plenty for Me)': Television's Politics of Abundance," *Flow,* 2, no. 5 (May 27, 2005).

YouTube, Use, and the
Idea of the Archive

Lauren Shohet

"AFTER" SHAKESPEARE ON FILM come desktop digital interfaces that put film—and films of theatrical performances, digital video, shots from mobile cameras, and other related technologies—on our laptops. As our titular "after" encapsulates, these downloadable texts are chronologically secondary, ontologically derivative, and commercially aggressive. These video-sharing sites, paradigmatically YouTube, act as an archive (of Shakespearean performances, among many other things) that in some ways contrasts with conventional archives, but in other ways reveals their long-standing but under-recognized aspects. Etymologically, "archive" conveys not only origin, but spatial fixity: the building wherein primary documents are kept. We now find ourselves with different kinds of mobile archives that we access through cyberspace—YouTube and Early English Books Online (EEBO) alike—and can ask what difference this peripatetic access makes, as the memorial function of these notebook-accessible digital archives replaces spatial *lieux de mémoire* with environmental *milieux de mémoire.*[1] Derrida claimed that "there could be no archiving without . . . the archontic principle of legitimization, without criteria of classification and of hierarchization."[2] Technology seems alternatively to have amplified or to have run around Derrida's sine qua non of archival principles.[3] How do the uses that video-sharing sites sponsor—nonspecialist access, wild heterogeneity, fragmentation of samples, and temporal leveling—impact ways we imagine what archives are, how we use them, and how they use us? What uses can Shakespeareans and their students make of YouTube? And what might early modern scholars bring to analysis of emergent broadcast technologies?

Teaching *A Midsummer Night's Dream?* YouTube offers almost

four thousand clips, many of the "Act 2, scene 3 for Mr. Green's English Class" genre. Others show snippets of full-scale theatrical productions, commercial films, and far-flung adaptations. Some longer productions are available as well; the size of YouTube's upload allowance has changed over time, as has the response of copyright holders to unlicensed use, so that maximum length varies, but the norm remains under ten minutes.[4] The proliferation of student scenes suggests a particularly lively operation of Derrida's "archontic principle" of the archive: although governed by set principles of inclusion and hierarchy, the archive seeks to enlarge itself. YouTube's users continually post new clips to the archive, replay what thereby becomes a repertoire, and add new performances into the mix. Thus, the click of a mouse brings up not only staggeringly myriad student projects, but also such varied morsels as the 1935 Max Reinhardt Warner Brothers' studio film (in sixteen sub-ten-minute segments); seven minutes of Diana Rigg and Helen Mirren, plus a separate one-minute-fifty-eight-second segment of "a seminude Judi Dench" from Peter Hall's 1900 Royal Chake speare Company film; motley offerings—frequently the trailer— from the 1999 Michael Hoffman film; Mickey Mouse and Donald Duck playing Demetrius and Lysander on 1960s television; and a Levis 501 jeans commercial rather incoherently set to Titania's ode to Bottom. Browsing the playlist reveals that searching a Shakespearean play on YouTube—presumably a significant, perhaps primary, encounter for many of our students—yields an experience that is striking for its variety, fragmentation, and temporal leveling.

The force of this accretion tends in multiple directions, rather than neatly aligning democratized access with subversion (or recuperation), remediation with fidelity (or innovation).[5] On the one hand, YouTube's archive foregrounds use (what people might do with a scene) before recovery (what the scene is "supposed" to mean: what Robert Scholes calls the "secrethiddendeepermeaning" that is taken to be the privileged province of English teachers).[6] YouTube reveals how very many ways there are to perform a single Shakespearean scene. This multiplicity of interpretation intersects with a homogenization of interface: scenes of different historical, geographical, and rhetorical provenance are all equally accessible, and present themselves to the user on a playlist sorted by frequency of use, without other indexical hierarchy.[7] Likewise, YouTube's bias toward brevity, plus the delivery of all selections on the same screen, homogenizes forms by presenting viewers with studio-film segments, Royal Shakespeare Company scenes, and high-schoolers' dialogues in material encounters of similar duration and dimension. The clips can be ordered, reordered, and/or reshuffled according to the user's needs: the twelve-year-old Mickey Rooney of 1935 delivers a line of Puck's the instant after Mr. Green's twelfth-grader plays the same scene in 2007, the instant before Stanley Tucci in 1999. YouTube privileges use above origin in its models of ownership as well as organization: posters frequently ignore copyright, and sometimes directly attack proprietary assertions, as when the poster of the Donald and Mickey *A Midsummer Night's Dream* prophylactically announces, even before the summary description, "I DON'T OWN THIS SHORT, [*sic*] IT BELONGS TO DISNEY."[8]

But, contra assumptions that democratized participation necessarily subverts cultural hierarchies, it is often a very conventionally fetishized "Shakespeare" that authorizes this proliferation of uses. The myriad student scenes derive from performance assignments dependent upon Shakespeare's canonical place in compulsory schooling, and many are set in a pseudo-Tudor past, replete with vaguely empire-waisted gowns and men in tights, exalting a transhistorical simulacrum of pastness that vitiates the historical specificity that is required for most modes of rigorous analysis. The grand accretion of student scenes is interesting; most of the individual performances are not.

Possibilities for more robust engagement on the part of students and scholars alike come not from students' historical fidelity to details of the scenes, settings, or even language, but rather from the generic revelations sponsored by performance itself. The laptop- and lectern- availability of YouTube, as well as curated video sites like the exemplary Bardbox or the Folger Shakespeare Library YouTube channel, suggest that students may now be experiencing a reversal in the customary accessibility of drama-in-performance as opposed to printed drama. Watching scenes, and performing their own, embroils students in the generically precise—and historically accurate—phenomenon of Shakespearean drama as primarily performance texts. Digitally reproduced past events may not count as "performance" according to criteria central to performance theorists interested in the dynamic quiddities of embodied encounter.[9] But the differences between YouTube and live theater do not merely register loss; they also reveal alternative ways of thinking about performance based on different kinds of use. In its amenability to sampling, reposting, and especially remixing, YouTube troubles the distinction between dynamic "repertoire" and relatively stable "archive" by locating performance *in* re-use. Ekaterina Haskins notes that digital technologies generally blur this distinction: "digital memory, more than any other form of mediation, collapses the assumed distinction between modern 'archival' memory and traditional 'lived' memory by combining the function of storage and ordering on the one hand, and of presence and interactivity on the other."[10] This blurring of distance/storage and presence/use is not an innovation of digital technology, but rather inheres (in different proportions) in the range of ways that expressive forms catalog past uses. For instance, YouTube channels recall commonplace books, commenting on and transmitting performances when they use digital technology to remix the performances they sample, perhaps most commonly cueing a voice-over of professionally declaimed Shakespearean dialogue to original visuals, in the mold of music videos.[11]

Indeed, YouTube clips bring a variety of codex technologies to filmed performances. YouTube facilitates practices of cross-referencing, fast-forwarding, and replaying that allow students to work with performances in ways that scholars habitually work with texts. This moves performance history from a recondite scholarly province into a more public domain (suggesting that we prioritize teaching it: if students are going to practice performance history, it's best that they do it well). Moreover, the aggregation of past performances available on YouTube fosters historical consciousness even when individual student performances do not. YouTube clips work as what Bruno Latour calls "immutable mobiles": mobile, they render 1920 as readily at hand as 2007, as YouTubers post them across the globe; immutable, their content remains intact.[12] YouTube puts specific performances into the relative stability of the "archive," as opposed to mutable "repertoire."[13] Although they are available for remixing and reuse, the clips that link past and present visibly belong to different eras. The broadcast technologies that make this intact content available to receivers in different times and places enable viewers to recognize their distance from the performance context, sponsoring historical consciousness—just as Goody and Watt argued of the advent of alphabetic technology—in the face of the innate evanescence of theatrical events.[14] Thus, even as students mine YouTube's capabilities to "broadcast *themselves*" in ways that vitiate historical difference, they also use it for *other-*

broadcasting, retrieving performances from days long past, in ways that bring hard nuggets of alterity before viewers' eyes.

Some of these past performances were very difficult to find, usually due to copyright disputes or commercial unviability, before the advent of YouTube. We now can watch and teach the storied but rarely accessible 1936 WPA Federal Theater Project *Macbeth,* directed by Orson Welles and set in Haiti with an African American cast, or Pasolini's 1968 *Othello* adaptation *Che cosa sono le nuvole.* Another previously hard-to-find Shakespearean performance that has enjoyed hundreds of thousands of views on YouTube exemplifies a way for YouTube Shakespeare to sponsor rigorous historical work in the classroom, even as it violates historical propriety, with a scene that is neither present-day nor specifically past: a 1964 BBC program of the Beatles performing the mechanicals' play from *A Midsummer Night's Dream.*[15] This clip presents an anachronistic dynamic that teaches history not through fidelity, but through the ways it involves receivers in performance relationships appropriate to early-modern drama. Linguistic and bardolatrous barriers to enjoying comic scenes present a continual frustration in teaching Shakespearean drama; Paul Rogers's hilarious, and plausibly Elizabethan, Bottom in the 1968 Peter Hall Royal Shakespeare Company film elicits few chuckles without extensive teacherly intervention. The Beatles, by contrast, are exuberantly anachronistic despite the scene's pseudo-Tudor properties. Visibly themselves at the same time they don their Shakespearean roles, the Beatles' mechanicals thematize seams between the players' offstage identities and their assigned roles. For students, this transliterates popular elements of Elizabethan theatergoing. Wes Folkerth has argued that, in 1964, the Beatles' performance worked counterhistorically, in counterpoint to pious Shakespearean quatercentenary commemorations: "the Beatles' television skit anticipates a large-scale transformation in the forms of adoration commonly associated with Shakespeare in contemporary mass culture, from the august object of bardolatry to a figure more our contemporary, like the Beatles themselves."[16] But in 2008, this plays rather differently: not so much making Shakespeare our contemporary (the Beatles are not our students' contemporaries either) as involving students in the repertoire in a way that places them in historical problematics of the Shakespearean theater. Paul McCartney is clearly his 1964 self as he clumsily winks at the camera; a player wanders out of character to wonder if a local pub is still in business. Embroiling students in the dynamic of the canny celebrity clown paradoxically lets them access Shake-spearean drama as popular culture in ways more homologous to early modern experience, if not historically authentic, than the piety and unfamiliarity that make Shakespeare into elite text rather than plebeian play. Here, anachronism itself foregrounds tradition as use, rather than as recovery, allowing audiences to access historicity, if not history.

*   *   *

In some ways, YouTube works as the dark double of other archives: its principles of selection are determined entirely by users and uses, and at present it has no mechanism for the erasure that may be half the archive's task.[17] That is, YouTube is specifically haunted by the inherent archival threat of "uncontrollable textual proliferation . . . a discourse without order or limits" that "stifle[s] thought beneath the weight of accumulating discourse."[18] The user-curated YouTube foregrounds the morphology of attention that subtends all archives: whatever principle of collection might catalyze the archive, attention shapes the hierarchy of needs that makes data visible. The most used items in traditional archives are the most indexed, and hence the most retrievable, whether explicitly (the more readers page a certain item, the more search terms are found to attach to it) or implicitly (the most cited items become part of a discourse, stimulating further readings, which reveal more uses for the source). "Archive" generally entails teleology, an implication of matter gathered for a reason, but archival researchers know that archives (plural, as used) are more heterogeneous and more accidental than "the archive" (singular, as imagined) connotes. The history of archival research is one of previously trivial items abruptly becoming significant under changing analytic regimes—regime change sponsored by those very items, as they catch the eye of a researcher who collaborates with the item to forge a new critical paradigm. YouTube registers this way that use carves meaning, extending the archive both materially (adding new items) and conceptually (multiply indexing existing items).

YouTube distinctively promises to replace traditional one-to-many commercial broadcast interfaces with many-to-many broadcasting: "Broadcast yourself," its motto invites. The lure of unmediated access is a dream we entertain about archives generally. Archives are curated by professionals who filter acquisitions and evaluate retention, and they often are built upon collections assembled for a particular proprietor's interests. Yet archives also sponsor a fantasy of heterogeneous authenticity because their copiousness promises an unfiltered density of data. We long for them to yield not only play scripts, but also laundry lists and bills and pins. We imagine traditional archives to be motivated and ordered, but in practice, researchers often find the spandrel—the unconsidered by-product that, once constituted, offers itself for elaboration—the most enticing element of the archive.

This crossing of intent and use is only one chiastic element that early modern scholars can recognize in relationships between archival practice and YouTube, and that our field might contribute to the nascent (excellent) anthropology of YouTube.[19] Broadcasting and archiving also operate chiastically. At our historical moment on the cusp of postprint culture, to publish is to archive (our articles resting in the unvisited bound-journals room); conversely, the proliferation of electronic archives means that to archive, today, is to broadcast. Moreover, although archiving ostensibly preserves a text inviolable for later consultation in its uncontaminated state, modes of use and even categories of storage dynamically alter the shape and meaning of these texts (materially, conservation practices of one era are considered radical deformations in another; conceptually, trivia become exampla). When archiving preserves information for potential future broadcast, YouTube users find that an ephemeral broadcast—perhaps a teenager filing a social lament—is preserved irretrievably in the archive, any single archival act of downloading preserving forever the possibility of future broadcast.

In Michael Wesch's ethnography of YouTube, a participant-observer muses that the YouTube video-logger (vlogger) speaks "as if to everyone," when in fact "there is no one there."[20] When vlogging on YouTube, before "broadcasting [one's] self," one must produce a self through the fiction that the metal eye of the camera is an other ready to engage. Or, more precisely, one produces the self through faith in the technology's capacity to shrink time and space after the solitary moment of soliloquy: the vlogger creates social relationships once others receive the posting and, usually, respond to it. At the moment of production, however, reception is only potential, and the technological mediation required to bring together self and other (present and future, Kansas and the Ivory Coast) is nakedly undeniable: a camera hovers before the speaker, demanding speech. While posting preexisting clips might soften this encounter somewhat, the technological mediation required to call up, replay, and often remix the archive remains significant. Researchers also use archives to create social relationships: we hope to speak with the dead (homologous to the vlogger's "conversations" with "others," always in the optative and the future) or to use the dead to speak with one another (homologous to YouTube replaying, remixing, and posting). Our own efforts are likewise heavily mediated by the technologies and institutions on which we depend for access. Perhaps we too easily forget these mediations, equating digitized access with material encounter, bracketing out the institutional investments that shape the sources we can access.[21] If we early modern archival scholars can find ourselves dismayed by the naive undifferentiation of what counts as "Shakespeare" among YouTube postings, perhaps we have something to learn from the relative media sophistication these same amateur fans bring to understanding the intertwinings of medium, archive, and use.

Notes

1. Pierre Nora, "Between Memory and History: Les Lieux de Mémoire," *Representations* 26 (1989): 7–25.

2. Jacques Derrida, *Archive Fever: A Freudian Impression,* trans. Prenowitz (Chicago: University of Chicago Press, 1995), 40.

3. Twenty years ago, Leah Marcus contrasted the "chatter of cyberspace" to the "silence of the archive," shrewdly remarking the ways that "the noise of cyberspace reproduces the conditions of early modernity more closely than the hush of the library can." We now are in a position to extend Marcus's questions about "hearing" archives into questions about *using* them ("The Silence of the Archive and the Noise of Cyberspace," in *The Renaissance Computer: Knowledge Technology in the First Age of Print,* ed. Neil Rhodes and Jonathan Sawday [London: Routledge, 2000], 18–28).

4. When in the fall of 2008 YouTube began offering copyright holders the option of having unlicensed fan clips pulled, or authorizing YouTube to run advertisements alongside them, the vast majority opted to remain posted.

5. The "democratization" of access enabled by YouTube (like EEBO) must, of course, be taken with the caveat that it applies to only one side of the digital divide (and for EEBO, only for those with institutional subscriptions).

6. Scholes, *Textual Power: Literary Theory and the Teaching of English* (New Haven: Yale University Press, 1985).

7. Use also sponsors YouTube's related functions of commentary and sorting with playlists that enable users to evaluate clips and channels allowing users to link their own selection of clips for subscribers.

8. "A Mouse's Tales Cartoon," YouTube, www.youtube.com/watch?v = WMI AGXDyN-s.

9. Peggy Phelan, *Unmarked: The Politics of Performance* (London: Routledge, 1993).

10. Ekaterina Haskins, "Between Archive and Participation: Public Memory in a Digital Age," *Rhetoric Society Quarterly* 37 (2007): 401–2.

11. For this understanding of commonplace books as exemplary instances of reading-writing, see Scott Black, *Of Essays and Reading in Early-Modern Britain* (New York: Palgrave, 2006).

12. Latour, *Science in Action: How to Follow Scientists and Engineers Through Society* (Cambridge, MA: Harvard University Press, 1987). The geographical and temporal collage that YouTube presents daily is truly astonishing. One YouTube hit of September 2009 (which then enjoyed over 300,000 hits by mid-September, and over 400,000 by early October) replayed a Kaddish from a Normandy battle-field of 1944; another recorded a former shepherd from Tajikistan who has become well known for his performances of Bollywood songs. Paul Vitello, "A Soldier's Voice Rediscovered," *New York Times,* September 18, 2009; Ellen Barry, "On Web, Storefront Crooner from Tajikistan is a Star," *New York Times,* September 11, 2009.

13. On the distinction between archive and repertoire, as well as nuancing of the opposition, see Diana Taylor, *The Archive and the Repertoire: Performing Cultural Memory in the Americas* (Durham, NC: Duke University Press, 2003).

14. Jack Goody and Ian Watt, "The Consequences of Literacy" [1968], repr. in *Perspectives on Literacy* ed. Kingten, Kroll, and Rose, 3–27 (Carbondale: University of Southern Illinois Press, 1988).

15. The BBC refused Wes Folkerth this clip in 2000. See "Roll over Shakespeare: Bardolatry meets Beatlemania in the Spring of 1964," *Journal of American and Comparative Cultures* 23 (2000): 75–80.

16. Ibid., 75.

17. Chartier, *Inscription and Erasure: Literature and Written Culture from the Eleventh to the Eighteenth Century,* trans. Arthur Goldhammer (Philadelphia: University of Pennsylvania Press, 2007).

18. Ibid., vii. Voss and Werner remark that "the archive's dream of perfect order is disturbed by the nightmare of its random, heterogeneous, and often unruly contents." Voss and Werner, "Poetics of the Archive," *Studies in the Literary Imagination* 32 (1999): ii.

19. See especially Michael Wesch, "An Anthropological Introduction to YouTube" (2007), www.youtube.com/watch?v = TPAO-lZ4_hU; Wesch, "The Machine is (Changing) Us" (2009), www.youtube.com/watch?v = X6eMdMZezAQ; Barry Wellman, "Connecting Community: On- and Off-Line," *Contexts* 3 (2004): 22–28.

20. Wesch, "Anthropological Introduction."

21. On consequences of remediating archives, see Meredith L. McGill, "Re-mediating Whitman," *PMLA* 122 (2007): 1592–96; on institutional shaping of both archives and fantasies about archives, see Suzanne Keen, *Romances of the Archive in Contemporary British Fiction* (Toronto: University of Toronto Press, 2001).

Looking for Mr. Goodbard: Shakespeare Films as Countermemory

Courtney Lehmann

> Yes, in the old days people never show their paintings. . . .
> Now we want to show our paintings to everybody. . . .
> We want to tell people that this is a most important place
> to us. This is land! They have taken it away from us
> and they didn't even think about it! This is the reason
> why we want to show the world our Dreamtime culture. . . .
> They are probably starting to think back now on what has
> been happening to Aboriginal people. So this *Possum
> Dreaming* is not just a beautiful wall in The [Sydney] Opera
> House—it will make people think.
>
> —Michael Jagamara Nelson

> I believe we make universal stories for the world, it [the film]
> has an Australian voice, and to maintain that voice you must
> be connected to your land.
>
> —Baz Luhrmann, quoted in Goeff Andrews, *The Guardian*

THE FINAL PICTURE in what is now known as "The Red Curtain Trilogy," *Moulin Rouge!* (2001) is the film that evinces the above comment from Luhrmann, long before he *really* made a film about being connected to his land in the epic *Australia* (2008). The "Australian voice" to which Luhrmann refers is, of course, a *visual* voice, comprised of his trademark cinematographic language. Due to its manic energy, complex tropes, and apparent originality, this language has long been the subject of intrigue and inquiry on behalf of scholars and critics. When confronted, the director is quick to acknowledge that he is perennially "stealing from culture all over the place to write a code so that very quickly the audience can swing from the lowest possible comedy moment to the highest possible tragedy with a bit of music in the middle."[1] Hence, if the infamous raison d'être of the Phillip Henslowe character in *Shakespeare in Love* (John Madden, 1998) is to produce "comedy—and a bit with a dog," then Luhrmann's cinematographic "code" may be easily summarized as "comedy, tragedy—and 'a bit of music.'" In fact, this is precisely the formula he employs to varying degrees in all three of the "Red Curtain" films, *Strictly Ballroom* (1992), *William Shakespeare's Romeo + Juliet* (1996), and *Moulin Rouge!* But when pressed to elucidate—more precisely—the source of his "cinematic language," this self-proclaimed "culture thief" tends toward mystification. Although Luhrmann readily identifies Shakespearean theater and Hindi cinema as the dual progenitors of his unique "code," or, in his exact words, the "theatricalized cinematic form that we now call the Red Curtain,"[2] he does not so much as hint at the source of the "Australian voice"—let alone its connection to "the land"—which is so integral to the filmic vision he articulates above. In fact, it is not until the film *Australia* that he guardedly insinuates the key to this code in the film's opening disclaimer, which reads: "Aboriginal and Torres Strait Islander viewers should exercise caution when watching this film as it may contain images and voices of deceased persons."

Set against a black screen, this "fine print" has much to tell us about the only film in Luhrmann's oeuvre that does *not* have a connection to his homeland—*William Shakespeare's Romeo + Juliet*—while simultaneously intimating why the "genre" of the Shakespeare film may have its brightest future in the past.[3] Though several of my colleagues have pronounced the Shakespearean film "dead"—just as others have declared the same fate for cinema itself in an outpouring of memento mori for 35- and 70-millimeter[4]— Luhrmann's adaptation is not just any dinosaur wandering through the long-gone graveyard known as the nineties. It is, rather, the highest-grossing Shakespeare film of all time, as well as a changeling that has morphed into more than ten different "special editions" on DVD—with the latest version released in 2007. As a film that anticipates the "death of cinema" while simultaneously offering a template for employing Shakespeare adaptations as a form of "countermemory," Luhrmann's *Romeo + Juliet* is uniquely situated to comment on the debate over film's future. Countermemory, in Foucault's words, is "a transformation of history into a totally different form of time."[5] For Australia's Aboriginal and Torres Strait Islander population, this counterhistory is known as the "Dreamtime," which, in perfect keeping with Luhrmann's "red

curtain" formula, is the story of how the ancestors " 'sang' the universe into being so as to make it consubstantial with themselves."[6]
This, I will argue, is the unavowed source of Luhrmann's cinematic
language in *Romeo + Juliet.*

                          *   *   *

Although I am not willing to concede the "end" or "death" of
cinema-proper in the age of Second Life, YouTube, Virtual Reality
(VR), and digital multimedia, I am willing to entertain the possibility that "film" as we know it may soon be relegated to the status of
a cultural artifact. Hence, for the purposes of this forum, I will treat
Romeo + Juliet as such—not as the cultural marker of a then-emer-
gent teensploitation genre, but ethnographically, in the Foucal-
dian sense, by undertaking a "search for descent" that "disturbs
what was previously considered immobile; it fragments what was
thought unified; it shows the heterogeneity of what was imagined
consistent with itself."[7] In an earlier essay on Luhrmann's *William
Shakespeare's Romeo | Juliet,* titled "Strictly Shakespeare?" I un-
dertook a similar approach to this film at the level of textual origins, discerning therein a counterhistory of resistance to the
tragedy embedded in Shakespeare's play. In so doing, however, I
found that Luhrmann's adaptation became inescapably trapped in
a web of allusions to *Shakespeare's* principal source, Arthur
Brooke, as well as even earlier articulations of the "Romeo and Juliet" legend from Matteo Bandello and Luigi Da Porto.[8] Others,
such as Alfredo Michel Modenessi and Peter S. Donaldson, have
used *William Shakespeare's Romeo + Juliet* to undertake rather
different quests for origins; Modenessi explores the distinctly Mex-
ican influences on the film (based on its location shooting in Mexico City and environs), while Donaldson discerns images that
invoke uniquely Australian (non-Aboriginal) traditions such as the
annual gay Mardi Gras parade in Sydney.[9] No one, however, has
employed this film in its implicit future-anterior mode—as a crystal ball, that is, into the distant past that *will have been* by the time
we catch up with it—for in so doing, we find that countermemory
keeps the Shakespeare film alive as a moving palimpsest, if only by
exposing film itself, like Foucault's "author," as its own "other."[10]

                          *   *   *

Though we have long ceased to concern ourselves with the idea
of authorial (or auteurial) convention, it is, nevertheless, important

to establish that Luhrmann's relationship to Aboriginal culture is at once personal and political—before and after his creation of *Romeo + Juliet*. For example, most recently, in conjunction with *Moulin Rouge!* Luhrmann produced a platinum-selling record, the proceeds of which went directly to what he bluntly describes as "the Aboriginal cause in Australia."[11] Likewise, during the planning stages of *Romeo + Juliet,* Luhrmann orchestrated the reelection campaign of Australian prime minister Paul Keating (Labour), whose political agenda included the restitution of land to the nation's indigenous peoples, as well as public acknowledgment of the years of "social death" to which this population had been subject (formerly 100 percent of the population, the Aborigines and Torres Strait Islanders now constitute less than 2.6 percent, based on more than two hundred years of separating indigenous children from their families). But the most provocative connection between Luhrmann and "the Aboriginal cause" occurred well before *Romeo + Juliet,* when he directed *La Boheme* in 1990 for the Sydney Opera House. Here, in Australia's most famous building, Luhrmann would have had ongoing encounters with an enormous wall mural painted by Aboriginal artist Michael Jagamara Nelson, titled *Possum Dreaming* (1987–88). Although Luhrmann has never acknowledged a debt to this work, the significance of the Dreamtime creation story it engages has not been lost on astute observers, who recognize that the subject of the painting is nothing less than "star-crossed" or, as Vivian Johnson puts it, "skin-crossed" lovers:

> Down the long central axis of the painting [i]s a line of
> large concentric circles, the campsites of the fleeing
> possum lovers, flanked on either side by long double arcs—
> the impressions left by their bodies lying next to one another
> and close to the fire for warmth. . . . The themes of love,
> transgression, retribution and death which dominate the
> Mawarriji Possum Love Story depicted here could not have
> been more appropriate for the painting's intended setting
> in the foyer of the Opera [House], for what libretto does
> not revolve around these same drives and outcomes?[12]

According to the Dreamtime narrative pertaining to Nelson's personal history, the painting is a representation of "star-crossed lovers" whose dead bodies make impressions in the earth, and, in so doing, create the Mawarriji Hills of Nelson's birthplace. Hence, in this culturally specific context, art imitates land and land, in turn, imitates life, that is, the ancestry detailed in the Dreamtime. Framed by the bodily impressions of the lovers, the concentric circles that figure so prominently in *Possum Dreaming* not only represent campsites where the lovers convene, but also places where rival clans clash, evocative of the Capulet and Montague feud. Still another "genealogy" of the concentric circles (particularly given the rampant use of blue paint in and around them) is their function as "water holes"—a site of sustenance and secrecy for the doomed lovers. Water plays precisely this role in Luhrmann's film—as the lovers' medium of courtship, commitment, and cover—the latter occurring when Romeo and Juliet plunge beneath the water of the Capulet pool to avoid the surveillance cameras. Early in the film, Romeo and Juliet will be shown in parallel scenes with their heads submerged in water, as the camera is positioned to "look" at them from the bottom up. Appropriately, Luhrmann has the lovers meet through opposing sides of a fish tank, playfully flirting with each other between the fleeting fish. The Capulet pool, in addition to providing camouflage, is the site of the lovers' initial exchange of vows; and, in the final montage that concludes the film-proper, the camera freezes on Romeo and Juliet kissing underwater, as if it were, paradoxically, the locus of their resurrection—already hinted at in the "sea" of neon blue crosses that is their final resting place. Indeed, Luhrmann himself is at a loss for words when confronted about the significance of water for the lovers; he can only borrow a desperate cliché from *West Side Story* to explain that it represents "their 'there's a place for us' moments."[13] As we will see, this loss for words is exactly what I would refer to as an example of the aboriginal "voice" in *Romeo + Juliet,* a locus of the strange supplementarity or " + " that marks the spot where traditional communication fails. In other words, what I will assay here is the point at which *extra*textual dialects—languages that are not necessarily predicated on words—prevail as representative of the "Aboriginal cause."[14]

Thus, what is so distinctive about this "discursive" terrain in both the Dreamtime story told by Nelson's painting and the Romeo and Juliet legend featured in Luhrmann's film is the dance it performs between disclosure and secret. Luhrmann's cinematic language functions in precisely this fashion—in his own words, as a "code"—a "genre" of communication that is predicated on some form of constitutive exclusion. Aboriginal dialects are similarly coded. In the first place, built into the very structure of their language are two versions of the first person, as well as parallel versions of the dual and plural form. Based on *inflection*—an "extra-diegetic" register that exceeds words—speaking to oneself, another individual, or a group may call for language that excludes others, including, paradoxically, the person to whom one is speaking. These linguistic features are often referred to as "mother-in-law" tongues, functioning as a means of establishing insider communities even in public spaces. (A classic, easily accessible example of this practice is the "reunion" scene that concludes the film *Rabbit-Proof Fence* [Phillip Noyce, 2002], or, somewhat less powerfully, the scene involving the "half-caste's" taming of the stampede in Luhrmann's own *Australia*.) "Code-switching," as John B. Haviland has shown, is essential to Australian Aboriginal communication and to self-disclosure in particular. In his study, Haviland shows how the articulatory senses of sight and sound effectively change places in Aboriginal autobiographical narratives, which reconstruct ancestry and identity from *seeing the voices* of relatives in the land and its silent recitation of their stories.[15]

Naturally, film demands the cultivation of a similar faculty, one that "hears" through "seeing," as the spectator attempts to make sense of both the spoken and visual language. In classical narrative cinema, sight and sound are synchronized, both literally and semantically. Luhrmann's films do not diverge significantly from this formula, for the diegesis is underscored by a sound track and complemented by imagery. And, yet, there is something so insistent about his camera—the sense that there is something more to say, indeed, a kind of surplus suggested by the reoccurring (+) image in *Romeo + Juliet*—that cannot be reconciled with or reduced to the story that the film ostensibly tells. In point of fact, when pressed to describe the camerawork employed in this film, Luhrmann cannot help but lapse into superlatives, converting the traditional close-up into "super-macro-slam-zooms," a simple fade or wipe into "360-degree blurs," jump cuts into "lightning cuts," and a standard tracking shot into "static super-wide shots."[16]

Space constraints do not allow here for a detailed reading of what we might think of as the "*geo*political unconscious" of Luhrmann's film; however, I would liken Luhrmann's frequent use of fireworks—another instance of *wordless* communication—to the "dance machines" of Torres Strait Islanders, machines that employ the image of exploding stars to represent the rise and set of the Southern Cross constellation, while conveying more sacred meanings to "insider communities." Indeed, the figure of the cross itself, used relentlessly throughout *Romeo + Juliet,* has multiple valences that have yet to be considered in this context. In addition to being a sign of excess, the cross functions powerfully in Aboriginal art, both as a symbol and as a technique. On an obvious level, the cross or plus sign is religious, invoking the brutal proselytism that led nearly half of all Aboriginal children to be violently torn from their families and forced into missions, where they would be converted to Christianity and groomed for "assimilation" into white culture as domestic servants, among other positions requiring menial labor. On another level, however, this quintessentially Western symbol betrays more subversive, indigenous meanings. Banned from representing their own symbolic traditions, Aboriginal artists used techniques such as cross-hatching and dot splatters to create paintings that "utter" one story to outsider communities while conveying an entirely different meaning—beneath the palimpsestic layers—to "insider communities." So, too, in Luhrmann's film, the cross functions both traditionally, as a symbol of religious devotion, and iconoclastically, appearing on guns and knives that underscore the violence of the colonial mission.

*   *   *

The search for origins, from Foucault's perspective, "is directed to 'that which was already there,' the image of a primordial truth fully adequate to its nature." "However," Foucault adds, "if the genealogist *listens to history,* he finds that . . . at the historical beginning of things is not the inviolable identity of their origin; it is *the dissension of other things.*"[17] In listening to the disparate histories embedded in Baz Luhrmann's *Romeo + Juliet,* I "see" both Luhrmann-as-auteur and "William Shakespeare" as "author" trumped by the silent dissent of a distinctly Aboriginal voice. This voice is most conspicuously registered in Luhrmann's unique treatment of natural land "marks" in this film—water and, even more explicitly, "Sycamore Grove." If, as Foucault observes, genealogy "is thus situated within the articulation of the body and history," and "[i]ts task is to expose a body totally imprinted by history and the process of history's destruction of the body,"[18] then "the body," for the purposes of this analysis, is "the land": the "voice" through which both Luhrmann and Australia's indigenous peoples relay their stories.

A phrase that implies lush vegetation, Sycamore Grove in Luhr-

mann's film is not a forest but a beach. Appropriately, for the indigenous population, sand is the locus of ground paintings that mark the "ceremonial 'sites' . . . linking people and places with stories and songs."[19] So, too, for Luhrmann, the burned-out cinema of Sycamore Grove that rises from the sand is a place where a ceremony for the "death of cinema" is daily enacted by shots like the one above that produce the very provocative image of a movie-house with a giant hole in the middle. This structure, in other words, is defined by negative space. Like the circular dots in Aboriginal paintings that hide the sacred images from Westerners and other "outsider communities," this circular void operates on a number of levels as a locus of cathexis. But the result is not a straightforward "moving picture," for by creating a space for projection *inward,* Luhrmann effectively reverses the ontology of cinematic production, envisioning the "death of cinema" as a violent act of implosion in a future that, paradoxically, has already come to pass. In so doing, Luhrmann invokes the disequilibrium of the "future-anterior," or, the uncanny presence of *"what will have been."* Importantly, as Sylvia Kleinert and Margo Neale write, "[t]he indigenous experience of time is not linear: rather it is multi-layered, expanding in an ever-lengthening time frame categorized—in Western thought—as, 'past', 'present', and 'future'"—or, in the words of W. E. H. Stanner, "everywhen."[20] Luhrmann's Sycamore Grove thus functions as space where what is "now showing" is counter-memory, for what we see in this image is what was already there, namely, an allusion to the most sacred natural landmark for Australia's Aboriginal population: Uluru, known by non-Aboriginal Australians as Ayers Rock, which became permanently renamed *what it already was*—"Uluru"—when the landmark was "officially" handed back to the Aborigines in 1985.

In the extremely popular commemorative poster, Uluru, eerily akin to Luhrmann's bizarre conception of Sycamore Grove, is defined by negative space—a reminder of the historical implosion of Australia's indigenous peoples, as well as an allusion to the forcible silencing of the Dreamtime story "voiced" by the giant rock. In fact, the artist (radical screen-printer Chips Mackinolty), is known for playing with this type of imagery—along with its future-anterior implications—most memorably in his exhibit, with Therese Ritchie, titled *If you see this exhibition you'll know we have been murdered* (1998). This literal speech-act, like the Uluru poster and the burned-out specter of Sycamore Grove, tells stories about the "Ab-

original cause" that subsume the "now" in "what will have been," forcing us to find "disparity," as Foucault reminds us, in memory, or, better put, *counter*memory. But the deaths that scream from both spaces—Sycamore Grove and Uluru—are, oddly enough, brought back to life by the specter of spontaneous graffiti inscribed at the bottom of the poster, which, with the repeated use of a single sign (+), tell us that there is *more, much more,* to be gained from the Shakespeare film when it is wanted, dead or alive, as a means of listening to history.

Notes

1. See Geoff Andrew's interview with Luhrmann in the *Guardian* at http://www.guardian.co.uk/film/2001/sep/07/2.
2. "Quotations," http://www.imdb.com/name/nm0525303/bio.
3. I place the term "genre" in quotation marks because Richard Burt and Scott Newstok contend in this forum that "the Shakespeare film" does not warrant the status of being its own genre; I disagree.

4. See, for instance, Timothy Murray's entire volume of *Wide Angle* devoted to the death of cinema, especially his lead essay, "By Way of Introduction: Digitality and the Memory of Cinema, or, Bearing the losses of the Digital Code," *Wide Angle* 21 (1999): 2–27. See also Jon Lewis, ed., *The End of Cinema as We Know It* (New York: New York University Press, 2001).

5. This is literally Foucault's definition of "countermemory" in Douglas Bouchard, ed., *Language, Counter-Memory, Practice* (Ithaca: Cornell University Press), 160.

6. John Morton, "Aboriginal Religion Today," in *The Oxford Compantion to Aboriginal Art and Culture*, ed. Sylvia Kleinert and Margo Neale, 11 (Oxford: Oxford University Press, 2000).

7. Foucault, *Language*, 147.

8. See Courtney Lehmann, *Shakespeare Remains: Theater to Film, Early Modern to Postmodern* (Ithaca: Cornell University Press, 2002).

9. See Modenessi's, "(Un)doing the Book 'without Verona walls': A View from the Receiving End of Baz Luhrmann's *William Shakespeare's Romeo + Juliet*," in *Spectacular Shakespeare: Critical Theory and Popular Cinema*, ed. Courtney Lehmann and Lisa S. Starks, 62–85 (Madison: Fairleigh Dickinson University Press, 2002), and Peter S. Donaldson's "'In Fair Verona': Media, Spectacle, and Performance in *William Shakespeare's Romeo + Juliet*," in *Shakespeare After Mass Media*, ed. Richard Burt, 59–82 (New York: Palgrave, 2002).

10. There are numerous examples in Foucault's essay, "What is an Author?" that expose the erasure of the authors based on the succession of another idea—for instance, when they "clea[r] a space for the introduction of elements other than their own. . . ." (132).

11. See Geoff Andrew's interview.

12. Vivien Johnson, *Michael Jagamara Nelson* (Sydney: Craftsman House, 1997), 79.

13. A much lengthier discussion of this topic appears in Lehmann, *Shakespeare Remains*, chapter 4.

14. I am citing Worthen's "Drama, Performance, Performativity," *PMLA* (1998): 1093–1107. W. B. Worthen has read the ubiquitous cross or "plus" sign as a source of negation—of "what the performance is not, what no performance can be: Shakespeare's *Romeo and Juliet*" (1104), by arguing that the plus sign "makes visible what most performances work to conceal: that dramatic performance, like all other performance, far from originating in the text, can only cite its textual 'origins' with an additive gesture, a kind of ' + '" (1104).

15. See John B. Haviland's brilliant essay, "'That was the Last Time I Seen Them, and No More': Voices through Time in Australian Aboriginal Autobiography," *American Ethnologist* 18 (1991): 331–61.

16. See Baz Luhrmann and Craig Pearce's screenplay, in *William Shakespeare's Romeo + Juliet: The Contemporary Film, The Classic Play* (New York: Bantam Doubleday Dell, 1996).

17. Foucault, *Language*, 142.

18. Ibid., 148.

19. See http://www.fireworksgallery.com.au/Artists/MNJ/MNJ.htm.

20. Preface to *The Oxford Companion to Aboriginal Art and Culture*, ed. Sylvia Kleinert and Margo Neale, v–ix. (Oxford: Oxford University Press, 2001).

Certain Tendencies in Criticism of Shakespeare on Film

RICHARD BURT AND SCOTT L. NEWSTOK

> Sovereign is he who decides on the exception.
> —Carl Schmitt, *Political Theology*

> The more precisely the empirical is investigated
> as extreme, the more profoundly it will be penetrated.
> The concept takes its point of departure [*Ausgehen*]
> in the extreme.
> —Walter Benjamin, *The Origin of the German Tragic Drama*

I. Specters of Shakespeare and Film Histories

> I am rewriting Shakespeare . . . The wretched
> fellow has left out the most marvelous things
> —Early French filmmaker Ferdinand Zecca

WHILE THE OCCASION HERE is to contemplate "After Shakespeare on Film," we are perhaps not yet done with "Shakespeare *on* Film." In addition to the resurgence of film adaptations that began with Kenneth Branagh's *Henry V* in 1989, subsequent Shakespearean film criticism managed to gain much wider currency in part because of the convergence of New Historicism and cultural studies in the 1980s and '90s. The analysis of Shakespeare and film as a legitimate field of study under the umbrella of Shakespeare studies has had many advantages. Yet a longer view of the history of Shakespeare studies and film studies reveals a forgetting of their mutually constitutive origins. As a professional field in US academia, film studies itself in the 1960s and '70s often found its advent in English departments, an institutional fact residually manifested

today by the presence of film studies professors in such departments, or by film studies programs that first emerged from literature
programs.[1] More specifically, it was often Shakespeare professors
who launched such courses.[2] Indeed, a number of scholars who
have since published widely in film studies were trained during
graduate school in medieval or early modern literature (Michael
Anderegg, Leo Braudy, Timothy Murray, Kaja Silverman, and
Linda Williams, to name a few). It is telling that the first edition of
Mast and Cohen's influential anthology of *Film Theory and Criticism* (1974) included a section devoted to "Shakespeare and Film";
it is further symptomatic that these essays were dropped from subsequent editions.[3]

By calling up this twinned, spectral history of Shakespeare and
film, we call attention to certain tendencies for Shakespeare to disappear in film studies and for film studies to disappear in Shakespeare film criticism. Shakespeare studies might thereby advance
beyond reading films the same way we read texts, with little attention to cinematic form or to film theory.[4] An impasse arises because
Shakespeare on film criticism too often amounts to a series of
flourishes, entrapped by the transcriptional impulse. Lacking a
stronger theory *across* films, it instead isolates itself to momentary
scenes, often only adding up to predictably thematic attacks that
argue by coincidence and associative implication.

Of course, this intertwined disciplinary genesis recapitulates the
earlier reflections on the status of film in the relation to theater
(among other arts) that so preoccupied European classical film theory. Here, Shakespeare tended to stand as a kind of touchstone,
even if a disjunctive one, for those seeking to articulate the parameters of an emergent medium in tension with prior performance
practices. Consider Rudolf Arnheim's 1932 aspirations not only for
film but for film criticism itself:

> The contemporary film critic must, since he deals with such new
> things, operate in just the opposite manner from the paleontologist,
> who deals with the ancient. He must preconstruct film art from occa-
> sional fossilizations, from impressions of sometimes not very noble
> parts; the laws of construction with which the films of the future will
> perhaps, in happy moments, completely comply must also be applied
> to contemporary film. The "Shakespeare of film" is yet to come, but the
> laws of his work already apply today. Without exception. Even to good
> films.[5]

Or, even earlier, Hugo Münsterberg's 1916 yearning for

> an original literature of real power and significance, in which every
> thought is generated by the idea of the screen. As long as the photoplays
> are fed by the literature of the stage, the new art can never come to its
> own and can never reach its real goal. It is surely no fault of Shake-
> speare that *Hamlet* and *King Lear* are very poor photoplays. If ever a
> Shakespeare arises for the screen, his work would be equally unsatis-
> factory if it were dragged to the stage.[6]

One need only to gesture toward Bazin's essays on the status of theater in *What is Cinema?* many of which were drawn into relief specifically by Shakespearean adaptations of Olivier and Welles, or
toward Cavell's lifelong meditations on film and Shakespeare
(which have been almost studiously avoided by those working in
this field, with Rhu as an exception).[7] There is a need for a study of
how film criticism itself was shaped from within by its engagement
with Shakespeare, which would in turn help complicate our be-
lated struggles with some of the same issues from the Shakespearean side of things.[8]

What follows is a reading of Quentin Tarantino's anti-Nazi exploitation film *Inglourious Basterds* (2009) in order to pursue this
spectral history of Shakespeare on film: its uncanny interruptions,
doublings, and returns that cannot be reduced to chronological linear history. Tarantino's figuration of the film frame in *Inglourious
Basterds* transforms reading into a question of characterological
(*letter*al), narrative, and generic framing. Understanding the frame
as figure is to understand that the film demands a double reading,
both of its infrastructure and of its sometimes furtive allusions to
films, film actors, film criticism, film theaters, film posters, and film
directors; these in turn furtively force open metaphorical window
frames through which one may read Tarantino's film as an account
of the spectral history of film as history. While *Ingloriuous Basterds*
makes but one passing citation of Hamlet (the character), such a
film proves itself the extreme case of where the critical action really
is, as opposed to the routine or normal "Shakespeare film."[9] The
study of Shakespeare (barely) in film may shed high-contrast light-
ing not only on Shakespeare (fully) in film but on Shakespeare
across media. (Shakespeare textual studies and Shakespeare media
studies might engage in dialogue, for example, to produce a mode
of film philology.) The spectral history of the medium of film invites a broad rethinking about aesthetics and politics in Shake-

speare criticism *tout court,* by conceiving politics in the context of
a resistance to reading generated through framing and irony that
dissolves seemingly obvious distinctions between Allies and
Nazis.[10] The now-dominant material culture studies seems to imagine (howsoever unreflectively) that positivism and empiricism
have triumphed in such a way as to negate philological reflection
on the practice of reading and the philosophical considerations of
reading as resistance to comprehension. Yet perhaps the *Geist* of
History has not been fully exorcised and haunts us still.

II. The (Anti)-Nazi Film(ed) Frame

> We cannot assume, try as we may, an Elizabethan seriousness.
> Yet we shall err grievously if we do not take that seriousness into
> account or if we imagine that the Elizabethan habit of mind is
> done with once and for all. If we are sincere with ourselves we
> must know that we have that habit in our own bosoms some-
> where, queer as it may seem. And, if we reflect on that habit, we
> may see that (in queerness though not in viciousness) it resem-
> bles certain trends of thought in central Europe, the ignoring of
> which by our scientifically minded intellectuals has helped not
> a little to bring the world into its present conflicts and distresses.
> —E. M. W. Tillyard, Epilogue to *The Elizabethan World Picture*

From the perspective of some anti-Nazi Germans before the
United States entered World War II, Hollywood film posed a prob-
lem even as it began to turn out propaganda films. Used by both
Allied and Germans, Shakespeare predictably made an appearance.
In 1941, Klaus Mann published a scathing review of Hollywood's
inadequacies in an essay entitled "What's Wrong with Anti-Nazi
Films?" which begins with the film business's trashy use of Shake-
speare:

> We have to accept the fact that among hundreds of moving pictures
> there are hardly two or three worth any serious consideration. The
> rest—the overwhelming majority—is glaring trash: pretty legs and idi-
> otic faces. Ziegfeld girls in techni-color, tough guys and Merry Melo-
> dies, angels with dirty faces. Marlene Dietrich with sunken cheeks and
> no talent, Mickey Rooney as Romeo, Mickey Mouse as Hamlet, Shirley
> Temple as Polonius, Stokowsky as prima ballerina, Silly Symphonies
> by Bach and Beethoven, the board of directors in their fascinating act
> as Last Gangsters, the writers' department as Dead End Kids, Mae West
> and Norma Shearer as Blossoms in the Dust. Dust . . . dust . . . Gone

with the Wind . . . box office dust. . . . So far so good. The trick works all right. People in Shanghai, Rio and Kansas City get a kick out of it, Sammy runs and Hollywood makes money. Everybody is pleased. But then comes Hitler.[11]

Films in which Allies mimed the Nazis in order to resist them include Ernest Lubitsch's *To Be or Not to Be* (1942) and Nick Grinde's low-budget film *Hitler—Dead or Alive* (1942). Whereas the latter film's serious and "patriotic" narrative frame segregates its Three Stooges–like plot about criminals actually killing Hitler (but to no avail as a Hitler double takes his place more audaciously), *To Be or Not to Be*'s tricky use of multiple frames within frames risks turning humor into "friendly fire." Yet neither film in any way questions the political differences between the Nazis and their resisters when it comes to violence, as does Tarantino's film by drawing parallels between American and German history. In *Inglourious Basterds,* the failed British plot to blow up the theater by having Allied soldiers dress as Nazi officers echoes the plot of *To Be or Not to Be* (in which there are two actors playing Hitler, one impersonating him, one the "real" thing, and two almost identical photographs of Hitler and his impersonator; neither Hitler nor his impersonator is confused with the other by the audience).[12]

III. Irony and the Character of *Inglourious Basterds*

> *Laertes:* Know you the hand?
> *Claudius:* 'Tis Hamlet's character.

Hamlet makes a brief appearance in Quentin Tarantino's *Inglourious Basterds,* a kind of verbal cameo.[13] A film actress and several Nazi soldiers on leave in Occupied Paris are getting drunk in a bar. They are playing a game that involves guessing the names of characters written on cards they have each stuck on their own foreheads. When one Nazi soldier fears that his character may be controversial because the character is American, the German film actress Bridget von Hammersmark (Diane Kruger), who is secretly working as a double agent for the Allies, declares that "it's not controversial. The nationality of the author has nothing to do with the nationality of the character. The Character is the character. Hamlet's not British, he's Danish." Although *Inglourious Basterds* makes no other overt references to *Hamlet* or Shakespeare,[14] the way that the film references Hamlet in the context of literary character criticism has productive implications for Shakespeare film criticism. For some time, Shakespeare on film criticism has been trying to leave behind considerations of *Shakespeare* and effectively read a given film *as a film.* In practice, however, this apparently film-centered criticism has meant that a given film related to Shakespeare is read as if it were a *text,* and thereby historicized the same way New Historicists might historicize the text of *Hamlet.* More recently, the tendency to historicize Shakespeare films as discrete ideological reproductions inadvertently coincides with a tendency in Shakespeare textual criticism and "New New Historicism" (or material culture criticism) to divorce the Shakespeare text (considered as *physical,* not metaphysical) from its performance history.[15]

The Hamlet reference in *Inglourious Basterds* implicitly calls into question an ontological distinction that historicism requires in order to situate its object of study in a narrative sequence and map: seemingly transparent paratextual distinctions between title and character, and author and character, author and title are subject in Tarantino's film to a medium-specific spectralization that divides sound from script and demands a careful attention to Tarantino's allegorization of film in relation to its (re)projection and its shooting script. Consider Bridget von Hammersmark's statement "Character is character." Two interpretations arise from an inaudible but scripted difference between lower-case-[c] "character" and capital-[C] "Character" when the line is delivered in the film and when it is printed in the screenplay. In the former, *inaudible* case, the statement may be understood as merely tautological ["c" is "c"]; in the other, *scripted* case the "Character" is only the character (independent from the other). In either case (lower or upper), the repetition of the word *character* calls attention, for it is spoken by a character in the film who is herself an actress playing a role in order to help the other side in a film. By extension, the difference between a letter "c" in character also calls up the meaning of "character" as *letter* in a film that deliberately misspells its own title, perhaps in order to call attention to its own inaudible but scripted difference from Enzo G. Castellari's earlier film of the same name, *Inglorious Bastards* (1978).[16]

By putting the "character of 'character'" in play through a reference to *Hamlet, Inglourious Basterds* systematically unfolds oppositions between Allies and Nazis, and between Nazis and Jews, in ways that bear similarity to Jean-Luc Godard's retrospective montage, in *Histoire(s) du Cinema,* of Hollywood films and stills, and World War II documentaries of the Nazis at war.[17] That is, like Godard's a-chronological film about history, the cinematic self-consciousness of *Inglourious Basterds* implies that history since the twentieth century cannot be understood apart from the history of film.[18] In addition to linking war and cinema (as Godard, Paul Virilio, Friedrich Kittler, and others have previously done), by literalizing silver nitrate film as an explosive device to be burned at a film premiere attended by Hitler, Tarantino metaphorizes film as a spectral medium that both precedes and follows "real" history.[19]

Loosely parallel to *Hamlet*'s inscription of Senecan tragedy and Elizabethan tragedy through the play-within-the-play, *Inglourious Basterds* uses a series of film-within-the-film references that invoke a history of cinema and film media. Beyond the nitrate footage, overtly metacinematic aspects include the shooting, development, and splicing of a 35 mm film print with a soundtrack into the final reel of *Stoltz der Nation* (*Pride of the Nation*); and the character of British Lieutenant Hicox, who is recruited for a sabotage plot not only because he is fluent in German but also because he's a film critic with a bimonthly column and two published studies (*Art of the Eyes, The Heart, and The Mind: A Study of German Cinema in the Twenties* and *Twenty-Four Frame Da Vinci,* described as "a subtexual film criticism study of the work of German director G. W. Pabst"). Additional cinematic citations abound: the German actor Emil Jannings attends the premiere of *Stoltz der Nation;* references are made to UFA (the German film studio taken over by propaganda minister Joseph Goebbels in 1933); at the Parisian theater, marquees are shown for *Le Corbeau* (*The Crow,* dir. Henri-Georges Clouzot, 1943—filmed during the Occupation, giving rise to contentious critiques about the degree to which it ought to be considered pro- or anti-Nazi), and the German "Berg" film starring Leni Riefenstahl, *Die weiße Hölle vom Piz Palü* (*The White Hell of Pitz Palü,* 1929), is to be shown for "German Night."

In Tarantino's self-conscious hands, film history becomes a principle of divisibility and misdirection, tearing and taking down the political differences between characters on opposing sides. In some cases, the divisibility is literal, or *letter*al. For example, Shosanna Dreyfus (Melaine Laurent) is the solitary Jewish survivor from the massacre of her family in the film's opening sequence, who turns revenger.[20] Years later, in Paris, she takes down letters from the marquee in a cinema she owns when she first meets the Nazi-turned-film-star, private Frederick Zoller (Daniel Brühl); in a subsequent scene, she is in the process of putting up letters on the same marquee for a new film when she is picked up by Frederick's adjutant and taken by force out to lunch.

The division between political sides unfolds through a vertiginous, ironically corrosive series of references to films that link both sides. For example, Frederick Zoller compares his role as a sniper in *Pride of the Nation* to *Sergeant York* (1941), which is to say both the World War I American soldier of the same name and the title of a Hollywood film based on his life, made by Howard Hawks during World War II as propaganda. Similarly, Frederick says he will become the equivalent of the Hollywood actor Van Johnson after *Pride of the Nation* is released. In other words, a Nazi character in the diegesis stars in a film in the diegesis based on a historical event outside the diegesis that resembles an American film. Yet this reversibility follows from asymmetrical relations between sides rather than from a straightforward mirroring. Whereas Frederick plays himself, Sergeant York is played by film star Gary Cooper (near the end Senator Hull tells York about ten job offers—the first to be in a Hollywood film about himself, the second to be in the Ziegfeld Follies, but he turns them all down and returns to his rural home); and whereas the anachronistically edited *Pride of the Nation* focuses entirely on the soldiers killed by the sniper, *Sergeant York* is mostly a romantic melodrama about the rakish Quaker Alvin York finding his religious faith (a comparable scene with York in a machine-gun nest fighting off Germans takes place near the end of the film). Tarantino's double flip on fiction and history, American and German, is echoed by an internal split in the characterization of Frederick, who at times seems very charming: when watching *Pride of the Nation,* he reacts like an ethically conflicted soldier out of *All Quiet on the Western Front* (1930), while the rest of the audience laughs and cheers wildly as American G.I.s get quickly and brutally shot down. Yet Frederick also turns out to be a sadistic would-be rapist and murderer.

These divisions are corrosively ironic in that they open up frames that double back on the film's audiences. Heroic Sergeant York morphs into the demented killer Charles Whitman.[21] Ethan (John Wayne) in *The Searchers* (1956) morphs into the part-Apache leader Lieutenant Aldo, who demands soldiers meet a scalp count (taken from Nazi corpses), echoed in turn by the Nazis referring to

German novelist Karl May's character, Winnetou Chief of the Apaches. Goebbels is compared to Hollywood producer David O. Selznick. The story of King Kong, in chains in New York, opens up the story of "the negro in America." Shosanna's projected film image in the movie theater, after *Pride of the Nation* ends, recalls less Big Brother in *1984* (as the screenplay says it will) or even the Great Oz, than the end of Stephen Spielberg's *Raiders of the Lost Ark* (1981) when the face of a feminine-looking ghost released from the ark by a Nazi archaeologist turns into a skull and then kills (by cremation) all the Nazis. In each case, the framing opens up a seeming exception, authorizing paralegal violence in the name of justice that turns out to be (or always already to have been) the norm.

The most controversial irony concerns Jews and Nazis. Unlike Lubitsch's *To Be or Not to Be, Inglourious Basterds* does present explicitly Jewish characters, and they too are divided. On the one hand, we have the G.I. "Jews," as it were, some of whom are first-generation European immigrants, and all of whom act in Germany as terrorist guerrilla fighters; these are the characters promoted by the trailers for audiences expecting an "action" film. Yet on the other hand we have the French Shosanna, who is excepted from the mass murder of her Jewish family by Hans Landa, who laughs as he decides not to shoot her after aiming his pistol at her as she flees.[22] The failed British plot to blow up the theater, which echoes *To Be or Not to Be,* is called Operation "Kino," which means "movie theater" in German.[23]

The least obvious parallel in the film (between a child and Shosanna) is also the most destructive of political oppositions between normal, lawful violence and the exceptional violence authorized in wartime. When Shosanna explains to her lover and projectionist how the nitrate films in the theater will serve as the explosive, the screen splits in half and on the right appears a sequence from Alfred Hitchcock's *Sabotage* (1936), based on Conrad's *The Secret Agent.* The sequence involves the child Stevie getting on a bus with a film canister that contains a bomb. Stevie, unaware that he is carrying a bomb, is delayed several times, and the rest of the people are killed when the bomb explodes. The survivor Shosanna at this point in the film appears to be an exception since, unlike Stevie, she was spared being murdered by Landa as a child. Yet the scene cancels her exceptionalism in that we see that she has become a "sui-decider," so to speak, as an adult, a kind of "no Sho-ah."

IV. *Hamlet* (Out of Film) and the Irony of the Political

> The so-called immortal works just flash briefly through every present time. *Hamlet* is one of the very fastest, the hardest to grasp.
>
> —Walter Benjamin, "Notes (II)" (285)

A reading of the film frame as ironic bombshell opening up spectral history in Tarantino's film may be productively deployed by turning to the unexpected, even embarrassing dialogue between Walter Benjamin and Carl Schmitt about the state of exception as it bears on political theology, tragedy, and temporality.[24] From our perspective, the main interest of Schmitt's *Hamlet or Hecuba: The Intrusion of Time in Play* is Schmitt's spectralization of history:[25] Schmitt says he doesn't expect the audience to see James I onstage. James I (carrying the baggage of his beheaded mother, Mary Queen of Scots) intrudes, but only as a ghost, in other words. Schmitt is not doing a conventional old historicist Henry Paul reading,[26] since his is a notion of intrusion and formal imperfection. Instead, he is writing a spectral historicism *avant* Jacques Derrida's *Spectres of Marx* by implying that sovereignty is always already weak sovereignty (that is, Schmitt's own reading self-deconstructs and becomes a Benjaminian *Trauerspiel*). Schmitt's book is not a detour away from his political writings (into aesthetics), but rather reveals the spectral, uncanny relation between theology and politics that haunts *Political Theology*.

Apart from the Appendix written to Walter Benjamin, by then long dead, who in 1928 had sent a kind letter to Schmitt along with a copy of his *Trauerspiel* book, *Hamlet or Hecuba* is a spectral book that haunts the history of political thought in which Schmitt engaged (Locke vs. Hobbes). Schmitt's book is gaining new attention from Shakespeareans now that an authorized translation has been published, but may best be read within the wider context of the relation between force and justice that concerned Benjamin and Schmitt. With the exception of Derrida's explosive essay "The Force of Law," critics have tried to salvage Benjamin's conception of violence and dismiss Schmitt. Yet perhaps Schmitt's value lies in his repetition in the Hamlet book in a more extreme manner: the implicitly paradoxical discussion of sovereignty and the state of exception he had made explicitly paradoxical in his political writings. To put it another way, to what extent is Schmitt's book on

Hamlet overtaken by irony? Whether *Hamlet* is a tragedy and *Trauerspiel* matters to Schmitt because he wants to separate politics from play: politics is what interrupts play. To demonstrate this point, Schmitt returns to *Hamlet,* a play Benjamin classified as a *Trauerspiel* about indecision. Schmitt ironically demonstrates, however, that the state of exception is everywhere in *Hamlet,* leaving Schmitt unable to make his argument and necessitating an Appendix in which he returns to Benjamin's *Trauerspiel* book.[27] But that is a matter to be taken up some other time.

Notes

Epigraphs at the beginning of the article were taken from the following: Carl Schmitt, *Political Theology: Four Chapters on the Concept of Sovereignty,* trans. George Schwab (Chicago: University of Chicago Press, 2006), 5; Samuel Weber, "Taking Exception to Decision: Walter Benjamin and Carl Schmitt," in *Benjamin's -abilities* (Cambridge, MA: Harvard University Press, 2009), 179; and Siegfried Kracauer, *Theory of Film: The Redemption of Physical Reality* (Princeton: Princeton University Press, 1997 [1960]), 223. Epigraph to Section II taken from Walter Benjamin, "Notes (II)" [1930], in *Walter Benjamin: Selected Writings Volume 2, Part 1, 1927–1930,* ed. Michael W. Jennings, Howard Eiland, and Gary Smith, 285–87.

　　1. Dudley Andrew, "The Core and Flow of Film Studies," *Critical Inquiry* 35 (2009): 914.

　　2. David Bordwell, "Contemporary Film Studies and the Vicissitudes of Grand Theory," in *Post-Theory: Reconstructing Film Studies,* ed. David Bordwell and Noël Carroll (Madison: University of Wisconsin Press, 1996), 3.

　　3. Gerald Mast and Marshall Cohen, *Film Theory and Criticism: Introductory Readings* (New York: Oxford University Press, 1974), 302–52. The five entries were Geoffrey Reeves's interview with Peter Brook, Frank Kermode's essay on "Shakespeare at the Movies," James Agee's extended review of Olivier's *Henry V,* selections from André Bazin on Welles's *Othello,* and John Blumenthal's article on Kurosawa's *Throne of Blood.*

　　4. Or worse, an overreliance on a hyper-canonized essay, such as the reiterated invocation of Laura Mulvey's 1975 piece on visual pleasure, from which Mulvey has long since distanced herself. See Laura Mulvey, "Visual Pleasure and Narrative Cinema," *Screen* 16, no. 3 (1975): 6–18; and Mulvey, *Death 24× a Second: Stillness and the Moving Image* (London: Reaktion Books, 2006).

　　5. Rudolf Arnheim, "Answer" [1932], in *Film Essays and Criticism,* trans. Brenda Benthien (Madison: University of Wisconsin Press, 1997), 194.

　　6. Hugo Münsterberg, *The Photoplay: A Psychological Study* (New York: D. Appleton, 1916), 196.

　　7. André Bazin, "Theater and Cinema—Part One and Part Two," in *What is Cinema?* vol. 1, trans. Hugh Gray (Berkeley: University of California Press, 1967), 76–94 and 95–124. See Stanley Cavell, *The World Viewed: Reflections on the Ontology of Film* (Cambridge, MA: Harvard University Press, 1979); "*North by North-*

west," Critical Inquiry 7, no. 4 (1981): 761–76; *Disowning Knowledge in Seven Plays of Shakespeare* (Cambridge: Cambridge University Press, 2003); "Shakespeare and Rohmer: Two Tales of Winter," in *Cities of Words: Pedagogical Letters on a Register of the Moral Life* (Cambridge, MA: Harvard University Press, 2004), 421–43; and "Seasons of Love: Bergman's *Smiles of a Summer Night* and *The Winter's Tale*," in *Cavell on Film*, ed. William Rothman (Albany: SUNY Press, 2005), 193–204. See also Lawrence Rhu, *Stanley Cavell's American Dream: Shakespeare, Philosophy, and Hollywood Movies* (New York: Fordham University Press, 2006), reviewed by Scott L. Newstok in *Shakespeare Bulletin* 24.4 (2006): 57–63.

    8. As an analogue, see the first half of Richard Wilson's *Shakespeare in French Theory: King of Shadows* (New York: Routledge, 2007), which explores how the intellectual careers of figures such as Bourdieu, Cixous, Deleuze, Derrida, and Foucault were formed in part by their engagement with Shakespeare. For such a project, we might first require an anthology of Shakespeare-within-film-theory along the lines of Paul Kottman's recent edition of *Philosophers on Shakespeare* (Stanford, CA: Stanford University Press, 2009). Filmmakers themselves have, of course, often produced critical reflections on Shakespeare; it remains instructive to read, for instance, Kozintsev on *Lear* and *Hamlet* (see Grigori Kozintzev, *Shakespeare: Time and Conscience*, trans. Joyce Vining [New York: Hill & Wang, 1966] and *King Lear: The Space of Tragedy, The Diary of a Film Director*, trans. Mary Mackintosh [Berkeley: University of California Press, 1977]), or Hitchcock's 1936 debate with Granville-Barker regarding realistic locations (see Anthony Davies, "Shakespeare and the Media of Film, Radio and Television: A Retrospect," *Shakespeare Survey* 39 [1987]: 2). But have we yet begun to consider more oblique engagements? How do we account, for instance, of an Eisenstein who was himself a close interpreter of Shakespeare, as is discussed in Turi Tsivian, *Ivan the Terrible* (London: British Film Institute, 2008)? See also N. M. Lary, "Eisenstein and Shakespeare," in *Eisenstein Rediscovered*, ed. Ian Christie and Richard Taylor (New York: Routledge, 1993), 140–50.

    9. Practically speaking, the Shakespeare film remains a "phantom genre," weaker even than film noir since it is never used as a generic marker. Barbara Hodgdon uses the phrase in her Editor's introduction to the first (and thus far only) *Shakespeare Quarterly* special issue on "Screen Shakespeare" ("From the Editor," *Shakespeare Quarterly* 53, no. 2 [2002]: iii–x), following Rick Altman's 1999 reflections on "the woman's film" (see *Film/Genre* [London: British Film Institute, 1999]; Altman, in turn, deploys a chapter heading ("Postmortem for a Phantom Genre") that Russell Merritt applied to melodrama in 1983 (see Russell Merritt, "Melodrama: Postmortem for a Phantom Genre," *Wide Angle* 5, no. 3 [1983]: 25–31), and two years before that Jeffrey Sammons skeptically postulated that only a handful of works could rightfully be considered a *Bildungsroman*, which hence for him ought to be considered a "phantom genre" (Jeffrey L. Sammons, "The Mystery of the Missing *Bildungsroman*, or: What Happened to Wilhelm Meister's Legacy?" *Genre* 14, no. 2 [1981]: 229–46).

    10. By invoking irony in relation to aesthetics and politics, recall Paul de Man's provocative assertion that "nothing can overcome the resistance to theory since theory *is* itself this resistance" (Paul de Man, "The Resistance to Theory," in *The Resistance to Theory* [Minneapolis: University of Minnesota Press, 1996], 19) and to de Man's corrosively ironic essay "The Concept of Irony" in the posthumously published *Aesthetic Ideology* (de Man, "The Concept of Irony," in *Aesthetic Ideol-*

ogy, ed. Andrzej Warminski [Minneapolis: University of Minnesota Press, 1996], 163–84). Attempts to recuperate de Man after his collaborationist Belgian journalism came to light have tended to bypass de Man's resistance to being read and to reading in favor of preserving a seemingly more palatable and accessible Derridean form of deconstruction (as if Derrida himself were not interested in spectrality and the uncanny of the political). However, both Derrida and de Man are engaged in similar kinds of textual self-ruination; note, for instance, de Man's deferral of actually reading Kierkegaard on irony in an essay putatively about Kierkegaard on irony, instead declaring that the reader will learn nothing from de Man's essay. One cannot decide whether de Man is giving his reader indirect directions (stop reading me, don't bother with Schlegel, just go to Kierkegaard) or is just playing out the logic of the buffoon he (through Schlegel) identifies with the ironist to the end.

11. Klaus Mann was the son of Thomas Mann and author of the 1936 novel *Mephisto: Roman einer Karriere,* a thinly veiled account of the Nazi actor Gustaf Gründgens, including Gründgens's interpretation of *Hamlet,* which characteristically rejected the version of this play as one troubled by delay and inaction, instead enacting Nazi scholars' "various odd ways of bringing the obvious contradictions in Hamlet's character into line with the requirements of a heroic and Nordic ideal figure" (Wilhelm Hortmann, *Shakespeare on the German Stage,* volume 2, *The Twentieth Century* [Cambridge: Cambridge University Press, 1998], 157). See an interview with the Gründgens-like actor in *Mephisto:* " 'Hamlet wasn't a weak man,' he said to journalists when interviewed. 'There was nothing weak about him. Generations of actors have made the mistake of viewing him as a feminine character. His melancholy wasn't hollow but came from real motives. The prince wants to avenge his father. He is a Renaissance man—a real aristocrat and something of a cynic. I want to strip him of all the melancholy traits with which he has been burdened by conventional portrayals' " (Klaus Mann, *Mephisto,* trans. Robin Smyth [New York: Penguin, 1977], 255). (See also Mann, "What's Wrong with Anti-Nazi Films?" [1941], *New German Critique* 89 (2003): 173.

12. For an acutely informed analysis of the homeopathic use of mimesis in Lubitsch's *To Be or Not to Be,* see Stephen Tifft, "Miming the Führer: *To Be or Not to Be* and the Mechanisms of Outrage," *Yale Journal of Criticism* 5, no. 1 (1991): 1–40; on Nazism, cinema, and Shakespeare, see Richard Burt, "SShockspeare: (Nazi) Shakespeare Goes Heil-lywood," in *Companion to Shakespeare and Performance,* ed. Barbara Hodgdon and William B. Worthen, 437–56 (Oxford: Blackwell, 2005); see also *Enemy of Women* (dir. Alfred Zeisler, 1944), which includes a scene with Joseph Goebbels's auditioning and failing to seduce an attractive young actress who performs lines from Juliet's balcony scene.

13. The Hamlet cameo echoes the uncredited audio cameos of prior Tarantino stars Samuel L. Jackson and Harvey Keitel.

14. It does, however, self-consciously divide itself into five "chapters," which we might consider a displacement of the more conventional five-act structure of a play. The Austrian actor who plays S.S. officer Hans Landa, Christoph Waltz, has, when interviewed, taken to likening *Inglourious Basterds* to "Shakespearean" drama (see Fred Topel, "Equal Time for All in *Inglourious Basterds,*" *EDGE Boston,* http://www.edgeboston.com/index.php?ch = entertainment&sc = movie s& sc3 = &id = 95204&pf = 1), as did David Carradine before him when speaking of

Kill Bill, and Bruce Willis when talking about *Pulp Fiction.* In a 2007 *GQ* interview, Tarantino gamely suggested that he's

> always had a thought maybe that I might have been Shakespeare in another life. I don't really believe that 100 percent, and I don't really care about Shakespeare, I've never been into Shakespeare, but then people are constantly bringing up all of these qualities in my work that mirror Shakespearean tragedies and moments and themes. People have written lots of pieces about the parallels of my work and Shakespeare. I remember in the case of *Reservoir Dogs,* writing this scene where the undercover cop is teaching Tim Roth how to be an undercover cop, and when the actors came in to rehearse it, Harvey Keitel read it, and he thought I had just taken Hamlet's speech to the players and broke it down into modern words. I'd never read Hamlet's speech to the players.

(Chris Heath, Interview with Quentin Tarantino, *GQ,* April 2007, 212–17 and 259).

15. Patricia Fumerton, "Introduction: A New New Historicism," in *Renaissance . Culture and the Everyday,* ed. Patricia Fumerton and Simon Hunt (Philadelphia: University of Pennsylvania Press, 1999), 1–20. See, for example, Margareta de Grazia, *"Hamlet" without* Hamlet (Cambridge: Cambridge University Press, 2007).

16. Indeed, one is tempted to speculate further that such a wayward spelling (or, to use the language of the First Folio *Macbeth,* "weyward" [see Ayanna Thompson, "What is a 'Weyward' *Macbeth?"* in *Weyward Macbeth: Intersections of Race and Performance,* ed. Scott L. Newstok and Ayanna Thompson (New York: Palgrave, 2010), 3–10]) additionally evokes the erratic precedent of "Renaissance" (or, as our students often imagine, "Old English")-style orthography. While "inglourious" is not an extant orthographic alternative from the early modern period, "basterd" certainly is—in Shakespeare alone, the Quarto *Henry V* has Burgundy cursing "Normanes, basterd Normanes," and the First Folio version of the same play has MacMorris's "What ish my nation?" speech read: "Ish a Villaine, and a Basterd, and a Knaue, and a Rascall"; likewise, line 2 of Sonnet 124 speaks of "fortunes basterds" in the 1609 Quarto. (For bastardy in early modern drama, see Michael Neill, " 'In Everything Illegitimate': Imagining the Bastard in Renaissance Drama," *Yearbook of English Studies* 23 [1993]: 270–92; and Nicholas Crawford, "Language, Duality, and Bastardy in English Renaissance Drama," *English Literary Renaissance* 34 [2004]: 243–62.) Note that the only instance of "inglorious" in Shakespeare's works is uttered by the Bastard in *King John* in reply to the King's peace treaty with the Pope's legate:

> Oh inglorious league!
> Shall we, upon the footing of our land,
> Send fair-play orders, and make compromise,
> Insinuation, parley, and base truce
> To arms invasive?
>
> (5.1.65–69)

Underscoring a need to read film history recursively with the history of Shakespearean performance, Enzo G. Castellari directed *Romeo and Juliet,* as well as a Western version of *Hamlet,* entitled *Johnny Hamlet* (1968); furthermore, Castellari's *Inglorious Bastards* itself mentions Elsinore. Castellari and original *Inglorious Bastards* lead actor Bo Svenson both appear in Tarantino's film, in a characterological nod to the earlier version.

17. Hélène Cixous, "The Character of 'Character,'" trans. Keith Cohen, *New Literary History* 5, no. 2 (1974): 383–402. For Godard's other films also related to the Holocaust, see the prologue "Hell" in *Notre Musique* (2004) and *In Praise of Love* (2001).

18. For Tarantino's biographical analogue to Godard's a-chronology, note that

> as a struggling young actor, Tarantino chose to put films on his resume that he had never acted in, but he chose obscure films by great directors, figuring casting agents would never have the time to confirm his claim while being impressed by the famous director. One of Tarantino's favorite directors is Jean Luc Godard (Tarantino's production company, A Band Apart, is named after Godard's film *Bande À Part*). He credited himself for playing a part that he never played in the film Godard made in 1987. That film was *King Lear.*

Eric David, "Kill Will: The Rough Magic of Quentin Tarentino," *The Ooze* (http://www.theooze.com/articles/article.cfm?id = 1247)

19. Paul Virilio, *War and Cinema: The Logistics of Perception* (New York: Version, 1989); Friedrich A. Kittler, *Gramophone, Film, Typewriter* (Stanford, CA: Stanford University Press, 1999). The finale's *coup de cinema* is thus a kind of *Mousetrap* inset that actually *works,* instead of the somewhat uncertain results of Hamlet's production of *The Murder of Gonzago.* Earlier in the film, Landa had characterized Jews as rats—"How now! a rat? Dead, for a ducat, dead!" Yet the grandiosely theatrical ending is perhaps more Marlovian than Shakespearean, akin to what Barabas had planned in *The Jew of Malta.*

20. Along with many other orthographic irregularities, Tarantino drops the second "h" from the conventional Jewish spelling of Shos*h*anna.

21. That is to say, the plot of *Pride of the Nation* resembles *Sargeant York* less than it does *Targets* (1968), based on the University of Texas student-turned-sniper Charles Whitman.

22. In Lubitsch's film, the character named Greenberg wants to play Shylock, and twice recites the "Hath not a Jew" speech; yet the speech is carefully revised to omit references to Jews, and is instead delivered as "Have *we* not eyes?" Mel Brooks gave the Jewish characters yellow stars in his 1983 remake of Lubitsch's film. On the non-representation of Jews in 1940s Hollywood films, see Ruth Karpf, "Are Jewish Themes 'Verboten'?" [1943], *New German Critique* 89 (2003): 183–84.

23. As Ryback has demonstrated, Hitler "owned the collected works of William Shakespeare, published in German translation in 1925 by Georg Müller . . . He appears to have imbibed his *Hamlet.* 'To be or not to be' was a favorite phrase, as was 'It is Hecuba to me'" (Timothy W. Ryback, *Hitler's Private Library: The Books that Shaped His Life* [New York: Random House, 2009], xi–xii).

24. For a return to Schmitt in relation to the George W. Bush administration, see Scott Horton, "State of Exception: Bush's War on the Rule of Law," *Harper's Magazine,* July 2007, 74–81.

25. Carl Schmitt, *Hamlet or Hecuba: The Intrusion of Time into the Play* [1956], trans. David Pan and Jennifer Rust (New York: Telos Press, 2009). For further reflections, see also Victoria Kahn, "Hamlet or Hecuba: Carl Schmitt's Decision," *Representations* 83 (2003): 67–96; Samuel Weber, "Taking Exception to Decision: Walter Benjamin and Carl Schmitt"; Julia Reinhard Lupton, "Hamlet, Prince: Tragedy, Citizenship, and Political Theology," in *Alternative Shakespeares 3,* ed. Diana Henderson (New York: Routledge, 2007), 181–203; Giorgio Agamben, *Homo*

Sacer: Sovereign Power and Bare Life (Stanford, CA: Stanford University Press, 1998), 15–30 and 75–112; and Jacques Derrida, *The Politics of Friendship* (New York: Verso, 1997), 165–67 and 169–70n32. For an argument that whether Old Hamlet's visor is open or as closed when appears on stage has no bearing on sovereignty (defined as seeing without being seen), see Jacques Derrida, *Spectres of Marx: The State of the Debt, the Work of Mourning, and the New International* (New York: Routledge, 1994), 7–8; and Jacques Derrida, *The Beast and the Sovereign* (Chicago: Chicago University Press, 2009), 6, 293.

26. See Henry Paul, *The Royal Play of "Macbeth"* (New York: Macmillan, 1950).

27. Kahn criticizes Schmitt for not being able to tell the difference between a decision to declare a true state of emergency from a decision to declare a fake state of emergency but she the more important point that the truth of any state of exception can never be determined; indeed, any decision will immediately be attacked by enemies of the state as a fraud, and no one will in turn be able to decide whether the critics are provocateurs, paranoid, or correct (or all of the above). Aesthetics and politics cannot rightly be separated out and reduced to truth and fraud, if only because fraud is part of history.

Recent Shakespeare Adaptation and the Mutations of Cultural Capital

Douglas Lanier

LIKE ECONOMIC CAPITAL in the age of globalization, Shakespearean cultural capital in the age of mass media is restless. Pierre Bourdieu's original conception of cultural capital tended to stress its relative stability. That is, for Bourdieu the cultural capital manifested in, say, the ability to recognize Shakespearean citations or appreciate a performance of *Macbeth,* remained a relatively fixed marker of cultural difference. Cultural capital preserves a system of social stratification based on cultural distinctions, without that system relying primarily on economic status or traditional ideas of "class." However, in a postmodern age, when supposedly distinctions between highbrow, middlebrow, and popular culture have collapsed, the cultural prestige attached to Shakespeare, residual now though it may be, has undergone a recuperative transformation. Shakespearean cultural capital now moves freely from investment to investment, from one cultural arena or medium to another, in a search for renewed value. That value accrues from a process of reciprocal legitimation, whereby Shakespeare's association with a mass-cultural product, medium, or genre lends that item a moiety of highbrow depth, "universality," authority, continuity with established tradition, or seriousness of purpose, while at the same time the association with mass culture lends Shakespeare street credibility, broad intelligibility, and celebrity.

Three qualities characterize this reciprocal relationship between Shakespeare and mass culture. First, it is rhizomatic. Deleuze's classic example of a rhizomatic relationship is of the wasp and the orchid. Both beings maintain their relative autonomy, but both evolve in the direction of the other so that the wasp can be said to be "becoming-orchid," and the orchid "becoming-wasp." The relationship is not symbiotic—one does not depend on the other—so much as mutually catalytic of dramatically new directions in development, what Deleuze calls "lines of flight." The recent relationship between Shakespeare and mass culture has had this rhizomatic quality, particularly so in the case of Shakespeare on film. Second, Shakespeare's relationship with specific media or arenas of culture tends to be invested with energy at certain moments and social contexts, and that energy shifts from medium to medium, context to context, over time. Shakespeare's relationship with advertising was highly charged in the Anglo-American sphere in the last quarter of the nineteenth century, only to wane quickly in the new century; in the United States in the 1930s, radio drama and costume film formed potent rhizomes with Shakespeare; the 1960s was the era of Shakespeare and the record album. That is, to speak generally of Shakespeare and mass culture is to risk not attending to how a rhizomatic frisson tends to be specific to Shakespeare's relationship with certain pop genres or mass media within particular sociohistorical milieus, or to how this transformative energy migrates and mutates over time. Last, speaking now particularly of the post–World War II era, an overarching determinative element in many of these rhizomatic relationships has been the educational market. One of the many reasons there has been a drive to recuperate the nature of Shakespearean cultural capital is that Shakespeare remains so integral to the curriculum, and that centrality guarantees a market. By recasting Shakespeare in terms of mass media and genres, producers could at once supply a ready-made market (schools), use pop Shakespeare to reinforce modes of mass-cultural reception, and minimize the extent to which Shakespeare might actively conflict with or interrogate mass culture.

It has become clear that the boom period of investment in the Anglo-American mass-market Shakespeare film has passed, and that despite a continuing trickle of new projects, the adaptational energy once associated with Shakespeare on film has migrated elsewhere. Indeed, the fact that it has moved on might be seen as a mark of its ideological success, even though most of the Shakespeare films produced during this period were hardly box-office bonanzas (with the important exceptions of Luhrmann's *Romeo + Juliet* and Madden's *Shakespeare in Love*). It's appropriate, then, to pause and think about what the collective cultural investment in 1990s Shakespeare on film accomplished, that is, how the rhizomatic relationship between Shakespeare and mass-market cinema changed (or sought to change) the nature of Shakespeare and the cultural capital he represents.

Three recalibrations of Shakespeare seem of particular importance. First, Shakespeare film pushed hard against the textual conceptualization of Shakespeare that was the dominant keynote of much of the twentieth century, the notion that Shakespeare's essence is to be found in the particularities of his language. One of the main achievements of the nineties was to bring Shakespeare in line with late twentieth-century visual culture and in the process loosen the equivalence between Shakespeare and text. Through film of this period Shakespeare became definitively post-textual. This was not just a matter of the proliferation of new Shakespeare films, the easy availability of older Shakespeare films through VHS and DVD, and the astonishing speed with which screen Shakespeare became a means for teaching Shakespeare in secondary schools, but it is also a matter of how visuality becomes a principal value in many of the cinematic styles of this period. Branagh, for example, often resorts to an illustrational style, feeling the need to show us on the screen what is mentioned or reported in the text—we *see* the accoutrements of royal power piled in a cart in Henry V's "Idol ceremony" speech, the supposed seduction of Hero, which is only reported in *Much Ado,* the sexual tryst between Hamlet and Ophelia, only hinted at in *Hamlet.* In his *Midsummer* Hoffman returns the play to Victorian visual traditions of grand spectacle and Victorian painting; in his *Romeo + Juliet* Luhrmann creates a postmodern hodgepodge of MTV video style and pop visuals, even turning snippets of the Shakespearean text into advertising slogans; and though in a very different register, Peter Greenaway's *Prospero's Books* and Julie Taymor's *Titus* draw on arresting images drawn from high and avant-garde art. In these and other Shakespeare films of the day, the range and density of pictorial allusiveness, the visual literacy they assume of their target audiences, firmly resituate Shakespeare in the regime of the (moving) image, not that of the word. One consequence of this is that by decades' end, the presence of Shakespeare's language is no longer the essential element it once was in Shakespeare film—witness *10 Things I Hate About You* or *O.*

Second, Shakespeare film in the nineties popularized the practice of resituating Shakespearean narrative in a new setting or time period. Anyone who has attended a Shakespearean stage performance in the last thirty years is familiar with this sort of time- or place-shifting of the action. Yet for the non-playgoing, cinematic audience, this practice for Shakespearean production was still novel in the early nineties, particularly since the photorealistic aesthetic of so much mass-market film had been until relatively recently antipathetic to anachronism. It is noteworthy, then, that nearly every major Shakespeare film of the nineties after Zeffirelli's *Hamlet* and Branagh's *Henry V* made a break, whether small or large, with traditional period production. Teen Shakespeare films were symptomatic of the cinematic impulse to recontextualize Shakespearean narratives in a new place and/or time. Earlier, as in *West Side Story,* where that recontextualization of Shakespeare had occurred, Shakespeare's language was also jettisoned in order to maintain a consistency of mise-en-scène, but in the nineties, films that re-sited Shakespeare's narrative also felt free to recite Shakespeare's language. The effect was to recast the relationship between fidelity to Shakespeare's language, period performance, and photorealistic mise-en-scène, so that cinematic Shakespeare might (or might not) include Shakespeare's language and almost certainly would resituate the narrative. Instead of being particular texts, "Shakespeare" thereby becomes a collection of narratives highly mobile from context to context, verbal style to style, genre to genre, media platform to platform.

Last, mass-market Shakespeare films of the nineties worked to recalibrate Shakespeare to the concerns and screen styles of youth culture, still the most lucrative market segment for film producers. This is not the entire story for Shakespeare film of this period, but the "teening" of Shakespeare was nonetheless one of its key drives, one most certainly driven by commercial considerations. Cher's correct attribution of "to thine own self be true" in *Clueless,* on the basis of her scrupulous attention to Mel Gibson, succinctly captures how youth market Shakespeare on film works to yoke Shakespearean and pop-cultural literacy. Though Luhrmann's *Romeo + Juliet* established the template for teen Shakespeare adaptations, the signature genre of the period, one can detect this impulse in many Shakespeare films of the decade. Indeed, the decade begins with Zeffirelli's recasting of Hamlet as a youthful action hero and Branagh's recasting of Henry V as a callow young king who comes of age through war. Arguably Branagh's later box-office and critical problems spring from his failure to address the youth audience he aimed at in *Henry V* and *Much Ado,* even though he cast young stars in key roles. The beginnings of this shift in demographic target audience for film Shakespeare may be traced to the sixties with *West Side Story,* Zeffirelli's *Romeo and Juliet,* Richardson's *Hamlet,* and Polanski's *Macbeth,* but it is only in the nineties that this shift was pursued with collective vigor. What is more, this change is also indicative of producers' increased awareness of the relationship between film Shakespeare and the captive market of the classroom, as witnessed by the nearly mandatory study guides accompanying releases of even unfaithful Shakespeare adaptations.

I've dwelt on these general elements of nineties film adaptation because they reveal how while individual Shakespeare films pursue particular agendas, those films, functioning collectively, are at the same time catalyzing more general changes in the nature of Shakespeare we experience and the forms of cultural capital he can represent. This aggregate of Shakespearean adaptations energizes particular collocations of qualities at particular moments, which are then themselves taken up (or left behind) and changed by subsequent adaptational aggregates. In the first years of the new millennium the energies associated with mass-market Shakespeare film of the nineties have been refocused in two directions. One is globalization of film Shakespeare. While Anglo-American production of Shakespeare films has sharply tailed off since 2000, production of Shakespeare films outside centers of Anglo-American film production is notably up. In the past ten years, Shakespeare films have been produced in areas as varied as Tibet, New Zealand, India, Lapland, Singapore, Spain, Mexico, Malaysia, Canada, Israel, Germany, Chile, and Russia. This globalization springs from and extends the logic of Shakespeare's cinematization in the nineties. The shift of gravity from text to image, for example, paves the way for Shakespeare to go fully global. Once Shakespearean narrative could be disembedded from Shakespeare's words, it became far more readily available for translation into all manner of languages and cultural contexts. The increasingly transnational nature of youth culture, epitomized by the postmodern pop style of *Romeo + Juliet,* also helped ease Shakespeare's passage across cultural borders. Through this adaptational process Shakespeare's work has become increasingly detached from its imbrication in Britain's colonial past, and so Shakespeare can be relocalized in new cultural contexts without filmmakers needing to address the politics of adapting the master texts of a former master. At the same time, Shakespeare's cultural stature, recuperated by its thorough cinematization, still offers certain forms of cultural authority to projects

within national or local film traditions. Even when radically transformed, recognizably Shakespearean narratives provide the added
legitimacy and prestige of "universality" or to use its less essential-
ist alternative, "globalization." Thus, the phenomenon of Vishal
Bhardwaj, a Shakespearean cinematic auteur in India whose brilliant films *Maqbool* and *Omkara* graft Shakespearean narratives
onto Bollywood genres, styles, and themes, relocalizing Shakespeare, universalizing Bollywood, and all without engaging Shakespeare's place in India's colonial history at all.

A second development is equally intriguing, one that also
springs from the logic of Shakespeare's cinematization in the nineties: the rise of the Shakespearean graphic novel. Shakespeare in
comic book form is nothing new. Albert Kantner issued five Shakespeare plays in his Classics Illustrated comics series of the fifties,
and a handful of imitators went on to capitalize upon Kantner's
idea. In the eighties Oval Projects published six full-length Shakespeare adaptations in quite different styles, three by the Brazilian
artist Von (*Macbeth, Romeo and Juliet,* and *A Midsummer Night's
Dream*), Oscar Zarete's *Othello,* Ian Pollock's *King Lear,* and John
Howard's *Twelfth Night.* But these pale in comparison with the
scope of recent graphic novelizations of Shakespeare. In addition
to reprintings of the Classics Illustrated series in the late nineties
and the Oval series in 2005, the last decade has seen a proliferation
of educational series that convert Shakespeare to comic book form.[1]
A new Classical Comics series produces three different versions of
each of its titles with different texts; so far *Henry V, Macbeth,
Romeo and Juliet,* and *The Tempest* are out, with *Julius Caesar* and
A Midsummer Night's Dream scheduled for 2010. Three different
English-language Shakespeare series in manga style are currently
publishing, the Manga Shakespeare series (fourteen titles to date),
Shakespeare: The Manga Edition (four titles to date), and Puffin
Graphics (one title); several Japanese Shakespeare manga series
have also appeared, including Yoko Shimamura's *Tenamon'ya
Shakespeare* (*Something like Shakespeare,* 2000) and Hiromi Mori-
shita's *Osaka Hamlet* (2005–6), along with many series referencing
Romeo and Juliet, a favorite manga scenario. There is also a spate
of nonseries graphic novelizations of Shakespeare, some faithful,
others quite free. Among them are Antony Johnson and Brett Wel-
dele's *Julius GN* (2004), Chuck Austen and Salvador Larroca's *She
Lies with Angels* (2004), Norris Burroughs's *Voodoo Macbeth*
(2006), Gareth Hinds's *King Lear* (2007) and *The Merchant of Ven-*

ice (2008), Brooke McEldowney's *Pibgorn Rep: A Midsummer Night's Dream* (2008), and the ongoing series *Kill Shakespeare* (2010–). Nick Craine, a Canadian artist, is at work on a graphic novel version of Shakespeare's life, titled *Parchment of Light,* an excerpt of which has been recently published. And this is not merely an exclusively Anglo-American phenomenon; to the Japanese manga examples mentioned above, one might add Gianna de Luca's *Hamlet* and *Romeo and Juliet* (Italy, 1995), Ralf König's *Jago* (Germany, 1996), and Olivier Louis and Rodolphe's *The Battle of Agincourt* (France, 2001), among several others.

How to understand this boom in the Shakespeare graphic novel? One way is to see it as a migration to a new, cheaper-to-produce medium of the adaptational energies once devoted to Shakespeare film. Certainly the graphic novelization of Shakespeare takes up and extends the conversion of Shakespeare to visual form so central to film Shakespeare of the nineties. Indeed, the graphic novel format allows the artist much fuller "directorial" control over that visualization, since one is not working with actors' performances and production designers' concepts as raw materials, as one must in film. Particularly with manga, graphic novel readers are used to a more expressionistic approach to visual style, well outside norms of cinematic realism. The skillful artist can exercise precise control over tone, pacing, and emphasis through quite free treatments of panel size and placement, relative size of figures, drawing styles, and reduction of the image to its essentials. Though a few series—most notably the Classical Comics series—opt for "period performance" treatments of the narrative, it is noteworthy how many graphic novel treatments resituate Shakespeare in new contexts. *Julius GN,* for example, recasts *Julius Caesar* as a "gangsta" tale; *She Lies with Angels* assimilates *Romeo and Juliet* to the X-Men universe, focusing on a forbidden romance between a human and a mutant; Gareth Hinds's *Merchant of Venice* is set in the contemporary business world of modern Venice; and *Pibgorn Rep* reimagines *A Midsummer Night's Dream* as a forties backstage musical. Self-MadeHero's Manga Shakespeare series has been especially creative in finding novel settings for its adaptations, placing *King Lear* in colonial America (with Lear as a king gone "native") or *Hamlet* in a postapocalyptic world of cyborgs and holographs.[2] We might understand this as consolidating the mobility of Shakespearean narrative across contexts that were popularized in nineties film, in this case extending Shakespeare tales to pop contexts once thought incompatible with the Bard. And undoubtedly one reason for shifting from film to the graphic novel is that the graphic novel has gained a cultural cachet among youth audiences—it is in many ways an emblematic medium for hip geek culture. Where once Albert Kantner stressed that enjoying the Classics Illustrated version was no substitute for reading the "real thing," now, in an age where visual culture is the new cultural dominant, graphic versions of Shakespeare have lost their former stigma and are becoming texts in their own right.

Even so, the graphic novelization of Shakespeare changes several of the energies it has inherited from nineties Shakespeare film. Even though Shakespeare graphic novels continue the process of converting Shakespeare to visual form, at the same time they represent a curious retextualization of Shakespeare. No doubt as a result of the needs of the educational market, many of the Shakespeare series feature full or lightly edited texts. Thus the Shakespearean text is reintroduced, but now not in terms of traditional scholarly protocols but rather in terms of popular visual media and their modes of reception. What is more, the relationship between the text and the image is variable across various series. In some cases, where long blocks of Shakespearean language threaten to overwhelm the visuals (as they do in the Comic Book Shakespeare series), the texts become an unintended allegory of the conflict between visual and textual Shakespeare. Other series strike different ratios between image and word. The Classical Comics series, for example, issues three different versions of the text—"original" (Shakespeare's language), "plain text" (modern paraphrase), and "quick text" (a much-reduced modern paraphrase)—for each of its Shakespeare plays, but the visual presentation of the narrative remains the same across all three versions. This approach—dictated by the desire to appeal to different market niches—strikes me as akin to dubbing films into different languages. Interestingly, the traditional relationship between text and performance is here reversed. On the stage, the text remains stable while performances of it differ from one another; here, the visual narrative remains the same while the texts that attach to it differ. Despite the fact that Shakespeare's language is available as one of the options, the text's authority within the graphic "performance" is notably reconfigured—Shakespearean language becomes one of three "sound track" options or, to change the metaphor, a styling option, not a primary source of the narrative.

Notable too in these works is the interplay of Shakespeare's cultural authority and the cultural status of the graphic novel as a form. The "comic book" has long played a symbolic role in twenti-eth-century debates about the effects of popular culture; comics, so the argument goes, are by their nature reductive, sensationalistic, and puerile, appealing to infantile heroic fantasies and primitive impulses to violence and sexuality, emblematic of how mass cul-ture caters to the lowest common cultural denominator. By renam-ing the form "graphic novel" in the late seventies, producers sought to signal both a change in length and type of narratives, but more important, the capacity for this form to address subject matter with a complexity and depth that rivals accepted literary media. The Shakespeare graphic novel, then, represents an example of re-ciprocal legitimation. The graphic novel format offers Shakespeare an extension of the project nineties film pursued, the recalibration of Shakespearean cultural authority to fit the demands of youth cul-ture, and in such a way that the resulting production also meets the needs of the educational market. Shakespeare offers the graphic novel the opportunity to demonstrate the format's capacity to han-dle complex, serious material. The Shakespeare graphic novel ap-pears at a crucial moment in the medium's history, when it has garnered some critical respect but in limited quarters and when it is moving away from superhero sagas and tales of adolescent angst toward a much wider range of narratives. Graphic Shakespeare thus suggests the graphic novel's continuity with traditional liter-ary culture, providing a means for consolidating and extending its critical acceptance as a legitimate art form.

The "mangafication" of Shakespeare is a special case of this process. In Japan, manga is a highly developed, critically respected medium whose appeal reaches across generations and other social divides; outside Japan, however, though manga has gained popu-larity in recent years, especially as translations have appeared more regularly, it nonetheless remains a genre for a niche market for youth. Adapting Shakespeare to manga, then, is a means for assimi-lating manga conventions and visual styles to a larger Western au-dience. Manga Shakespeare becomes a means to "universalize" the form for a broader audience, showing manga's potential power and value as a global lingua franca. And, reciprocally, since manga is still coded as Japanese, the very fact that Shakespeare can be trans-lated into the form is yet another demonstration of Shakespeare's status as a global author.

I've purposely avoided offering close readings of individual examples in this discussion. In much recent criticism the institutional imperative to generate close readings has tended to focus our critical attention on individual acts of Shakespearean appropriation. While there is certainly value in attending to the dynamics at work in those examples, it is equally important to acknowledge that individual works also always participate in collective acts of Shakespearean adaptation, acts that considered as an aggregate are reshaping our conceptions of Shakespeare in response to energies, paths of flow, tensions, pressures, and blockages within the larger social and cultural matrix, itself constantly in flux. Often an important issue in those collective acts is how to recuperate Shakespearean cultural authority when the cultural preconditions of that authority are undermined or challenged by new media or social systems. The history of the last twenty years suggests that adaptors are collectively ingenious and tenacious in finding means for reconceiving and thereby preserving that authority, even in the face of the enormous challenge of global mass-media culture. By attending to how our Shakespeare is constituted as a specific collection of qualities, intensities, and tendencies in flux at any moment in history, in short, by thinking of Shakespeare as a collectively created, adaptational rhizome rather than a body of texts appropriated by single adaptors, we may be better able to chart the ever-nomadic paths of Shakespearean cultural capital.

Notes

1. See, for example, Pendulum Illustrated, Graphic Shakespeare, Picture This!, Comic Book Shakespeare, Livewire Shakespeare, No Fear Graphic Shakespeare, and Wonderland Illustrated Classics, to name a few.

2. The relationship between the visuals of film versions and graphic novel versions can sometimes be quite direct. Igarashi Yumiko's manga *Romeo and Juliet* (1995) is deeply indebted to Zeffirelli's film adaptation in setting and costuming; Emma Vieceli's Manga Shakespeare *Much Ado About Nothing* clearly references elements of mise-en-scène—colonnades, arched doorways, interiors, the garden—from Branagh's 1993 film.

Applying the Paradigm: Shakespeare and World Cinema

MARK THORNTON BURNETT

FROM THE EVIDENCE OF THE art houses and multiplexes, at least, it might appear as if we have witnessed the death of Shakespeare and film. After a flurry of cinematic activity mainly spearheaded by Kenneth Branagh in the 1990s, and a few gusts of representation in the following decade, the "boom" of the Bard on-screen ground to a halt. Yet if we turn the coin over, so to speak, and attend to alternative systems of production and distribution, a more nuanced picture emerges. For, during this period, seemingly dominated by an Anglophone tradition, there has been a corresponding plethora of Shakespeare films developed outside immediate UK and US fields of circulation. Hence, *William Shakespeare's "A Midsummer Night's Dream"* (dir. Michael Hoffman, 1999) is often cited as a title that illustrates the enduring popularity of the play, yet it has rarely been linked to *An Athens Summer Night's Dream* (dir. Dimitris Athanitis, 1999), a Greek film that plays searching variations on the theme of a stage production of the drama affecting "real life." Such a comparison would surely yield pertinent findings touching upon the local complexions of *A Midsummer Night's Dream* and its cultural translatability.

Similarly, coming toward the end of a run of television productions was the Baz Luhrmann–inspired *Macbeth* (dir. Geoffrey Wright, 2006): an opportunity exists here for discussing the film in relation to another version of the play, *Yellamma* (dir. Mohan Koda, 2001), a Telegu-language recreation of Shakespeare's story of ambition set in India during the time of the Sepoy Mutiny. Dialogue between the two films could prompt us to reflect anew upon *Macbeth*'s political resonances and to query critical assumptions about the universality of its analysis of power relations. More generally, paying attention to what resides outside the mainstream allows us to explore the ways in which current templates for filmed Shakespeare agree or disagree inside or across national boundaries. And by bringing into the arena of debate an international sense of filmic interpretations of Shakespeare's plays, we may yet arrive at a richer construction of "Shakespearean" significances. A "Shakespeare and World Cinema" line of inquiry is all the more urgent in that, by and large, criticism has tended to concentrate on a narrow sample of Anglophone Shakespeare films.[1] By contrast, extending the purview complicates the centrality of English-language film and inscribes a more representative and ethically responsible Shakespeare canon. The effect is to offer a new understanding of Shakespeare and his relevance, one that allows for interrogation of the channels through which we have access to Shakespearean production and insists upon a reengagement with plurality.

Pursuing the paradigm sketched here, I offer in this essay a working discussion of *The Banquet* (dir. Xiaogang Feng, 2006), a Chinese retelling of *Hamlet*, and use the film to ask questions about what might be entailed in a "Shakespeare and World Cinema" critical project. *The Banquet* declares its generic affiliations via the evocation of a bloody moment in Chinese history: an on-screen announcement informs us that the action is set in "China, 907 B.C. . . . the period [of] . . . the 'Five Dynasties and Ten Kingdoms' . . . an era plagued by widespread turmoil . . . and a bitter struggle for power within the imperial family." Lush cinematography reinforces the film's epic dimensions, as in the sumptuous opening where the extravagantly attired empress Wan/Gertrude (Ziyi Zhang) is filmed from behind processing toward the throne: the sequence recalls a similar back-view image of the protagonist in *Hamlet* (dir. Kenneth Branagh, 2006) and positions *The Banquet* as a continuation of this earlier production in ambition and scale. Framing devices, then, consort with filmic content to establish recognizable interpretive parameters for *The Banquet*. Among them is perhaps the film's boldest rereading in which the Shakespearean family is reconfigured so as to highlight culture-specific questions about female agency. The Gertrude figure is situated at the center, and female sexuality is constructed as the lynchpin or underlying spur to the narrative. Thus, in the film, Empress Wan/Gertrude is involved in a love affair with her stepson, Wu Luan/Hamlet (Daniel Wu), despite her power-brokering marriage to Emperor Li/Claudius (You Ge): the authority she wields stems from her combined roles as stepmother and ruler. More generally as part of its "Shakespearean" engagements, *The Banquet* places its lineage on display, dwelling repeatedly upon forms of theater as genres enjoying a powerful utility. In this application, Shakespeare is the instrument with which "Asia," broadly conceived and multiply understood, reflects upon itself at a key stage of its recent global emergence. Crucially, self-consciousness in the film assumes local complexions that both answer to the transposition imperative and express divergent political responses to the contemporary.

Expressions of a Shakespearean kinship are part and parcel of how *The Banquet* is immediately structured and distinguished. For instance, *Hamlet,* and reinventions of the play across time, are repeatedly evoked in the highlighting of questions or images and readings that have gained widespread critical currency. Whenever Qing Nu/Ophelia (Xun Zhou) appears, the sound of running water is heard: this diegetic signature is picked up in the song associated with her about the boat girl and stamps the character (who dies via poisoning rather than drowning) with the memory of her counterpart's means of death in Shakespeare's "original." The play—in particular, the protagonist's role as "soldier" and "poet" in Ophelia's estimation—returns more forcefully in the representation of a Wu Luan/Hamlet who is a practitioner of martial arts and a student of music and calligraphy (here, as elsewhere, *The Banquet* implicitly elects to privilege the textual traces of a female character's perspective). At the same time, *The Banquet* prioritizes the play's Oedipal dimension: because Wu Luan/Hamlet is figured as having lost not only his father but also his former lover (Empress Wan/ Gertrude), an obvious rationale is offered for his melancholy and subsequent reification of paternal bereavement. *The Banquet* investigates the question of who or what inhabits the armor of the dead Hamlet by figuring the ghost as a chain-mailed carapace that is empathetically occupied. In the scene where Wu Luan/Hamlet investigates his father's armor, a point-of-view shot from inside the casing's eyeholes suggests a still-sentient presence, while an accompanying glimpse of blood trickling from the sockets points out the idea of harm or injury. As in the play, this ghost is offended: something is not yet satisfactorily settled. Later, Wu Luan/Hamlet grasps at a handkerchief that falls from the air: on it is illustrated a dark figure puffing poison into a victim's ear with a quill. Because the sound of background breathing is heard in this sequence, too, the suggestion is that the ghost's inhaling and exhaling motions have blurred with the murderer's blowing: father and uncle are briefly Oedipally synonymous. Or, looked at slightly differently, the sequence exposes the moment when the emperor expires and the usurper assumes his living privileges. These episodes are largely wordless, yet they have the virtue of communicating in a powerfully economic way the richness of the text and a powerful history of Shakespearean interpretation and debate.

To confess to Shakespearean debts, *The Banquet* suggests, is also to be self-conscious about the processes through which the Bard is reanimated for twentieth- and twenty-first-century cinema audiences. Revealing, then, is the film's opening, which takes place in an outdoor theater, "under the protection of the Crown Prince," in the "southern heartlands." The correlation with the King's Men and early modern royal patronage posits performance in *The Banquet* as a kind of descendant of Shakespearean playing practices. In its circular shape the film's theater resembles the Globe: from the start, then, *The Banquet* imagines itself as a reconstruction of Shakespeare that is for the world. Inside his retreat, Wu Luan/Hamlet, seeking "solace in the art of music and dance," acts out through mime impressions of sufferings and disappointments, suggesting theater as recuperative and physicality as a way of coming to terms with romantic rejection. The multiple uses of playing are further instanced when the outdoor theater serves simultaneously as a space for martial arts and a highly theatricalized form of combat. Later, we see Empress Wan/Gertrude ascending a dais to view her late husband's armor (costume is a political spectacle) and taking a bath in another circular enclosure (the eroticized body is placed on display). The theatrical is also figured in *The Banquet* in the ways in which the film conjures various permutations of *The Mousetrap*—in a rehearsal for the performance (in which Wu Luan's parrying of the swords of his attackers refracts Hamlet's verbal dexterity), in the performance itself and in the lengthy banquet scene. Here, Qing Nu/Ophelia sings the "Song of Yue" and, unwittingly drinking the poisoned wine intended for Emperor Li/Claudius, dies before she has completed her performance. Throughout, via her love of embroidery and handiwork, Qing Nu/Ophelia has been tied to Wu Luan/Hamlet and his theatrical preoccupations. It is telling, then, that the protagonist reveals himself at this point, stripping off his mask—and his "antic disposition"—to cradle his dying lover: in another gesture to Shakespeare's play, a celebratory banquet becomes an impromptu funeral.[2] A powerful distinction is drawn between the unwavering commitment of a lover and a context of court treachery: throughout, *The Banquet* suggests an intense evocation of drama as reparation and of the ways in which theater and politics are intimately intertwined.

Emerging from an encounter with Shakespeare defined in self-conscious terms is a concentration on the local. Typical are Empress Wan/Gertrude's reflections on her training with the "sword of the Yue maiden," which make sense inside a culture historically associated with education and mentorship. The evocation of Empress Wan/Gertrude's studenthood connects her to Wu Luan/Hamlet, particularly in the opening, where he, too, is discovered as schooling himself. The stillness of his body in these sequences, coupled with the care with which he performs individual gestures, bespeaks a conjunction of body, mind, and spirit: as Sheng-mei Ma states, in Asian chivalric stories, "the protagonist's arduous apprenticeship and later combat is predicated upon a philosophy of stringent self-discipline."[3] Skillfulness in music and dance prepares the way for the discovery of Wu Luan/Hamlet's proficiency in calligraphy. Because this form of writing was thought to define masculine strength, Wu Luan/Hamlet is thus envisaged as particularly empowered. Brush strokes in calligraphy imitated parts of the bamboo plant, and following hard upon orange-filtered battle scenes comes the introduction of Wu Luan/Hamlet in a swaying bamboo grove: the juxtaposition analogizes the ways in which families can be pushed by politics and fortunes fluctuate in times of war. Flexibility, probity, and righteousness, qualities that bamboo is said to incarnate, are also, of course, the distinguishing markers of a Wu Luan/Hamlet who, dressed in white and consummately executing expertise in martial arts, outwits his dark armored opponents and acrobatically avoids injury: body and plant are imagined as one. *The Banquet* commences, to adopt a formulation of Gary G. Xu, with a "poetic sense" of "*yiying* . . . the harmony between the human mind and . . . surrounding nature."[4] Yet such a balance is immediately upset in the spectacle of the armed assassins sent against Wu Luan/Hamlet by a conspiratorial uncle: here, the Confucian virtues of loyalty and camaraderie (*zhong* and *yi*), which were commonly tied to the bamboo, are conspicuous by their absence.[5] A conjuration of the local visualizes a Shakespearean preoccupation; at the same time, such a procedure is key to establishing the moral polarities of the particular filmic universe.

Key to *The Banquet*'s moral polarities is its foregrounding of female character: remodeled as a villainous Claudius, Empress Wan/ Gertrude is discovered as a proactive and scheming aspirant in a *Hamlet* that places her, and not her male counterparts, at center stage. Contests for privilege are at work in the scene where Empress Wan/Gertrude and Emperor Li/Claudius play, half-threateningly, half-erotically, with each other's ties and titles: relational terms are bandied in tit-for-tat fashion, while the mutual insistence on the "correct" forms of "address" being employed ("Your Majesty" and "Empress") suggests a jockeying for advantage. At the same time, as the accompanying dialogue reveals, union with Emperor Li/ Claudius is the price Empress Wan/Gertrude must pay to secure her own needs and requirements. "Will brother-in-law let the prince go free?" she asks, her question highlighting not only Wu Luan/Hamlet's imprisonment but also her own: to effect release, Empress Wan/Gertrude barters in sexual favor. On a later occasion, Empress Wan/Gertrude reflects on her titular trajectory: "Little Wan . . . Empress . . . Her Majesty, the Emperor," she intones, tracing a historical journey from child to adult, from dependent to independent, from female to male. Simultaneously stated is an identification with the Chinese phoenix or *fenghuang,* a mythical creature embodying an empress's powers and abilities. "I shall rise," exclaims Empress Wan/Gertrude in a promise that is as arresting for its glorification of singleness as it is for its exclusion of the male Chinese dragon with which the female phoenix was conventionally allied.

Ultimately, however, *The Banquet* offers an essentially dispassionate picture of the quest for female emancipation. Stabbed by an anonymous assassin as snow falls, Empress Wan/Gertrude fails in her political endeavor, the cold of the snow symbolically blanketing and changing the heated temperature of her "desire." White covers red (the spirit of Wu Luan/Hamlet returns) and effaces Empress Wan/Gertrude's "flame" of ambition. As petty human actions cede place to larger natural processes, the assembled maidservants quickly depart, suggesting both a clue to the identity of the killer and a sorority of women taking revenge. Writes Molly Hand of *The Banquet,* "chaos and death, darkness and despair, there is little hope for renewal or rebirth."[6] Yet the closing montage is not as definitive as this assessment allows. As the knife blade is seen being dropped into a mossy pool, a glimpse is afforded of koi carp swimming together beneath. Beyond the "unweeded garden" (1.2.135) of the court, it is implied, and past the knotty entanglement of mystery and motive, the beautiful and the rare are still discernible.

Linked in Chinese mythology to love and friendship, and associated with a state of bliss, the koi carp index an as-yet-unrealized
world of harmonious interaction that belies surface appearances.

Thanks to a screening at the 2008 meeting of the Shakespeare Association of America, *The Banquet* is beginning to have its creden-
tials approved as an appropriation of *Hamlet*.[7] This was an event
that helped to focus interest on Asian "Shakespeares"; as Alexander C. Y. Huang has argued in a different context, "the first decade
of the new millennium was for Asian cinematic Shakespeares as
the 1990s had been for Anglophone Shakespeare on film."[8] Yet the
fact remains that, for the most part, the kinds of films instanced in
my opening paragraph have slipped beneath the radar. Their relative absence from discussion prompts us to ask: What is a Shakespeare film, and what mechanisms do we use to assess its critical
afterlife? What factors shape the invisibility or visibility of Shakespeare films produced during the "boom" period from the 1980s
onward? In part, this critical imbalance is tied to the networks of
distribution and exhibition within which particular films are identified. But this requires us, as critics and consumers, to take greater
account of the global circuit that defines and determines reception
and to question the unidirectional cultural flow that invariably
travels from West to East or from North to South. For non-Anglophone Shakespeare films, such as *The Banquet,* to be properly appreciated necessitates a rethinking of Shakespeare's recent filmic
manifestations. It is no longer possible to talk about Shakespeare
within existing geographical and political parameters; instead, alternative paradigms that acknowledge exchange must be developed, paradigms that, in helping to expose current inequities of
space and place, stand as testimony to the ethical valences of a
global Shakespearean citizenship. Only then might ongoing questions about fidelity and authorship in Shakespeare studies, and
knowledge and authority, be adequately confronted.

Such a rethinking involves the application of a number of methodologies and practices—an attention to context, a deployment of
history, the utilization of gendered critique, a bringing to bear on
materials of theoretical awareness (the gap between the study of
Shakespeare on film and film studies is still pronounced), a distinguishing between various cultural perspectives, a sense of local and
global interchange. *The Banquet* is a case in point. If some parts of
Asia, for example, are now characterized by a move toward recognizing multiple points of reference, then *The Banquet* follows suit:

in discovering the self-immolation of a system and the impossibility of authority being concentrated in one figure, the film implicitly argues for a need for a more various and representative order. In its reading of *Hamlet,* moreover, *The Banquet* similarly recognizes that power can inhere in more than one location—the martial arts, the disciplines of art and music, the natural world.

Its utilization of a local register is, of course, underpinned by Shakespeare; that is, *The Banquet* shows how the Bard is the medium or conduit through which the political discussions, gendered disputes, cultural vexations, and social imperatives of twentieth- and twentieth-first-century Asia might best be conveyed and communicated. The force of Shakespeare is what is recognized here, and, indeed, in the film, the power of the Bard in performance is a recurring interest. Shakespeare, as the film conceives him, is a palimpsest for revision, a repository of meaning that facilitates the processes through which the new Asia also reassesses itself. And if this is a film that draws attention to itself as artifact (*The Banquet* is a theatrical object lesson in reconstruction), and reflects upon how Shakespeare has been relayed and transposed through writing and script, then this is because self-consciousness is a symptom of the encounter with modernity. The process of analogizing its relation to Shakespeare, a Western cultural phenomenon, becomes the means through which *The Banquet* ultimately contemplates the tensions and the energies, the initiatives and the instabilities, that constitute its own possibility.

Notes

1. An exception is Richard Burt, "Shakespeare and Asia in Postdiasporic Cinemas: Spin-offs and Citations of the Plays from Bollywood to Hollywood," in *Shakespeare, the Movie, II: Popularizing the Plays on Film, TV, Video and DVD,* ed. Richard Burt and Lynda E. Boose, 265–303 (New York: Routledge, 2003).

2. *The Norton Shakespeare,* ed. Stephen Greenblatt, Walter Cohen, Jean E. Howard, and Katharine Eisaman Maus (New York: Norton, 1997), 1.5.173. All further references appear in the text.

3. Sheng-mei Ma, *East-West Montage: Reflections on Asian Bodies in Diaspora* (Honolulu: University of Hawaii Press, 2007), 66.

4. Gary G. Xu, *Sinascape: Contemporary Chinese Cinema* (Lanham, MD: Rowman and Littlefield, 2007), 40.

5. Ma, *East-West Montage,* 66, 42, 65, 67.

6. Molly Hand, review of *Ye Yan/The Banquet* (dir. Feng Xiaogang), *Shakespeare* 4, no. 4 (2008): 433.

7. A "review cluster" of essays dedicated to *The Banquet* and *Maqbool* (dir. Vishal Bhardwaj, 2004), an Indian version of *Macbeth,* appears in *Borrowers and Lenders: The Journal of Shakespeare and Appropriation* 4, no. 2 (2009).

8. Alexander C. Y. Huang, *Chinese Shakespeares: Two Centuries of Cultural Exchange* (New York: Columbia University Press, 2009), 12.

ARTICLES

Black Shakespeareans vs. Minstrel Burlesques: "Proper" English, Racist Blackface Dialect, and the Contest for Representing "Blackness," 1821–1844

ROBERT HORNBACK

ONE AREA OF MARKED OVERLAP in examinations of race in Renais sance studies and of antebellum minstrelsy alike is an interest in whether or not early representations of blackness—however "early" is defined—might stage the authentic presence of black identities and perspectives. As Eric Lott noted in his study, *Love and Theft: Blackface Minstrelsy and the American Working Class* (1993), the earliest historians of minstrelsy "assum[ed] . . . that minstrelsy's scurrilous representations of black people were scrupulously authentic."[1] In response to generations of what Lott called "revisionist" critics who thereafter aimed at revealing "minstrelsy's patent inauthenticity, its northern origins, [and] its self-evidently dominative character,"[2] W. T. Lhamon Jr. has been one of the chief proponents in the last several years of what we might call a *counter*revisionist interpretation of minstrelsy by which he sees any racist elements in supposed white egalitarian critiques of elitism as accidental or even as entirely absent. Before the rise of full-blown minstrelsy in 1843, Lhamon indeed finds only "cross-racial attraction or mutuality," "anti-racist dimensions," and wholly inclusive, "integrative" impulses in American blackface, particularly in T. D. Rice's famed impersonation of blackness through the character of "Jim Crow."[3] Before we turn to reexamining this romanticized view, such recent counterrevisionist work must be distinguished at the outset from the previous, more subtle criticism of Lott, which granted "minstrelsy's oppressive dimension" while simultaneously aiming to complicate the previous dualism of inter-

125

pretations reading the tradition as either "wholly authentic or wholly hegemonic."[4] Noting that beyond the pervasive grotesque racial parody and racial domination was an occasionally "sympathetic (if typically condescending) attitude toward black people" in blackface minstrelsy, Lott pointed to particular moments in which we may sometimes observe a paradoxical, "dialectical flickering of racial insult and racial envy, moments of domination *and* moments of liberation, . . . a pattern at times amounting to no more than the two faces of racism, at others gesturing toward a specific kind of racial danger, and all constituting a peculiarly American structure of racial feeling."[5] Unfortunately, in the inevitable pendulum swing of criticism, Lott's subtle revision has given way to some views in recent work that Lott clearly aimed to differentiate himself from: "I am not one of those critics who see in a majority of minstrel songs an unalloyed self-criticism by whites under cover of blackface, the racial parody nearly incidental."[6] He seems here to have anticipated Lhamon's argument that Rice's stereotypical representations do not constitute racial parody but rather an unambiguous, unambivalent acknowledgment of the presence of black culture and perspectives—Rice is, for instance, said to have been "translating black experiences for whites" in "ethnographic skits" in which he was "copying black gestures to identify . . . *with* them"—even as, dubiously, the presence of some black audience members in the now newly *segregated* "upper gallery reserved for blacks" (in the very period in which "Jim Crow" was already becoming synonymous with segregation) is here somehow recast as "partially integrated in the compromise then permissible" in order to suggest some remarkable inclusiveness in Rice's representations.[7]

Without intending to refute Lott's nuanced arguments finding moments of attraction and ambivalence in some minstrelsy (especially since audience interest is, in fact, a major concern in this essay), recent critical excesses warrant a corrective reexamination of the limits of assuming identification and presence via mere representation. Writing in a different, yet ultimately highly relevant context in her work on the representation of race in Renaissance England, Dympna Callaghan challenged "the fetishistic insistence on presence" in readings of black or Africanist Shakespearean characters like Othello and emphatically cautioned that "*presence cannot be equated with representation any more than representation can be equated with inclusion.*"[8] Callaghan's healthy "skepti-

cism about the benefits of representation" offers, I want to suggest,
an antidote to what finally amounts to distorting "fantasies of presence" in recent minstrel criticism.[9] What an application of Callaghan's argument cannot address, however, is the struggle of African
American actors to *be present* on the antebellum stage out of a desire to *represent themselves,* remarkably enough, by performing
Shakespearean plays like *Othello.* Though Callaghan's insistence
that originally onstage, "Othello *was* a *white* man" might make a
willingness to consider the impact of a later black actor's race upon
the role seem ironic in hindsight,[10] a key issue in the history of racial representation was nonetheless the contest between black and
white Americans (and Englishmen, too) for representing and con-
structing both what "blackness" and "Shakespeare" meant in precisely the period in which minstrelsy developed, between 1821
and 1844.

Prior investigations of the representation of blackness have overlooked the degree to which literary blackface dialect and the foolish, misspeaking minstrel stereotype emerged in response to black
Shakespeareans claiming Shakespeare as part of their American
cultural heritage while using representation in order to affect perceptions about blackness. Indeed, while I have worked elsewhere
to uncover a protoracist Renaissance blackface comic tradition underlying pseudoscientific racism,[11] another untold story about the
influence of Renaissance drama on the blackface tradition is the degree to which the rise of minstrelsy had much to do with racist
responses to nineteenth-century African American actors' performances of Shakespeare. As we will see, it was the eloquence of the
Shakespearean tragic figures Othello and Richard III and, above all,
black actors' self-assertions as "Shakespeare's proud representative[s]" that presented a special challenge to nineteenth-century
racist assumptions. In response to black actors' representations of
Othello, white theatergoers required that the "noble Moor" be utterly degraded and that white anxieties about potential equality be
exorcized through demeaning minstrel burlesques of Shakespeare,
while one black actor's portrayal of Richard III even influenced the
characterization of Jim Crow. In fact, one of the most damning conventions of the American blackface tradition, a recognizably modern stage caricature of "black dialect," was standardized in the
1820s in reaction against—through grossly distorted, propagan-
distic representations of—black Shakespeareans, particularly ones
playing the eloquent outsiders Othello and Richard. In one way or

another, Shakespeare's language thus came to be implicated in a high-stakes contest for representing blackness in nineteenth-century America.

At the same time, burlesque Shakespeare in blackface played a significant role both in defining the American working class and in the transformation of "Shakespeare" from being a fundamental part of popular culture in nineteenth-century America to something identified by Lawrence Levine in his brilliant work *Highbrow/Lowbrow: The Emergence of Cultural Hierarchy in America* as, by the end of the century, increasingly "highbrow," that is, an untouchable, even sacred possession of elite/high culture and thus something rejected by an emergent, nativist working class as both elitist and un-American. Since Levine observes that "[i]t is easier to describe this transformation than to explain it," as well as that, "The more firmly based Shakespeare was in nineteenth-century culture, the more difficult it is to understand why he lost so much of his audience so quickly,"[12] I would add that such a phenomenon was already observable by midcentury, beginning in the wake of the blackface burlesques of Shakespeare and black Shakespeareans, which helped give rise to the flourishing of full-blown minstrelsy. After midcentury, the preface to one of E. P. Christy's minstrel songsters could thus already blare, "[O]ur countrymen confuted the stale cant of our European detractors that nothing original could emanate from Americans."[13] Touting blackface minstrelsy with characteristic jingoism as a "NATIVE" art form, Christy anticipates similar claims of originality and novelty that reverberate, oddly, even through modern criticism. Hence, the resulting "racial caricature," with its "conscious impersonation of the alien African," has been credited with creating an "absolutely native" American tradition, wholly "indigenous to our soil," a uniquely "native and national genre," that has recently been characterized as an utterly original and "emergent social semantic" that formed, quite simply, a "historically new articulation of racial difference," not in any way an "incarnation of an age-old" type.[14] If minstrelsy was—and still is—deemed a native form of American popular culture, we must recognize the degree to which it developed first through, then *against,* a highbrow "Shakespeare" it helped to create.

Contexts and Reception of the African Theater

In the decade that first embraced American blackface performance, the 1820s, as the slave population in the United States as a whole increased from 1,529,012 in the 1820 census to 1,987,428 in the 1830 census,[15] there appeared myriad expressions and assertions of freedom by manumitted black New Yorkers. The Gradual Manumission Act had freed all children of slaves born after July 4, 1799, and, by 1810, New York City could already claim the country's largest population of free African Americans.[16] Then, in 1817, New York State passed legislation decreeing the end of slavery in ten years.[17] As thousands of freed people were establishing a community in New York City (one that increased from a total in 1790 of 3,470 to 13,796 by 1830),[18] some of them formed the African Theater, specializing in Shakespeare. One reason no doubt, in keeping with the remarks of one newspaper critic of the era, was that "The playgoing portion of our negro population feel more interest in, and go in greater numbers to see, the plays of Shakespeare represented on stage, than any other class of dramatic performance."[19] The African Theater opened on Monday September 17, 1821, to a full house with *Richard III,* and remained open until 1824, undergoing sporadic revivals thereafter in the 1828–29 season and, apparently, ca. 1843, when an English traveler once again refers to "entertainment at the black theater" in performances of *Richard III.*[20] The company's star possibly reappeared at least as late as 1844, when, I will argue, a minstrel Shakespearean burlesque seemingly alludes to its lead actor and frequent solo performer, James Hewlett. For some twenty years, Hewlett and the African Company would intermittently perform a repertory of plays that included not only *Richard III* and *Othello* but *Macbeth* and *Julius Caesar* in a theater "seating as many as three hundred patrons."[21] Such performance prompted reactions ranging from enthusiastic admiration to bigoted contempt. But it was the latter of these responses that would leave behind the most familiar legacy as the members of the company met vehement resistance to their efforts to make Shakespeare theirs, to assert that, as Hewlett put it, "he is *our* bard as well as yours."[22]

Although George Thompson, in a move that appears analogous to the counterrevisionist minstrel critics' eagerness to emphasize cross-racial identification in blackface performance, discounts any assessment of the African Theater "as harassed with a continual and concerted persecution" and finds such claims simply "exaggerated,"[23] the evidence points elsewhere. As he outlines the first two years of a history that was thereafter sporadic, including the forced closing of the company's first and second theater, arrests right off the stage, a police raid on a performance that required yet another "forced . . . retreat to the outskirts of town," a riot by circus performers evidently paid by a rival theater, harassment of the actors onstage leading to performances being abandoned, a vicious assault and battery (never punished) on the teenaged Ira Aldridge, and beating of the manager William Brown, one wonders how much harassment would be required to be considered persecution.[24] In the end, however, one suspects that Thompson is not just playing with semantics when he imposes the qualifiers "continual and concerted," for he is also ignoring what we will see was dogged harassment in the press and from the stage.

The hostile response to the company's emergence came not just with considerable urgency but also with a retentive fervor sustained over the course of the next two decades. Throughout this period, the most bigoted white voices in the theatrical and political culture understood the stakes quite clearly. At a time when "Shakespeare" was associated with the best oratory—in a democratic nation hungry for rhetoric—that a group of free men and women were owning their freedom by voicing their claim to Shakespearean eloquence seemed an assertion that demanded some kind of response. The black community in New York gravitated to Shakespeare not merely for entertainment purposes (one motive), but also in support of a bolder agenda, in order to demonstrate that black Americans were in no way inferior to white Americans, a view at least one of their actors, Hewlett, overtly expressed in abolitionist speeches. Thompson notes, moreover, that the company staged at least four plays with overtly political content that ranged from resistance to colonial power to slavery.[25] But, overt politics aside, the company's very performances asserted that there was no essential difference at all between black and white, something further expressed when the company temporarily took, in response to attacks, to calling its playhouse the "American Theater." Not for the last time, American and British whites who favored slavery intuitively understood that such a demonstration of mastery of Shakespearean English, conventionally termed "the King's English" on both sides of the Atlantic, could also demonstrate *self*-mastery, rationality, and thus equality. The African Theater, then, had to be stopped or, lacking that, at least undermined at every turn.

Efforts aimed at undercutting the company turned quickly to misrepresentation, for reviewers could only satisfy their readers' desire to have their self-affirming stereotypes of black inferiority confirmed by distorting what they witnessed: white critics and par-

odists on both sides of the Atlantic consistently portrayed the acting style practiced across the company as grossly incompetent and
ineloquent (an account that flies in the face of many details). For
example, a "Simon Snipe" suggested in *Sports of New York . . .
Containing an Evening at the African Theatre; Also a Trip to the
Races! With Two Appropriate Songs* (New York, 1823) that white
audience members who pelted the African Company's stage with
"chestnuts, peas, apple-cores, &c." were, apparently justifiably,
outraged that *Othello* had been "transformed into mimic burlesques."[26] The Scottish traveler Peter Nielson, writing in *Recollec-
tions of Six Years' Residence* (Glasgow, 1830), only begrudgingly
conceded that Hewlett's "Othello may pass, and another character
or two" in the repertory, while he offered what would become a
common response, sneering that "it really is worth one's while to
go there for a few nights for the novelty of the thing," revealing
some of the stakes involved by archly warning that such a "novelty" would subject one "to hear[ing] the king's English mur-
dorod."[27] Likewise, in 1828 29, in a piece entitled "The Negroes
of New York" in the *Family Magazine* (1829), appears a claim that
dominated hostile reviews, an implication that dialect interference
made "the pronunciation" of the African Company "ludicrous."[28]
Challenging such demeaning characterizations, however, is evidence of the eloquence of the man who promptly became the lead
actor of the African Company, Hewlett, in his surviving letters,
which is only buttressed by the notice he received for solo performances in which he showed an uncanny ability to imitate, apparently convincingly, famed actors such as the Englishmen Edmund
Kean and William Macready, and several glowing reviews in the
white press. In addition, the company for which he worked initially included (though evidently in minor roles) a teenaged Ira Aldridge,[29] later to become one of the most famous Shakespearean
actors of the nineteenth century.

Even if more fair-minded accounts of the company had not survived, the intensity of the critical denunciations would make one
wonder: If the company's performances were really laughable, why
did white audiences not welcome them as an opportunity to confirm their worst opinions? Why were their performances on occasion met with violence rather than laughter? That is to say, why
didn't racists simply come to laugh at James Hewlett as they would
Jim Crow?

Apparently, they could not, a conclusion supported by other contemporary commentaries that allow us to discern very different kinds of responses. For one, there is the account in Ira Aldridge's *Memoir,* which includes the actor's proud observation that patrons "who went to [the theater to] ridicule, remained to admire."[30] Contemporary evidence confirms this remark. One hostile critic had to concede that Hewlett "gave imitations in tolerable style, of all the popular singers and actors of the age," just as, amid slurs, a George Stone acknowledged with surprise and enthusiasm in 1826 that "this darkey was *some* in Richard and Othello."[31] A less offensive (but still somewhat condescending) reviewer of a solo performance by Hewlett in the *Brooklyn Star* (Dec. 1825) observed that he had "a natural talent . . . and an excellent voice withal." Moreover, Hewlett "raised himself by the force of innate genius" to a point where "he would have done credit to any stage." In fact, were it not for his complexion, "a serious impediment," "he might rival some of the proudest actors who now tread our boards." "A Friend to Merit" concurred in the *New York American* (April 1826), calling Hewlett "one of the most astonishing phenomenas of the age," a man who "by the mere dint of natural genius and self-strengthened assiduity, [had] risen to successful competition with some of the first actors of the day."[32] And we have the frank assessment of African American activist Martin Robinson Delany, who, having witnessed what he called "a private rehearsal, in 1836," reported sixteen years later that although Hewlett "was not well educated," sometimes making "grammatical blunders," he was "a great delineator of character" who "possessed great intellectual powers."[33] Given overwhelming evidence that white audiences could not fully satisfy a desire to just come to laugh at the actors, it is clear that some white reviewers were intent on keeping empowering representations of African Americans—via Shakespearean English—from being seen not only by creating fictions about the performances, but by actually harassing the company.

After all, harassment took many forms. Notably, the *National Advocate* reported gleefully on September 21, 1821, the arrest of two of the company members so that, "though the sable audience retired peacable to their homes[,] Richard and Catesby were unfortunately taken by the watch." Given that the arrest of one of these actors on the charge of battery occurred "when [he was] engaged trimming the Public Lamps,"[34] it is clear that the so-called battery was provoked. In fact, company actors were attacked on several occasions. Hewlett himself was assaulted at the Park Theater on December 2, 1821.[35] And, on August 10, there was a riot at the African Company's American Theater when "a gang of fifteen or twenty ruffians," most of them white circus riders, attacked the stage, tearing the actors' costumes, destroying the scenery and curtain, breaking benches, cutting down the lamp over the pit, and assaulting the company manager William Brown.[36] Earlier, on July 19, a then not quite fifteen-year-old "Ira Aldridge, a black, of NO. 416 Broadway Street" (probably at or near Canal Street in the SoHo and Green-which area known as "Little Africa"), was savagely attacked in the sixth ward by one of the circus riders, a James Bellmont. The Indictment of August 12, a shocking document, which I now quote at some length, reveals that Bellmont:

UNLAWFULLY AND INJURIOUSLY, AGAINST THE WILL, AND WITHOUT THE CONSENT OF THE SAID Ira, AND ALSO . . . WITHOUT ANY LEGAL WARRANT, AUTHORITY, OR JUSTIFIABLE CAUSE WHATSOEVER, DID IMPRISON . . . [AND] FOR . . . THE SPACE OF FOUR HOURS THEN NEXT FOLLOWING . . . DID . . . BEAT, BRUISE, WOUND, AND ILL TREAT [Ira Aldridge] SO THAT HIS LIFE WAS GREATLY DESPAIRED OF; AND THAT THE SAID James WITH BOTH HIS HANDS . . . DID VIOLENTLY CAST, FLING, AND THROW THE SAID Ira TO . . . AND AGAINST THE GROUND; AND . . . IN AND UPON THE HEAD, NECK, BREAST, BACK, SIDES, AND OTHER PARTS OF THE BODY, WITH BOTH . . . FEET . . . VIOLENTLY DID KICK, STRIKE AND BEAT . . . THE SAID Ira. . . .[37]

Aldridge's *Memoir* would report, with not a little understatement, that whites "became actually *jealous* of the [company's] success . . . and emissaries were employed to put them down."[38]

On none of these occasions were any of the offenders ever punished; authorities can hardly have been said to be on the African Company's side. For example, late in 1821, when the company manager Brown rented space next door to the posh Park Theater, the police, led by that sheriff, journalist, and playwright, the industrious and ubiquitous Mordecai Noah (1785–1851), interrupted the opening night's performance and closed the theater for disturbing the peace.[39] Of course, the real disturbance was on the part of competing theatrical entrepreneurs such as Stephen Price of the Park Theater, located at elegant Park Row and newly rebuilt after a fire at considerable cost.[40] Price even paid thugs to bully the fledgling company, and, as the impresario Brown repeatedly moved his actors to different spaces, "Noah pursued, closing performance after performance, making some arrests right off the stage."[41] The company was finally driven back to its original location at the corner of Mercer and Bleeker streets,[42] just one block west of Broadway and two blocks north of Houston Street (now the neighborhood of New York University—where there is, remarkably, *no* historical marker of any sort). Although located on the outskirts of what was then the settled part of the city,[43] the harassment never ceased. Even so, as the *Commercial Advertiser* remarked with some admiration on January 16, 1822, and as others were to come to understand, "It seems . . . that they are not so easily to be driven from the field in which Shakespeare, Garrick, . . . and our . . . jolly Sheriff have reaped such harvests of glory."[44]

Legal harassment and looking the other way after physical attacks were not the sole means the "jolly" Sheriff Mordecai Noah exercised in policing the African Theater Company in order to maintain a sense of difference that accorded with his ideal social order. Part of the city's Tammany Hall Democratic political machine at a time when the party was working to deny voting access to the black citizenry, Noah carried out his most powerful enforcing of racial boundaries in his capacity as editor of the patriotically named *National Advocate.* As a Jewish American sometimes subjected in nineteenth-century America to bigoted stereotyping himself, it is possible that, in his falsified attacks against Hewlett and his company, Noah may have been driven in part by a keen desire to assert his own sameness with other white Americans by making a scapegoat of black Americans. Whatever the underlying motivations behind his purported reviews and mock-advertisements, he served up parodies representing the African Company's use of theater, and of Shakespearean English in particular, in denigrating terms that pioneered the stereotypical techniques that endured long thereafter. For example, deriding the African Theater in the *National Advocate* of August 27, 1823, he produced a mock playbill that simultaneously attacked African Americans' political activism/oratory and their artistic endeavors. The announcement of the "GRAND CONCERT OF DE BOB-LINK SOCIETY" ("bob-link" being an absurd malapropism for the more conventional "bobalition," itself a racist malaprop for "abolition" employed by racist white propagandists), was followed by a subtitle reflecting Noah's chief point about black New Yorkers: " 'De times hab changed,' But we hab not." The opening read, "In consequence of great couragement bin had at skunk point for dram-tick berformance, de managers will gib grand consert ebery evening dis week."[45] In 1827, another poster, "De Grandest Bobalition," singled out Hewlett ("an broder Hewlett sing dis song in he bes style"), making him likely "the only African American to achieve the dubious distinction of being featured, under his own name, in a Bobalition poster."[46] Clearly, the actors' politics and very existence presented such a challenge that racists were unwilling to let them be.

"To be or not to be, dat is him question": Shakespearean English vs. Minstrel Dialect

Allusions to the African Theater in "Bobalition" propaganda underscore the degree to which Shakespearean English, and opponents' misrepresentations of black actors' pronunciation of it, initially played a prominent role in defining the stereotypical dialect of the demeaning minstrel tradition. Noah's first significant, not entirely successful attempt to burlesque these new performers' dialect appeared in the *National Advocate* on September 21, 1821, in his parody of Richard III's first speech in the company's opening performance just a few nights earlier: "Now is de vinter of our discontent made / glorus summer by de son of New-York."[47] Noah's review characterized Richard's speech in the climactic episode in similarly inept terms with "Gib me noder horse." Supposedly describing the staging of the king's tragic fall, Noah went on to sneer: "[F]inally, the agony of the appalled Richard, the rolling eye, white gnashing teeth, clenched fists, and phrenzied looks, were all the author could have wished."[48] Within months, Noah standardized and Southernized his caricatured literary "black dialect," which thereafter regularly featured malapropisms, defamiliarized phonetic spellings, swallowed syllables or elided forms, broken English, and the transposition of *d*s for *th*s (e.g., "de," "dem," "dis," "dat") and *b*s for *v*s or *f*s (e.g., "riber," "eb'ry," or "ob")—rather than the obscure regional/native New York Dutch replacement of *v*s for *w*s— which then came to be a recognized convention. Thus, in 1824, the English actor and mimic Charles Mathews "first brought Noah's words to stage" in England, and, in the same year in New York, Noah "solicited the help of the [eventual star] actor Edwin Forrest (1806–72)" to represent his caricature onstage with "widened eyes, gaping lips, ill-fitting clothes, 'nigger' dialects, and contorted movements."[49] If, as theater historian Samuel Hay has argued, Noah was "the father of Negro minstrelsy,"[50] due to his standardization in print of the caricatured dialect that performers would subsequently popularize, then it is essential that we recognize the extent to which Noah developed, constructed, and defined the literary black dialect by contrasting Shakespearean English with a fantasy of an utterly different, inept "Negro English" spoken by the African Company.

That it was Shakespearean English that was originally contested in developing the fictional black dialect is all the more clear once we turn in some detail to another of the fathers of Negro minstrelsy, the just-noted English actor Charles Mathews (1776–1835). Famous for his "At Homes," solo performances featuring sketches told in persona and featuring elaborate impersonations, Mathews was feted in America (especially in New York City) during a nine-month tour, upon which he embarked on August 1822. While in America, Mathews wrote to a friend recounting the burlesque imitations he was preparing of African Americans' speech: "I shall be rich in black fun. I have studied their black English carefully. It is pronounced the real thing, even by the Yankees. . . . I have several specimens of these black gentry that I can bring into play, and particularly scraps and songs, and malaprops."[51] For a taste, his letter offered a parody of "a *black* Methodist!" sprinkled with "de," "dey," "den," "debbil," "ebery," and swallowed syllables, as in "de spiritable man" and "twelve 'postles."[52] Upon his return to England, however, Mathews would falsely claim inspiration from the African Company, supposedly reporting on visits to their theater. Indeed, he was to make allusions to fictional encounters with the African Theater the centerpiece of his London performances beginning on March 25, 1824, descriptions of which he had rushed into print in five volumes of *London Mathews* to capitalize on his sensational success. Two of the volumes, *Mathews in America . . . written for and intended to be delivered abroad* (London, vol. 3, ca. 1824 and 1825) and *London Mathews, Containing An Account of this Celebrated Comedian's Trip to America* (London, vol. 4, ca. 1824 and 1825), repeatedly allude to the African Company.

The fact that Mathews was, like Noah, engaging in gross misrepresentation is most evident when he describes in *A Trip to America* a performance at "a theatre called the Nigger's (or Negroe's) theatre" of a play the African Company had never performed, *Hamlet,* which Hewlett and contemporary records reveal was not even in the company's repertory. Mathews reveals his representation was based on a fantasy of a farcically stereotypical African American actor when he claimed to have entered the theater just as "a black tragedian" was "proceeding with the speech, 'To be or not to be? that is the question; whether it is nobler in *de* mind to suffer, or tak' up arms against a see of trouble, and by *opossum* end 'em.'"[53] Another account of Mathews's performance included even more distortions since he attributed the speech to a "Kentucky Roscius," clearly supposed to be Hewlett (who was probably born in Rockaway, Long Island).[54] The reported speech was, accordingly, supposed to be Kentuckified:

> To be or not to be, dat is him question,
> whether him nobler in de mind to suffer
> or lift up arms against one sea of
> hubble bubble and by oppussum
> end em.[55]

In both representations, when Mathews spoke the words "oppose 'em" in persona, it sounded like "opussum," a stereotypically "Kentuckified" mispronunciation that prompted the audience to demand a rendition of the "Original Negro Melody," "Opossum up a Gum Tree," featuring verses such as:

> Opossum up a gum tree,
> Him know not what to follow;
> Opossum up a gum tree,
> With nigger in de hollow.
> Opossum up a gum tree,
> Him know not what him ail;
> But Nigger go up de gum tree,
> And pull him down by de tail.
> Opossum, &c. &c.[56]

After rehearsing the song, Mathews makes his "Kentucky Roscius" slip into lines from *Richard III,* but as borrowed from Noah's description, "Now is de winter of our discontent, made de glorous summer by de sun of New York," before explaining "him tought of New York den."[57] This burlesque representation of the African Company was, however, not enough to satisfy Mathews's appetite for what he had called "black fun."

Elsewhere in *Mathews in America,* in what was to become a long-term fixation, the comedian focused on *Othello.* For example, Mathews devotes one piece to a Virginny-styled African American who, while auditioning for the part of Othello, is portrayed as freely adapting the Shakespearean lines to an African American slave's supposed frame of reference:

> Most potented sir reverences!
> My very good massas! dat I take away
> Old buckra man him daughter,
> It all true, true, no lie was;
> Den she marry, I make her my Chumchum,
> Dat all I do, cause I do no more was![58]

In another episode in this work, Mathews impersonates a white man trying to "get a situation as actor" who discovers that performance in blackface made him inherently laughable as Othello:

Now the part selected for my first appearance was Othello; and . . . I made my face as black as cork and grease could make it. . . . I . . . dressed and blacked my face . . . to personate the black hero, Othello; when I had the pleasure of playing to an audience who mortified me during the whole performance by laughing at my tragedy. . . . and as I could get little or nothing for my pains, I resolved to turn comedian, and give the public some cause for exerting their risible muscles. . . .[59]

Like many English writers, Mathews was determined to demean Americans generally but was especially focused on the efforts of black actors and/or the character of Othello.

If Mathews thereby intended to get the notice of Hewlett, with whom he had formed an acquaintanceship, he was not disappointed. The American actor seems to have genuinely admired Mathews but felt compelled to write a rebuttal to the comedian's distortions. Claiming that he believed that it would make his readers "smile," Mordecai Noah himself agreed to publish Hewlett's letter of rebuttal to Mathews, whom Hewlett addresses as "My Dear Mathews" (repeated thereafter with considerable irony), in the *National Advocate* on May 8, 1824, a little over a month after Mathews opened in London: "I lament to say, you have given me cause of complaint. . . . [You have] ridiculed our *African Theatre in Mercer Street,* and burlesqued me with the rest of the negroe actors, as you are pleased to call us—mimicked our styles—imitated our dialects—laughed at our anomalies—and lampooned, O shame, even our complexions. . . ."[60] Hewlett observes that Mathews is performing some imitations in England that he had developed "on this side of the Atlantic"—"This is all fair," he writes. But, he questions, in the case of his burlesque of the African Theater, both the inaccuracies in Mathews's "imitation" and the delay; "where is the justice in withholding a . . . roar at us [in America]?" Hewlett wondered, since Mathews had not performed attacks on Hewlett and company until he was in England. Far from mocking the African Company in America, Mathews had, as Hewlett observes, instead lavished praise and "approbation" after being treated to performances by Hewlett: "At your earnest and pressing solicitation, I performed several of my best parts; was perfect to the letter; . . . which met with your unqualified approbation."[61] Hewlett also points out Mathews's dishonesty in representing the company's dialect when he writes, "we were all unmercifully handled and mangled in your new entertainment." Finally, he pointedly compares Mathews to Shakespeare, via *Othello,* while claiming Shakespeare as his own:

> Our immortal bard . . . (and he is *our* bard as well as yours . . .) . . . makes sweet Desdemona say,
>> "I saw Othello's visage in his mind."
> Now when you were ridiculing the "chief black tragedian" and burlesquing the "real negro melody," was it my "mind," or my "visage," which should have made an impression on you?[62]

Mathews, however, was not to be persuaded by reason or eloquence. Instead, such a dignified representation of the "noble Moor" by a black Shakespearean would continue to rankle Mathews and be distorted in his own reports and representations of Hewlett's style.

"Break-speare" and Full-Fledged Minstrel Othellos

In England in 1833, as abolition was being debated and slavery was about to be abolished later that year, and as an African American actor was about to begin performing Shakespeare in the capital of the proslavery lobby, London, Mathews predictably resurrected the strategy of parodic distortion that he had earlier employed to stereotype Hewlett and his colleagues. Once again, Mathews tried to impose a perception of racial difference through Shakespeare, when he wrote, under the pen name "William Breakspeare," his burlesque, *Othello, the Moor of Fleet Street* (previously misattributed on dubious authority to Charles Westmacott).[63] This time, however, he would feature a blackface Othello in a complete play, though he reduced him to working as a crossing-sweeper. Curiously, instead of speaking in literary black dialect, this characterization, a stage direction tells us, was "*spoken in the manner of Kean*" (3.35):

> Most potent, very reverend, grave,
> My noble and approved good masters:
> Rather than speak, I'll sing a stave
> Relating to my strange disaster.
>
> (3.35–38)

Then, this Kean-inflected Othello sings, to the tune of "Madame Fig's Gala," "Ye potent men and grave, / My noble friends and masters" (ll. 39–40), and so on, before concluding ridiculously with the nonsensical "Tooral looral lay, te rol rumpti nay, /Tweedle deedle rem! Ri fol rumpti doodle em!" (ll. 47–48). As the *Spectator* remarked on February 2, 1833, "The Adelphi produced a vulgar burlesque of *Othello,* for the purpose of introducing imitations of KEAN and MACREADY in *Othello* and *Iago,* by REEVE and YATES . . . [which] are capital."[64] The imitation of Kean was thus not limited to scene 3. The review raises the question why, given his predilection for mocking black actors, had Mathews seemingly represented Kean in blackface?

In truth, Mathews's 1833 mockery of a blackfaced Othello in the style of Edmund Kean—who we must recognize had, by 1820, long since inaugurated the so-called "bronze age" of lightened, tawny Moors, "because he preferred not to risk the ridicule of the age toward a black skin and decided to substitute a light brown tint"[65]—was aimed primarily at African American actors, in this case for their self-conscious imitation of the greatest actor of the day. Hewlett was, in fact, widely known to have emulated Kean as his idol and was an apt imitator of his characterizations. In the fall of 1825 Hewlett even took to advertising himself thereafter, in imitation of a letter from Kean printed in a newspaper, as "Shakespeare's proud representative," a nickname that stuck for decades.[66] Hewlett also took the novel step of having his image engraved in 1825 above the words "Mr. Hewlett as Richard the third in imitation of Mr. Kean."[67] And a number of notices in Philadelphia and New York mention Hewlett's performances of "a scene in

Othello, in imitation of Mr. Kean."[68] Hewlett had even performed his imitations in England, after having gone there in 1825 to confront and expose Mathews for his earlier misrepresentation of the African Theater Company.[69] Although he seems to have received little press in England, Hewlett's Kean impersonations were noteworthy enough that in 1825 the *Brooklyn Star* remarked that "his imitations of Kean . . . were recognized as correct and evincing a nice discrimination and peculiar tact on his part."[70]

But by 1833, Mathews was facing a more immediate challenge than Hewlett in New York; a further connection between a black Othello and Kean had come to England by way of a new "Roscius," whom the journal *Figaro in London* referred to in the most offensive terms possible as a "vain glorious *Niger,*" "a stupid looking, thick lipped, ill formed African calling himself the African Roscius" who was "posting placards" advertising his appearances.[71] Significantly, this "African Roscius," not Hewlett but the younger and more educated Ira Aldridge, had come to England ca. 1825 and had begun performing in the provinces thereafter, apparently in imitation of Kean. After his arrival in England in 1825 Aldridge had begun to advertise himself as "Mr. KEENE, Tragedian of Colour, from the African Theatre, New York,"[72] a practice he continued for years. By 1827, he was "the Celebrated Mr. Keene, the African Roscius," and it was not until 1831 that he began to phase out the name Keene, styling himself, "F. W. Keene Aldridge, the African Roscius."[73] It seems likely, then, that like Hewlett and so many white actors from the period (including John Reeve in Mathews's burlesque), the young Aldridge was initially imitating Kean. Consequently, an 1831 advertisement in New York reported that Hewlett was calling himself, perhaps in tribute to an old hero and pupil alike, after both Kean and this new "Keene": "Hewlett for this night styles himself Keen."[74] Thus, Mathews's 1833 blackface Othello, performing "in the manner of Kean," in actuality touched upon *both* Hewlett and the young Aldridge. (The characterization became even more pointed when, following Kean's collapse during a performance of *Othello* on March 25, 1833, Aldridge actually replaced Kean in two performances at the Covent Garden Theatre on April 10 and 12, 1833.)[75]

Mathews's imitative blackface Othello is not just incapable of escaping a tendency to lapse into country songs, but Mathews could not resist making the racism of Roderigo more overt by having his version refer mockingly to "Massa Othello." Mathews also expands upon fears of sexual attraction between white women and black men in having Othello sing drunkenly:

> Buckra [white] wives, dey like Old Nick.
> Very fair to face, sir.
> Very black dey do de trick
> Dere hubbies to disgrace, sir.
>
> (7.20–24)

But Mathews's version was subtle compared to what was to come, for if Mathews was restrained about debasing the Shakespearean English of the "noble Moor" at great length, subsequent playwrights would be less so.

Shortly thereafter, in 1834, just seven months after abolition within England and the very year slavery was also abolished in British colonies of the Caribbean (freeing some 800,000 slaves), Maurice G. Dowling's more successful *Othello Travestie: An Operatic Burlesque Burletta in Two Acts* was performed in the slaving port of Liverpool, with Othello speaking in a Caribbean-inflected stage dialect.[76] Here, Othello speaks deferentially and stereotypically to "Good Massa Lieutenant," "Massa Duke," "Massa Iago," "Desdemony," and "Missee O." As in Mathews's play, Othello also speaks in close parodies of famous lines, such as, "Him nebber more be officer of mine" (24), "Him hear you say just now, 'me no like dat!' (28), "No, Massa, Iago, him prove before him doubt" (29), "Villain! be sure you prove my lub—" (32), and "put out de light" (40). Such degrading, supposed translation is most notable in Dowling's version of the senate scene, where Shakespeare's Othello demonstrates his eloquence and nobility, but where Dowling's Othello instead sings to the tune of "Yankee Doodle":

> Potent, grave, and rev'rend sir
>   Very noble Massa—. . . .
> Yes, it is most werry true
>   Him take dis old man's daughter
> But no by spell, him promise you,
>   But by fair means him caught her.
>
> (13)

Significantly, this burlesque of *Othello,* which was published in 1836, was seen by T. D. Rice, the most famous American minstrel, during his tour of England in that year. Indeed, Dowling's burlesque was to provide the source for Rice's most elaborate effort, his own adaptation, *Otello* [*sic.*], *A Burlesque Opera* (1844).

Deciphering T. D. Rice's *Otello*

W. T. Lhamon has argued that *Otello,* Rice's 1844 musical travesty of *Othello,* differed from other minstrel burlesques in that it skewered not blackness per se but rather "the Italian operas which the Brabantios of [Rice's] own era attended" as "a radical slam at effete life" and, further, that "The formal target . . . was Rossini's *Otello* (1816)," which was "performed in New York in 1826 during the formative years of Rice's earliest theatrical dreaming."[77] For Lhamon, class issues and elitist aesthetic tastes rather than ethnicity are the true, and novel, targets of this piece. It is true that beginning in November 1825 European opera star Manuel Garcia performed seventy-nine times, exclusively in New York, over the following nine months—works such as Rossini's *The Barber of Seville* and *Otello.*[78] It is also true that when Rice's *Otello* opened—in *Philadelphia,* however—in October 1844, a recent revival of Italian opera had appeared in New York, first in 1843 during a seven-night run at Niblo's Garden. However, Niblo's could hardly be considered an elitist space; it was an informal, open-air theater with moderate pricing and heterogeneous audiences, and it would still be serving a populist audience as late as 1863 when the editor of *Harpers*, George William Curtis, sneered at the way "it was crammed with people. All the seats were full, and the aisles and the steps. . . . And the people . . . hung upon the balustrade" when aforementioned (white) people's favorite Edwin Forrest, one who prompted the Astor Place Riot in 1849, employed what Curtis called the "boundless exaggeration" of "the muscular school; the brawny art; the biceps aesthetics; . . . the bovine drama; rant, roar, and rigamarole."[79] Moreover, in February 1844, when the Italian immigrant Ferdinando Palmo had opened "Palmo's," it too was a humble New York opera house that the *Herald* called "a little *bijou* of a theater," which, according to Karen Ahlquist in *Democracy at the Opera: Music, Theater, and Culture in New York City, 1815–1860,* "drew the least criticism for social ostentation" of any opera house in the period. Thus, contrary to Lhamon's implications of elitism among "the Brabantios of [Rice's] own era," both New York venues were in reality egalitarian in pricing, charging an affordable flat rate for admission before Rice's *Otello* appeared. Indeed, Palmo's was actually notable in being deemed "not exclusive enough" for elite audiences.[80] Further undermining an emphasis on class or elitism as the focus of Rice's *Otello* is the problematic fact that the Brabantios of the era did not yet attend Italian operas with any regularity by 1844, and it was not a fait accompli that Italian opera was then, or would eventually become, the exclusive possession of elites. It was actually not until the *late* 1840s that elite opera houses opened and employed restricted access, resulting in the increasing exclusivity that, far less so than nativist jingoism on behalf of American Shakespearean Edwin Forrest among the Bowery B'hoys and xenophobic antagonism toward English Shakespearean William Macready, contributed to the infamous Astor Place Opera House rioting of early May 1849 during Macready's run there.[81] It is therefore unlikely that Rice's parody primarily targeted the Brabantios of the early 1840s. And even if it did, we would at least be forced to conclude that Rice was pandering to the worst nativist prejudices of his audience in opposing foreignness, since the Italian American impresarios Niblo and Palmo had been markedly egalitarian themselves.

But even if we grant the application of subsequent class-based motives to Rice's burlesque in 1844, we still need to consider the fact that, as a "formal target," Rice's choice of Rossini's *Otello* would have been curious. After all, William J. Mahar's survey of playbills for the most popular minstrel operatic parodies prior to 1860 reveals that such burlesques targeted Italian operas that had *recently* and *frequently* been performed, especially *La Sonnambula* (premiering in New York in 1835 and a hit throughout the 1840s), *The Bohemian Girl* (New York premiere in 1844), and *Leonora* (Philadelphia premiere in 1845).[82] Performances of Rossini's *Otello* exclusively in New York in 1826 hardly offer a promising target for parody in Rice's *Otello* at Philadelphia's Chestnut Street Theater nearly two decades later in 1844, since parody, as Mahar discovered, depends on some familiarity. As Levine argues in *Highbrow/Lowbrow,* prior to midcentury, "as with Shakespeare, the familiarity of opera . . . was manifest by the large number of burlesques and parodies it stimulated," again citing Bellini's *La Sonnambula* (*The Roof Scrambler* [1839] and *Lo, Som am de Beauties* [1845]) and Donizetti's *Lucia di Lammermoor* (*Lucy-did-Sham-Amour* [1848]).[83] The audience composition for opera did not begin to change fundamentally until after midcentury, but there was no clean break even then for some years, since in 1853 *Putnam's Mag-*

azine could still praise P. T. Barnum and even advocate him being named manager of New York's opera, since "He comprehends that, with us [contrary to Europeans], the opera need not necessarily be the luxury of the few, but the recreation of the many."[84]

When we turn to the history of opera performance in Philadelphia, we find even less promising evidence in support of the formal parody thesis. In fact, the lone performance of Rossini's *Otello* in this city prior to the 1844 premiere of Rice's burletta was not just at the Chestnut itself—the populist site of Rice's own performance—but also over a decade earlier, on January 23, 1833.[85] While there were other Italian operas performed in the interim, among them *La Sonnambula,* Rossini's *Otello* did not appear again in Philadelphia until October 4, 1851.[86] In short, given that parodies were necessarily topical, requiring familiarity, and thus often appearing "within days of their [original's] premieres,"[87] the notion that Rice's public at the opening of his *Otello* in Philadelphia would have appreciated so remote a formal target as Rossini's opera in performance several years earlier is, to say the least, improbable. Rather, as we will see, Rice's burlesque was aimed at an all-too-familiar target: the famous Hewlett, who, ca. 1844, was evidently attempting yet another comeback. Such a satiric focus would explain the timing of Rice's opening; that is, Hewlett's return to the stage finally afforded an opportunity for Rice to make an *Otello* burlesque topical at last.

While little has been found of Hewlett following a stint performing in the Caribbean in 1839, the English traveler Mrs. Felton, observing ca. 1843 that "the blacks" of New York "contrive to keep open one, and sometimes two theatres," reports a fellow traveler's "account of his last night's entertainment at the black theater, where a sable 'Richard' was the point of attraction." As White suggests, based on this evidence, it seems likely that Hewlett took at least "a few last bows on a New York stage."[88] If an African American New Yorker starring as Richard was indeed the main attraction "at the black theatre," this star had to have been Hewlett (who was reported in 1852 to have "died in New York a few years ago"),[89] back performing his most famous part (Richard III), the one he could perform either in his own vein or in imitation of famous white actors like Kean and Macready, the one he had performed before thousands. So often had Hewlett performed the part and imitations of famous actors in the role of Richard during his solo performances that some newspapers claimed that he was "vulgarly called 'Dick Hewlett.'"[90] Furthermore, though his popularity had faded by the era of Jim Crow, Hewlett was nonetheless the most famous black American of the period, having achieved iconic one-name recognition as a "point of attraction" in newspapers across the country.[91] Partly for this reason, no doubt, Thompson finds it "very likely that he toured more extensively than is known, but that the records have not been found, or no longer exist."[92] It would seem, therefore, that when Rice's *Otello* opened, the indomitable Hewlett was again performing in New York and likely Philadelphia as he often had, no doubt capitalizing on Macready's U.S. tour taking place that year to do imitations of the famous Englishman and also sensing a revival in interest in Italian opera that afforded an opportunity to reprise his *Otello* imitations—and for Rice to mock him.[93]

Hewlett's noted talent for singing opera made Rice's *Burlesque Opera* all the more pointed. Hewlett had first turned his extraordinary skills in mimicry to Italian opera, and, significantly, Rossini's *Otello* in particular, beginning in March 1826, when, in solo performances, he began impersonating "Signior Garcia" in scenes from Rossini operas, especially the operatic role of Otello.[94] And, whereas Garcia had performed only in New York, within two weeks of that debut, Hewlett was already performing "Imitations of the Italian Opera Troop" for Philadelphians as well.[95] It is difficult to overestimate the impression such performances made, given the utter novelty and innovation of such a feat: "Very few are today aware of the fact that the debut performance by an American-born singer of Italian opera in front of a paying American audience was given by James Hewlett."[96]

Remarkably, just as Shakespeare's tragic Moor was a standard for Hewlett throughout his career, so was Rossini's character Otello, so much so that an 1830 review in the *Family Magazine* reported in a piece entitled "The Negroes of New York" that an African American company performed a bill that included *Julius Caesar* and "some pieces of Rossini."[97] Likewise, in 1839, notices of performances by "Mr. Hewlett" appeared in December 1839 in the *Port of Spain Gazette,* Trinidad, advertising "imitations, recitations, and songs, & c. &c. &c.," particularly of a "Garcia" who had performed at the "Theatre Royal, at Paris."[98]

Not only had Hewlett performed *Otello,* but his extraordinary singing had also become such an important part of his repertoire that he was performing twenty or more songs per "concert" (his term) late in his career.[99] And so, when the *Trinidad Standard* advertised Hewlett's performance as Othello, it had added, "in which character he will sing the songs of 'The Banner of Battle,' 'The Marseilles Hymn and the Parisienne,' in English."[100] Because Hewlett *sang* in his performances of *Othello,* and because he was noted for singing Rossini's opera in particular, Rice's offering of a burlesque *Otello*—concluding just after a song by Rice/Otello performed *Alma Opera,* that is, "in the spirit of opera"[101]—was not a remote formal parody aimed over the heads of his audience; it was instead a typically topical joke that degraded the famous Hewlett by parodying Shakespeare's tragedy while incorporating plenty of songs that mocked the actor's performance of both Othello and Otello via minstrel dialect.

Following his model of Dowling, but adapting Othello's speech to the stereotypically Kentuckified or Virginny-ized dialect standardized by Noah's mockery of the African Theater, Rice rendered the noble character's eloquence as mere "rude . . . talk": "Most potent, grabe, and rebsrend Signiors, my bory noble and approbed good Massas: Dat I hab tuck away dis old man's darter—is true and no mistake. True, I's married her. De bery head and tail ob my offence hab dis extent, no more: rude am I in talk. I cannot chat like some folks for, since a piccanninny two years old, I'b always been in rows and spreezes. Yet, by your gracious patience, I'll tell you how I won his darter."[102] In fact, even more than Dowling, Rice closely parodies Othello's most eloquent lines in demeaning fashion. And so, Otello declares, "Whar it my cue to raise a row, I should hab know it widout your telling me" (348); "To die would be most happy now. / I'd kick de bucket freely—" (363); "My life, upon her faith, dar's no mistake" (355); "Cassio neber more be ossifer ob mine" (370); "De way I lub her really is a sin / And, when I doesn't, chaos comed again" (374); "No, Massa Iago, I prove before I doubt; / And when I prove, why den I sarbe her out" (375); "More could Iago chat, / If he'd but let de bag out of de cat" (376); "Farewell to de banjo and de cymbals / . . . . Otello's occupation am gone" (379); "It am de cause, / It am de cause"—accompanied by a crow's "*caw—caw—caw*" sound effects (380); "Yes, she must die, dat is plain, / Else more niggers she'll betray again" (380); and "I done de state some sarbice / . . . . Noten extenuate" (382).

Other details, beyond Otello's grotesque stage dialect, are similarly degrading to the character of Othello. When Otello hears that *the towel* (in lieu of the handkerchief) has been lost, he enters with "*his wool all on end*" (378), that is, wearing the conventional "fright wig" of the minstrel show.[103] Then, in the dramatic climax, as Otello approaches to kiss his wife in the tragic smothering scene, Rice undercuts Otello's dignity yet again when the slumbering Desdemona starts and "*kicks him over*" (380). Worst of all, uncritically taking details from Dowling's racist antiabolitionist play, Rice represents Otello as a lusty rapist when Desdemona recounts how she swooned into unconsciousness at Othello's tales and that "When I came about—ah, me!" she was "Greatful for the scrape I'd missed" (354), with "scrape" suggesting both rape and abortion.[104] Whereas Shakespeare's character had broken with the stereotype of the "lascivious Moor" (*Othello,* 1.1.124), what Virginia Mason Vaughan describes in her study *Performing Blackness on English Stages, 1500–1800* as "a long line of black male [characters] . . . who flaunt their sexuality as a quality inherent in their blackness,"[105] Rice's *Otello* reinstates it.

Such dynamics inform the fact that in the era in which "Shakespearean travesties . . . dominated minstrel programs," "it was Othello that was most frequently parodied in nineteenth-century America."[106] Take, for instance, "Alexander Do Mar's" *Othello: An Interesting Drama, Rather!* (London, ca. 1850), in which Othello appears as minstrel with a banjo; G. W. H. Griffin's *Othello: A Burlesque* (New York, ca. 1870); *Desdemonum: An Ethiopian Burlesque in Three Scenes* (New York, 1874), in which Desdemonum resolves to "see Otheller's visage in his high-falutin' mind"; and *Dar's de money* [i.e., "Desdemona"], *Othello burlesque* (London and New York, ca. 1880), the latter originally performed in Wood's Minstrel Hall in New York and depicting would-be black actors attempting scenes from *Othello*.[107]

Minstrel burlesques of *Othello* underscore what Tilden G. Edelstein identifies as the keen anxieties and "continuing difficulties . . . that color-conscious Americans were having with the play," especially in the nineteenth century.[108] In serious drama, anxiety about a noble Moor and his relationship with a white woman in an era in which both Hewlett and Aldridge married white women contributed to representations of a markedly violent and irrational Othello but also to an increasingly lightened or whitened character when white actors undertook the role. Kean had started the trend in inaugurating "the bronze age," since his makeup was "greatly lightened" as a so-called mulatto.[109] But further steps were taken to "whiten Othello" when the famed Edwin Forrest—who had earlier presented racist blackface portrayals in Noah's staged antiabolitionist propaganda against the African Theater and who, not surprisingly, became the favorite of the nativist Bowery B'hoys— subsequently began playing Othello in New York as an "octoroon," one "looking white but having a trace of black blood and some tell-tale Negroid features." Forrest's Othello was also especially violent and irrational in keeping with his racist views about "telltale" black characteristics.[110] When Edwin Booth took up the part thereafter in 1849, "an Othello who bore no resemblance to a black African" took the stage.[111] In fact, Edelstein demonstrates that Booth "sought to expunge from the play any taint of miscegenation by becoming the lightest-skinned Othello ever." Booth himself claimed that he aimed to elevate Othello's character above a "brutal blacka-moor"—a stereotype Booth accepted as accurate. In the event, his Moor was, he said, "Arabian, not African," sporting a Tartar-like mustache for emphasis. As Edelstein concludes, "American audiences demanded whitewashed Othellos."[112] But they did so not merely because they could not abide miscegenation, but also because they would not believe and would not *tolerate* an elo quent, and therefore dignified, representation of a black man. Thus, white Americans simultaneously demanded a lighter Othello in so-called "legitimate" Shakespeare as they required a more stereotypi-cally "black" Othello in minstrel burlesques; both complementary representations were necessary to assure the majority white audi-ence that its racial fictions were true.

Consequences for Black Shakespeareans and for "Shakespeare"

It was inevitable that Shakespeare would be appropriated by the minstrel tradition generally, and by T. D. Rice in particular, given that Shakespearean plays were regularly on the bill with Jim Crow. In fact, "Shakespeare accounted for nearly a quarter of the plays performed in America during the nineteenth century."[113] At a time when Hewlett was one of the best-known African Americans in the country and sometimes even "vulgarly called 'Dick'" for his close association with *Richard III* in a period in which this work was the most popular play in America, Jim Crow would claim, "for you see I been born wid sharp set of grinders jis like dey say in de play King Dick hab."[114] Famously, it was said of Richard, "Teeth hadst thou in thy head when thou wast born" (*3 Henry VI*, 5.6.53). More important, both Richard and Jim Crow were deformed, improbable ladies' men and would-be dandies. In famous lines from *3 Henry VI* appropriated in *Richard III* during the nineteenth century, Richard points out his "shr[u]nk[en] . . . arm . . . like a wither'd shrub" (*3 Henry VI,* 3.2.156), an "envious mountain on [his] back" (l. 157), and "legs of an unequal size" (l. 159), and in *Richard III* he references one arm as "like a blasted sapling withered up" (3.4.70) and refers to himself as "Deformed" (1.1.20), made "lamely" (l. 22), and as "halt[ing]" (l. 23) or limping. However, he successfully woos Lady Anne, despite not being shaped for such "sportive tricks, / Nor made to court an amorous looking glass" (ll. 14–15), and then gloats, "I'll be at charges for a looking glass / And entertain a score or two of tailors / To study fashions to adorn my body" (1.2.276–78). Like Richard, the would-be but ragged dandy Jim Crow—depicted in *The Life of Jim Crow* (ca. 1835) by way of the illustration *Dandy Looking in a Mirror*—moved about with a limp (one reviewer described him as being "lame . . . [since] nature unkindly afflicts born fools with some co-operative deformity"), and illustrations actually depict the character, again like Richard, with one deformed arm and shoulder, just as a critic praised Jim Crow for "such a twitching-up of the arm and shoulder!"[115] One account went so far as to claim that Rice had modeled his dance on a deformed slave: "He was very much deformed . . . the right shoulder was drawn up high, and the left leg was stiff and crooked at the knee which gave him a painful but at the same time ludicrous limp."[116] Yet, rather than emulating a crippled slave—a myth of accuracy that maintained that this grotesque racist caricature was truth rather than a gross lie—it now seems that Rice was inspired to create Jim Crow partly to burlesque Hewlett's performance of Richard III, a character with an unequal gait, a hunchback, and a withered arm.

After all, Rice invited gratuitous comparisons between *Jim* Crow and *James* Hewlett, even when his plays had no overt connection to Shakespeare. In fact, in his earlier *Bone Squash Diavolo* (ca. 1834–35), a satirical farce focused on black dandyism, Rice did so most pointedly in the wake of Hewlett's humiliating, much-reported arrest in 1834. Hewlett was widely being mocked for both the arrest and a court appearance; contemporary newspaper accounts of the latter represented his interaction with the magistrate regarding his request to be released on his own recognizance as a mock-Shakespearean dialogue in which one highlight was an allusion to *Othello:* "*Hewlett:* Then is Othello's occupation gone. But I know you will take my word for my appearance here tomorrow."[117] In the wake of Hewlett's humiliation, Rice was sprinkling *Bone Squash Diavolo,* variously advertised as "a petite opera" or as "The Grand Opera in Two Acts,"[118] with gratuitous allusions to the operatic Shakespearean's repertoire. For example, in this play without swords, set in a modern-day New York, one character inexplicably mocks the dandy Spruce, who has taken up strutting full-time and "leff off scouring" (189)—Hewlett's day job at his Clothes Dressing Emporium on Warren Street near Broadway, where he offered "Steam pressing" and removal of "all kinds of Stains"[119]—with the *Othello* allusion "Put up dat sword, don't strike!" (189), a homely echo of Othello's "Keep up your bright swords, for the dew will rust them" (1.2.60). More gratuitous still is the following Shakespeare-laden gag:

> *Bone Squash:* Farewell all my calculation.
> For I'm bound to the wild goose station [*Snum*]
> Farewell, all your fancy balls. [*Start.* Brown *gives knife.*]
> . . . Farewell all, Bone Squash is gone.
> If only you would excuse me,
> And tomorrow you may use me,
> And tomorrow, and tomorrow,
> So please you let me stay.[120]

In this odd hodgepodge of allusions, Rice conflates Othello's eloquent farewell speech, Cassio's traditional stage business of giving Othello a knife to kill himself, another Hewlett role in an allusion to Macbeth's despairing "Tomorrow and tomorrow and tomorrow" speech, and the newspapers' court scene accounts ending in Hewlett's request to be allowed to return tomorrow.

Rice did not just mercilessly gloat over Hewlett's bad fortune but he was appropriating his roles, including *Othello,* to do so, contrary to the claim that "Rice resisted the connection [to Othello] before he bitterly took it on in 1844."[121] In fact, as even Lhamon is forced to concede, "Knickerbocker critics [took] Jim Crow to be a crude emulation of Othello." Moreover, in those plays written for Jim Crow, racial slurs against Othello also appear, as in the pronouncement in *Flight to America* (1836) that "All dese Othello fellow make very bad husbands."[122] New York critics, then, were making the direct comparisons that Rice himself invited.

During his European tours between 1834 and 1836, Rice likewise appropriated Shakespeare, but his attacks then probably had Aldridge in view in the verses entitled "Jim Crow's Description of Hamlet":

> I went to Surry Teatre,
>   To see de Hamlet play. . . .
> Out came Massa Hamlet
>   Wid his "Be, or not to be."
> Den Hamlet grab him uncle,
>   And choke him by de troat,
> And shake him like de debil,
>   De last button off him coat,
>   Veel about, &c.[123]

It seems that Rice also participated in a larger-scale *Hamlet* burlesque, later appropriated by Christy's Minstrels, in which he cleverly introduced his "Jump" theme song:

> Oh! tis Consummation Devoutly to be wished,
> To end your heartache by a sleep;
> When likely to be dished,
> *Shuffle off your mortal coil, Do just so,*
> *Wheel about and turn about and Jump Jim Crow.*[124]

In each of Rice's Shakespearean allusions, it is clear enough that Shakespeare was the vehicle and black Shakespeareans and their audiences the target, not vice versa.

Here, we must recognize that Shakespeare was not appropriated by Rice and the minstrel tradition because his work was thought to be elitist. On the contrary, "no one thought of removing Shakespeare to a separate category called Culture," since through the first half of the nineteenth century "his plays [remained] the property of every class and community from Indiana to New England."[125] (Lawrence Levine suggests that Shakespeare did not become synonymous with "Culture" until the early twentieth century.[126]) After all, the very "ubiquity of Shakespearean drama in the humor of the minstrels" and the "national penchant for parodying Shakespeare" in the nineteenth century demonstrate Shakespeare's popularity.[127] So passionate were the working-class Bowery B'hoys of New York about their Shakespeare that they spearheaded the Astor Place riots of 1849 against English Shakespearean Macready and in defense of their champion, the nativist Shakespearean Forrest; up to 15,000 rioters took to the streets, 113 were arrested, and 26 were killed as a consequence.[128]

As I have already suggested, what bardolatrous Americans admired most about Shakespeare was his eloquence. Nigel Cliff has noted in his analysis of Shakespeare's extraordinary appeal in the period that "nineteenth-century Americans were in love with oratory," "theatre was a showcase for oratory," and Shakespeare's oratory was recognized as the best.[129] According to Levine, "Shakespeare was taught in nineteenth-century schools and colleges as declamation or rhetoric, not literature."[130] Moreover, he explains, "The same Americans who found diversion and pleasure in lengthy political debates, who sought joy and God in the sermons of church and camp meeting, who had, in short, a seemingly inexhaustible appetite for the spoken word, thrilled to Shakespeare's eloquence, memorized his soliloquies, delighted in his dialogues." Thus, just as Shakespearean language became the property of minstrel burlesques, other popular forms of oratory, such as political speeches and sermons, were appropriated by minstrelsy in order to create a clash of idioms, an incongruous juxtaposition of what was presumed linguistically decorous with what minstrels constructed as indecorous. That is, "Shakespearean English" was depicted as essentially in opposition to "Negro English," so that a Shakespearean burlesque in blackface—or a performance by black actors—was constructed as an absurd amalgamation of extremes: eloquence and ineloquence, the beautiful and the grotesque.

It was thus the tradition of blackface and its attempt to impose a racist social hierarchy that became one wedge between what was thereafter constructed as the contrast between the highbrow and the lowbrow, so that Shakespeare and opera alike were actually beginning to be constructed in opposition to popular culture of the nativist stripe—via blackface burlesque constructions of African Americans' supposed pretension in appropriating such art forms—well before they were high/elite culture in reality. Ironically enough, contrary to counterrevisionist arguments, the blackface tradition was thus nonegalitarian, both because of its divisive assertions of white supremacy and in that it ultimately separated some art from populism by making what minstrelsy effectively constructed as black affectation to the "high," artful, beautiful, and cultured (here, Shakespeare and opera) contemptible to the working class.

Equally important, given that the self-consciously "low" idiom of blackface minstrelsy was defined in opposition to the eloquent language of Shakespeare, there is much reason to question recent revisionist assertions that the minstrels' literary dialect was not a grotesque caricature.[131] Against such assurances, in addition to the unrelentingly demeaning interpolations evident in the ubiquitous malapropisms, elisions, and misspelled phonetic "eye dialect" that represented standard pronunciations as ignorant error in print, we must now add reactions from the African Company; Hewlett himself mocked the emerging stereotype of black English on multiple occasions, showing that he did not accept what he had referred to as the "mangled" representations of his company by Mathews and other propagandists. On one occasion, after a smashing solo performance by Hewlett in February 1826, the white audience demanded a curtain call, at which time Hewlett first eloquently reported that "he was about fulfilling an engagement in London, and therefore would take a respectful leave of New York," before provocatively slipping into a stereotypical dialect and adding that since "de Atlantic Ocean would sipparate him from his 'merican bredren, he would soon be in dat country vere dey had no 'stinction of color' "—a political performance that the white crowd hardly found humorous, as it prompted a riot.[132] By contrast, Simon Snipe reported a very different reaction from a largely black audience when an actor, no doubt Hewlett, sang in dialect:

> Is dare a heart dat nebber lub'd
> Or felt soft woman sigh;
> Is dare a man cab marl unmov'd
> Dear woman tearful eye?

Snipe then recorded "peals of laughter" from the house but seemed puzzled as to exactly their source: "[S]ome laughed, perhaps, because it was sung well; others because it was an excellent song, but the principal part of the audience laughed at the pronunciation."[133] Snipe failed to get the humor because, as a racist himself, he assumed that this dialect was authentic enough. The joke here, however, was that Hewlett was parodying a white stereotype of "black English" that black New Yorkers, comprising the principal part of the audience, recognized as laughably inaccurate. Such evidence demonstrates powerfully that most black voices sounded little like Jim Crow, unless they were subverting such a stereotype or using irony at the expense of white rubes.

What drove the unceasing harassment of the actors, then, was that the African Theater presented a threat, in that, like Phillis Wheatley's elegant poetry, it disproved racist myths. As Harriet Martineau aptly explained, "As long as the slave remains ignorant, he is often . . . humoured," but "from the moment he exhibits the attributes of a rational being—from the moment his intellect seems likely to come into the most distinct competition with that of whites, the most deadly hatred springs up;—not in the black but in his oppressors."[134] It was just such hatred that fueled riots against, and the Shakespearean burlesques of, the African Company.

Noah's and Mathews's travesties resulted in the development of a literary black dialect that offered inspiration for T. D. Rice, whose performances were, in turn, to limit Hewlett's ability to perform. Shane White has even gone so far as to argue that Hewlett was "a casualty of the vogue for 'jumping Jim Crow'" after 1830. In fact, after Crow's appearance, Hewlett's popularity waned. He even had some difficulty appearing onstage in New York City and was eventually forced, as we have soon, to travel to the Caribbean to find acting work during the late 1830s. Tragically, when he attempted one of his many solo comebacks in 1831, Hewlett was allowed to perform under the most unusual circumstances: the advertisement in the *New York Evening Post* for his appearance at the New York Museum proclaimed ominously on July 12, 1831: "Mr. HEWLETT, *Shakespeare's proud representative* will appear this evening. . . . Mr Hewlett will take Exhilerating Gas."[135] The dignified Shakespearean, whether the victim of a cruel trick or simply desperate for money, could only suffer through such humiliation once. And, after Rice began to appear as Jim Crow, the bulk of American white audiences would for years only countenance representations of African Americans as mentally impaired, that is, as born fools rather than as "Shakespeare's proud representative[s]."

Whereas Rice's performances were representations of stereotypical foolishness that presented no challenge to a demeaning Africanist persona defined by irrationality, the surest sign of James Hewlett's excellence is the extraordinary lengths that his white antagonists had to go in order to prevent his dignified, eloquent representation of blackness. Because Hewlett had quite successfully made Shakespeare *his* bard onstage, many racists felt compelled to stop him, or, failing that, to undercut him. Hewlett's sometimes tragic career was thus, as contemporaries recognized, remarkably like the noble Othello's. Neither Hewlett nor Othello were "rude

... in speech," nor was either a fool, but Noah, Mathews, Rice, and other Iagos of their respective ages were determined to make them so. Still, Hewlett had paved the way for Aldridge, who actually replaced Kean at the Covent Garden Theatre in London and came to be recognized as one of the great actors of his day. Hewlett's enemies had been determined to deny "Shakespeare's Proud Representative" a legacy. In that, they failed, even if this theatrical pioneer—the first great autochthonous American Shakespearean and singer of Italian opera—has yet to receive the recognition he richly deserves.

Notes

1. Eric Lott, *Love and Theft: Blackface Minstrelsy and the American Working Class* (New York: Oxford University Press, 1993), 34.

2. Ibid., 35.

3. W. T. Lhamon Jr., *Jump Jim Crow: Lost Plays, Lyrics, and Street Prose of the First Atlantic Popular Culture* (Cambridge, MA: Harvard University Press, 2003), 2; Lhamon, *Raising Cain: Blackface performance from Jim Crow to Hip Hop* (Cambridge, MA: Harvard University Press, 1998), 6, 152.

4. Lott, *Love and Theft*, 35.

5. Ibid., 18; emphasis mine.

6. Ibid., 119.

7. Lhamon, *Jump Jim Crow*, 2, 20, 12, 84.

8. Dympna Callaghan, *Shakespeare Without Women: Representing Gender and Race on the Renaissance Stage* (New York: Routledge, 2000), 9; the emphasis is Callaghan's here. See also the essay version, "What's at Stake in Representing Race?" *Shakespeare Studies* 26 (1998): 21–26.

9. Ibid., 7 and 2, respectively.

10. Ibid., 76.

11. For discussion of the ways that early drama developed some of the central tropes of the blackface tradition, see my *The English Clown Tradition from the Middle Ages to Shakespeare* (Boydell & Brewer, September 2009), chapter 1, "Folly as Proto-Racism: Blackface in the 'Natural' Fool Tradition," 24–62; "'Extravagant and Wheeling Strangers': Early Blackface Dancing Fools, Racial Representation, and the Limits of Identification," *EXEMPLARIA* 20, no. 2 (Summer 2008): 197–223; "Blackfaced Fools, Black-Headed Birds, Fool Synonyms, and Shakespearean Allusions to Renaissance Blackface Folly," *Notes and Queries* 55 (2008): 215–19; "The Folly of Racism: Enslaving Blackface and the 'Natural' Fool Tradition," *Medieval and Renaissance Drama in England* 20 (2007): 46–84; and "Emblems of Folly in the First *Othello:* Renaissance Blackface, Moor's Coat, and 'Muckender,'" *Comparative Drama* 35, no. 1 (Spring 2001): 69–99.

12. Lawrence W. Levine, *Highbrow/Lowbrow: The Emergence of Cultural Hierarchy in America* (Cambridge, MA: Harvard University Press, 1988), 34 and 45, respectively.

13. Edwin P. Christy, *Christy's Plantation Melodies No. 4* (Philadelphia: Fisher, 1854), v.

14. Brander Matthews, "The Rise and Fall of Negro-Minstrelsy," *Scribner's* 58 (1915): 754; George F. Rehin, "Harlequin Jim Crow: Continuity and Convergence in Blackface Clowning," *Journal of Popular Culture* 9, no. 3 (Winter 1975): 696; Eric Lott, *Love and Theft: Blackface Minstrelsy and the American Working Class* (New York: Oxford University Press, 1993), 5, 6, and 24n9.

15. Harry Harmer, *The Longman Companion to Slavery, Emancipation and Civil Rights* (New York: Longman, 2001), 43–44.

16. Eric Homberger, *The Historical Atlas of New York City: A Visual Celebration of Nearly 400 Years of New York City's History* (New York: Henry Holt, 1994), 55.

17. Harry Harmer, *The Longman Companion to Slavery*, 84.

18. White, *Stories of Freedom in Black New York* (Cambridge, MA: Harvard University Press, 2002), 29–30, 12.

19. Nigel Cliff, *The Shakespeare Riots: Revenge, Drama, and Death in Nineteenth-Century America* (New York: Random House, 2007), 28.

20. Shane White, *Stories of Freedom*, 223.

21. Shane White, "African Grove Theater," in *Slavery in New York*, 174.

22. White, *Stories of Freedom*, 133.

23. George A. Thompson Jr., *A Documentary History of the African Theatre* (Evanston: Northwestern University Press, 1998), 30.

24. Thompson, *Documentary History of the African Theatre*, 32.

25. Ibid., 27.

26. White, *Stories of Freedom*, 114.

27. Ibid., 97, 100–101.

28. Ibid., 167.

29. *Memoir and Theatrical Career of Ira Aldridge* (London: Onwhyn, 1849), 10–11.

30. Ibid., 11.

31. White, *Stories of Freedom*, 168.

32. Ibid., 143–44.

33. Ibid., 181, 160.

34. Thompson, *Documentary History of the African Theatre*, 62, 64.

35. White, *Stories of Freedom*, 95.

36. Ibid., 93.

37. Thompson, *Documentary History of the African Theatre*, 99.

38. *Memoir and Theatrical Career of Ira Aldridge*, 11.

39. White, *Stories of Freedom*, 83.

40. Homberger, *Historical Atlas of New York City*, 64–65; White, *Stories of Freedom*, 83.

41. Shane White, "Black Life in Freedom: Creating a Popular Culture," in *Slavery in New York*, eds. Ira Berlin and Leslie M. Harris, 178 (New York: New Press, 2005); Samuel A. Hay, *African American Theatre: A Historical and Critical Analysis* (Cambridge: Cambridge University Press, 1994), 10.

42. White, *Stories of Freedom*, 83.

43. Homberger, *Historical Atlas of New York City*, 69–70; White, *Stories of Freedom*, 166.

44. Thompson, *Documentary History of the African Theatre*, 87.

45. White, *Stories of Freedom*, 205.

46. Ibid., 155.

47. Ibid., 109.

48. Ibid., 113.

49. Hay, *African American Theatre,* 13, 17, and 19.

50. Ibid., 13.

51. *Memoirs of Charles Mathews, Comedian, By Mrs. Mathews,* vol. 3, (London: Richard Bentley, 1839), 390–91.

52. Ibid., 390–91.

53. *London Mathews: Containing an Account of the Celebrated Comedian's Trip to America,* 4th ed. (Baltimore: Roninson, 1824), 9.

54. White, "James Hewlett, Actor," 176.

55. *Sketches of Mr. Mathews Celebrated Trip to America* (London: J. Limbird, n.d.), 9–10.

56. *Trip to America,* 25.

57. White, *Stories of Freedom,* 112.

58. *Mathews in America: A New Dramatic at Home; Written and Intended to Be Delivered by Mr. Mathews Abroad,* 2nd ed. (London: Duncombe, 1825), 16.

59. Ibid., 12–13.

60. Thompson, *Documentary History of the African Theatre,* 147.

61. Ibid., 147–48.

62. Ibid., 148.

63. M. Draudt, ed., *Othello, the Moor of Fleet Street (1833)* (Tubingen: Francke, 1993), 2–3.

64. Ibid., 26n53.

65. Errol Hill, *Shakespeare in Sable: A History of Black Actors* (Amherst: University of Massachusetts, 1984), 9.

66. White, *Stories of Freedom,* 140.

67. Ibid., frontispiece.

68. Thompson, *Documentary History of the African Theatre,* 167, 175.

69. Ibid., 153.

70. White, *Stories of Freedom,* 143.

71. Draudt, *Othello, the Moor of Fleet Street (1833),* 29.

72. Herbert Marshall and Mildred Stock, *Ira Aldridge: The Negro Tragedian* (Washington, DC: Howard University Press, 1993), 55.

73. Marshall and Stock, *Ira Aldridge: The Negro Tragedian,* 55.

74. White, *Stories of Freedom,* 170.

75. Marshall and Stock, *Ira Aldridge: The Negro Tragedian,* 117, 135.

76. Harmer, *The Longman Companion to Slavery, Emancipation and Civil Rights,* 78. On Dowling, see W. T. Lhamon Jr., *Jump Jim Crow: Lost Plays, Lyrics, and Street Prose of the First Atlantic Popular Culture* (Cambridge, MA: Harvard University Press, 2003), 73, 419n131.

77. Lhamon, *Jump Jim Crow,* 72, 79, 73.

78. White, *Stories of Freedom,* 146.

79. Levine, *Highbrow/Lowbrow,* 57.

80. June C. Ottenberg, *Opera Odyssey: Toward a History of Opera in Nineteenth-Century America* (Westport, CT: Greenwood Press, 1994), 93; Karen Ahlquist, *Democracy at the Opera: Music, Theater, and Culture in New York City, 1815–1860* (Urbana: University of Illinois Press, 1997), 131–33. On the popularity

of opera at the time, see also John Dizikes, *Opera in America: A Cultural History* (New Haven: Yale University Press, 1993), 3–12.

81. William J. Mahar, *Behind the Burnt Cork Mask: Early Blackface Minstrelsy and Antebellum American Popular Culture* (Chicago: University of Illinois Press, 1999), 5, 134; Cliff, *The Shakespeare Riots;* on anti–British sentiment generally, see 110–29, 141–47; on such antagonism directed toward the Shakespearean Macready, see especially 130–33, 136–37, 148–49, 165–67, 171, 206–8, 234–41.

82. Mahar, *Behind the Burnt Cork Mask,* 105.

83. Levine, *Highbrow/Lowbrow,* 92.

84. Ibid., 100–101.

85. W. G. Armstrong, *A Record of the Opera in Philadelphia* (Philadelphia: Porter and Coates, 1884; repr., New York: AMS Press, 1976), 21.

86. Armstrong, *Record of the Opera in Philadelphia,* 23–48, 70.

87. Mahar, *Behind the Burnt Cork Mask,* 5.

88. White, *Stories of Freedom,* 223.

89. Ibid.

90. Ibid., 166.

91. Ibid., 154, 158.

92. Thompson, *Documentary History of the African Theatre,* 39.

93. On Hewlett's imitation of Macready, see White, *Stories of Freedom,* 146, 148, 222.

94. White, *Stories of Freedom,* 146–47. White does not discuss Rice's *Otello.*

95. Ibid., 147.

96. White, "Black Life in Freedom," 178.

97. "Simon Snipe" reported in 1823 on a performance when "the play was Othello"; George Stone gushed in 1826 that Hewlett "was *some*" as Othello; Peter Nielson reluctantly admitted in 1830 that Hewlett's "Othello may pass"; and the *Trinidad Standard* advertised "MR. HEWLETT AS OTHELLO" on December 17, 1839. Thompson, *Documentary History of the African Theatre,* 224, and White, *Stories of Freedom,* 186.

98. White, *Stories of Freedom,* 221–22.

99. Ibid., 141–42.

100. Thompson, *Documentary History of the African Theatre,* 224.

101. Lhamon, *Jump Jim Crow,* 382, 450n74.

102. Ibid., 350.

103. Ibid., 449n63.

104. Ibid., 444n29.

105. Virginia Mason Vaughan, *Performing Blackness on English Stages, 1500–1800* (Cambridge: Cambridge University Press, 2005), 43. For discussion of Africans/Moors and stereotypical associations with sexuality and lasciviousness, see 4, 35, 43, 47, 53–54, 77, 84, 108, 111, 112, 116, and 122.

106. Gary D. Engle, *This Grotesque Essence: Plays from the American Minstrel Stage* (Baton Rouge: Louisiana State University Press, 1978), xxvii; see also Ray B. Browne, "Shakespeare in American Vaudeville and Negro Minstrelsy," *American Quarterly* 12, no. 3 (Fall 1960): 374–91; Tilden G. Edelstein, "*Othello* in America: The Drama of Racial Intermarriage," in *Region, Race, and Reconstruction: Essays in Honor of C. Vann Woodward,* ed. J. Morgan Kousser and James M. McPherson, 187 (New York: Oxford University Press, 1982).

107. Henry E. Jacobs and Claudia D. Johnson, *An Annotated Bibliography of*

Shakespearean Burlesques, Parodies, and Travesties (New York: Garland, 1976), 58, no. 163; 155, no. 149.

108. Edelstein, "*Othello* in America," 184.

109. Ibid., 183.

110. Ibid., 184.

111. Ibid., 186.

112. Ibid.

113. Cliff, *The Shakespeare Riots,* 13.

114. Ibid., 16; Lhamon, "The Life of Jim Crow," in *Jump Jim Crow,* 388.

115. Lhamon, *Jump Jim Crow,* 396 and 40–41; George Odell, *Annals of the New York Stage* (New York: Columbia University Press, 1928), 4:372.

116. Odell, *Annals of the New York Stage,* 3:632.

117. White, *Stories of Freedom,* 175.

118. Lhamon, *Jump Jim Crow,* 54.

119. White, *Stories of Freedom,* 116–17.

120. Lhamon, *Jump Jim Crow,* 203.

121. Ibid., 430n19.

122. Ibid., 72.

123. *The Humorous Adventures of Jump Jim Crow* (Glasgow, ca. 1836–44), 8.

124. "Hamlet," in *Christy's Nigga Songster, Containing Songs as Sung by Christy's, Pierce's, White's Sable Brothers, and Dumbleton's Band of Minstrels* (New York, n.d.), 261.

125. Cliff, *The Shakespeare Riots,* 15 and 18.

126. Levine, *Highbrow/Lowbrow,* 34.

127. Ibid., 4, 15.

128. Cliff, *The Shakespeare Riots,* 241, 285n11.

129. Ibid., 14.

130. Levine, *Highbrow/Lowbrow,* 37.

131. Mahar discusses the blackface stage dialect in terms of "authenticity" in "Black English in Early Blackface Minstrelsy," *American Quarterly* 37 (1985): 260, 284. Lhamon likewise maintains that "accurate is what Rice's performance seemed." Lhamon, *Raising Cain,* 169.

132. White, *Stories of Freedom,* 157.

133. Ibid., 114.

134. Harriet Martineau, *Retrospect of Western Travel* (London: Saunders and Otley, 1838), 1:152–53.

135. Thompson, *Documentary History of the African Theatre,* 191; emphasis added.

Edwin Booth and Melodrama: Writing the History of Shakespearean Elitism

Nora Johnson

ONE NIGHT IN 1887, Edwin Booth stood before an adoring San Francisco audience, attempting to star in *Hamlet*. According to his supporting actress, Katherine Goodale, the audience's response almost made the performance impossible:

> Mr. Booth held his sombre mood and posture as long as he could, then bowed gravely—not a trace of a smile upon his face. But they—out there—kept it up, until he was forced to step out of character and wanly smile upon them. More applause. He rose now, but in his dignity, and reseated himself. More applause. He rose again, and bowed a slightly more human smile this time, and sat down. . . . Again he rose, bowed and waited, but as the "reception" would not let up, he came down to the footlights and just stood there helplessly. As if he had forgotten he was on the stage, he looked out upon that wonderful and beautiful audience and his eyes filled with tears. Aggressive tears they were—no blinking them back. When his audience saw those tears, they began all over again. . . . I saw him utterly conquered by his audience and his audience utterly conquered by him before he had spoken one word. And how young he looked with the border lights shining upon his brown hair! Why, he's just a boy—San Francisco's boy—even the Fire Boy come again. How could he help it after that welcome![1]

The logic of Booth's performance in this scene is familiar to those who study the history of entertainment and cultural hierarchy. Straining nobly toward the elevation of Shakespearean performance to the status of high culture, Booth does everything he can to disavow the affection, the nostalgia, and the popular appeal of his relationship to the audience, but in Goodale's description, the au-

161

dience can only see him as a local boy made good.[2] In the mid-nineteenth century, there was no great difference between a Shakespeare play and popular entertainment, according to scholars like Lawrence Levine. Shakespeare doesn't become a figure for high culture, according to Levine's book *Highbrow/Lowbrow,* before late century, when cultural arbiters like Booth work to elevate him, distancing themselves as Booth does here from everything vulgar and popular.[3] Booth's attempt at "wan" austerity thus marks his relative proximity to the standards of modernist theater, as Goodale points out in her 1931 memoir: "Sometimes one hears it said, or reads it, that the methods of Edwin Booth would be too out of date to sway a modern audience. No one who saw his art as he *listened* to the new King's first speech from the throne could endorse such a mistaken estimate" (177).

But the impact of this tasteful restraint upon his audience in 1887 should introduce a note of caution about the inexorable march of theatrical refinement. As Goodale reports, Booth's very rejection of audience appeal turns the audience into something almost uncontrollable. She times the first applause at "more than five minutes," recording then a series of audience interruptions, including the incident above (178–79). Lines that now seem merely familiar rather than deeply moving inspire something like hysteria. "'The play's the thing' had sixteen calls and asked for more," Goodale writes, while "O cursed spite, That ever I was born to set it right" yielded eight (180–81).[5] When the play is done, the audience enacts what Goodale calls "refined Bedlam": "Ladies climb upon their seats, scream out for Booth! Booth! . . . and then more calls" (182). Unlike the rowdy and mostly male "gallery gods" of the earlier part of the century, this more modern audience reveres Booth because he represents a new sense of Shakespeare's inviolate elitism.[4] But Goodale's observation about the adoring fans' power ("That audience tonight had done something to him" [182]) reminds us that the new "high" Shakespeare may have unacknowledged affinities with the old "popular" one. When the canons of high culture stretch far enough to include screaming ladies climbing on their seats, we should suspect that something much more interesting than refinement as we know it is holding sway. This moment onstage powerfully combines elite refinement, vulgar popularity, and an implicit recognition of the crass commercialism that makes Booth's reputation for nobility so marketable. Like Booth's audience in 1887, Goodale's memoir in 1931 enshrines the great actor as a figure for elite Shakespeare even while "doing something to him," placing him firmly in the sentimental marketplace.

Booth's cooperative venture with the actor/manager Lawrence Barrett, the tour Goodale describes in her memoir, became a three-year series of tours throughout the states, offering mostly Shakespearean tragedy with the finest possible production values. With Barrett's skill at management and Booth's reputation for excellence, it seemed at last that America could support Shakespeare as he deserved. Audiences flocked to the productions all across the country and reviews were almost unfailingly positive.[5] Though these productions were emphatically on the high side of the cultural divide, they were economically sustainable—profitable and popular—in a way that, as Levine has argued, was to become almost impossible in the twentieth century. Goodale's memoir of the tour in 1886–87, however, suggests that even at this apparent high point of artistic integrity, there were telling disturbances.[6] Accompanying Booth as a supporting actress, Goodale was at that time a theatrical newcomer called Kitty Molony. The terms of her engagement by the company are particularly resonant for a study of Booth's position in the marketplace. Though Kitty's breathless story is somewhat removed from the usual registers of theater history, I want to take it seriously as a record of Shakespeare's place in American culture in the period under discussion. In her girlish obscurity and her fawning admiration, Kitty taps into an American structure of feeling about high and low, past and present, that resonates beyond the memoir itself. Inscribing Booth as the object of her youthful crush, Kitty inscribes herself as a figure for the popular and the sentimental. Studying her story helps us, ultimately, to read our own narratives of evolving Shakespearean elitism in surprising ways, finding hidden forms of connection between elite and popular. The story we usually tell of cultural modernization has been about a process of cultural stratification, but Kitty's project of traveling back in time from 1931 to 1887 to claim a privileged relationship to Edwin Booth helps us to test our very understanding of Shakespeare's elite position in the America we call "modern."

Through what appears to be a combination of Booth's planning and that of his managers, Molony and two other women became Booth's personal companions for the duration of the tour, taking their meals and even sleeping in his private car. Booth took to calling these specially chosen actresses his "Chickens," praising them for their lack of competitiveness, their tact, and their innocence: "It is my tonic that our profession breeds girls without jealousy. You make me happier than I expected to be again in the theatre. Three of a kind, and I have them in my company. Be kittens and puppies for a week. You are younger than one of you realizes, and this amuses me most of all. You do not have airs for one another—" (223). This was, the memoir makes clear, a perfectly chaste and proper arrangement. She presents Both as an aging (albeit devastatingly attractive), pensive, temperate man who simply needed pure and gracious female companionship in order to keep from slipping into a depression. Her own privileged position, she contends, is entirely contingent on her ability to refrain from falling in love with him. Though, as she gushes, it was "in the air to be 'insane on Edwin Booth'" (5) in 1886–87, her own desire for him is firmly subordinated—even more firmly, she suggests, than that of the other chickens—to her plucky common sense and virtue. Only Kitty, apparently, can withstand proximity, concealing her love like Patience on a monument, smiling at Booth's overpowering charisma. When she is finally overcome with grief at their ultimate parting, however, it becomes clear that the repressed intensity of her feelings for him was assumed and even encouraged by all parties. An assistant manager makes the expectation clear as Kitty "bawls": "If you, child, hadn't put your pride in your pocket and let Mr. Booth realize you were fond of him—after all he has done for you—for the three of you—I'd never have gotten over it!" (298). Kitty's purpose on the tour is to love Booth in a way that is starstruck, foolish, somewhat improper, and yet somehow morally edifying.

Though this form of intimacy is intriguing enough as an aspect of Booth's and Goodale's biographies, its resonances with the problems of art in the marketplace become so startling in Goodale's memoir as to outweigh other concerns. Not content, apparently, to use Kitty's relationship with Booth as a kind of general antidepressant for the great actor, the manager Mr. Chase contrives to deploy her in a series of encounters that are aimed at getting Booth to do what is commercially expedient. He takes her aside one day and enlists her aid in a delicate matter: "'Miss Kitty, I –we—Mr. Barrett is trusting you with a responsibility that will tax all your tact' . . . Boiled down, my plight lay in my selection to *persuade Mr. Booth to wear a wig in Hamlet*" (154–55). This is, apparently, an unthinkable suggestion. Booth *is* Hamlet, after all, sublime in his subjectivity, a pure artist, spiritual, beyond concern about the gray hair that ruins the verisimilitude of his performance. He knows not seems. Chaste, gracious, and co-opted by the management, however, Kitty effects a virtual seduction by asking very nicely, ultimately compelling Booth to surrender his principles: "I am not a clown to amuse in *Hamlet*—yet, I will try it on" (160). The wig is both attractive and natural, as it turns out, and Booth, Mr. Chase, and Kitty all manage to put the moment behind them. In fact, they seem collectively to have been experiencing amnesia about much of Booth's career, for in all the many decades he had been playing the part of Hamlet he had, of course, already experimented with wigs and other aspects of his costume.[7] The wig seems to have become unthinkable only as part of an intricate relationship between Chase, Booth, and Kitty, which, I will suggest, is also an intricate relationship between Shakespeare as high art, Shakespeare as a market commodity, and Kitty's indomitable, imperiled virtue.

Again, later, Kitty is called into action by Mr. Chase because Booth does not want to play the role of Othello during his triumphant return to San Francisco, though his publicity machine has created a powerful expectation that he will do so. On an afternoon when Booth has taken his chickens to Cliff House, Chase takes Kitty aside and asks her to make Booth more inclined to cooperate:

> "Is this another of your 'persuasions,' Mr. Chase?"
>
> "Just think how easy that wig was for you!"
>
> There is a courage born of despair. I soberly reasoned with him that in the case of the wig I had merely been up against Mr. Booth's hesitancy. "Really he had decided to wear it before I ever said one word to him—"
>
> "I know all about that wig! Will you try for Othello? Because you must get Mr. Booth to go on as Othello here. It should be done for the last week—say on Tuesday." . . .
>
> I told him I couldn't and wouldn't. It was too soon. Mr. Booth would resent it this time—and, anyway, it wasn't professional etiquette. I hoped this might floor him.
>
> But he drawled: "Being here today at the Cliff House eating with Mr. Booth, and driving from here in carriages with him doesn't exactly come under the head of professional etiquette, either. Now, does it? Mr. Booth never before took members of his company yachting on the Pacific that I have heard of." (201–2)

Directly impugning her integrity—in fact, Goodale takes an extraordinary risk as a narrator when she includes his insinuations—

Chase enlists Kitty as an accomplice: "So I weakly yielded to my desire. But I refused to violate hospitality. Not one word from me today. I would not be alone, even, with Mr. Booth, for the rest of this outing. But I was. . . . Mr. Chase saw to it" (202). Kitty's ostensibly unforced desires become the force by which Mr. Chase manipulates Booth's relationship to a popular market.

In light of the wig episode, it may be no surprise that the posters advertising Booth's appearance as Othello the following Tuesday were printed before Kitty and Booth ever discussed the topic. "She has done it," Booth announces to Chase after Kitty wins him over. Kitty herself is unable to explain his willingness, except to say that Booth knew "his acting was [her] chief pleasure in life": "perhaps he trusted his instinct to give me this pleasure for the reason that I had not fallen in love with him. He may have deemed it poetic justice to reward a girl who was unsentimental over him!" (204). These instincts and pleasures, these inexplicable surrenders by both Kitty and Booth, the strange business of acknowledging that Kitty is compromised by the intimacy even while she insists that she is a plucky heroine, deserving of his affection because she resists his charms: these are strategies for concealing the workings of the market, certainly. The great Booth has not transcended the marketplace but has rather shifted the focus of market forces onto a sentimental girl whom he manipulates in order to maintain a fantasy of transcendence. By extension, it is not Booth who is commercial, but rather his audiences. Kitty's memoir would seem to argue that high culture has simply learned to disavow its inevitable relationship to commerciality. Kitty's participation in the selling of Booth's greatness would complicate the narrative of gradual separation between Shakespeare and the market over the course of the nineteenth century.

But these strategies of disavowal seem to demand a richer affective language than terms like "high," "low," and "marketplace." The structures of desire, restraint, discretion, seduction, virtue, and reward that Kitty (and apparently Booth and Chase) rely on here come directly from melodrama. Kitty seems to double as the virtuous heroine and the fallen woman; Booth is both the hero and, as will become powerfully apparent, the seducer. Chase is only inches away from being a mustache-twirling villain. It is easy enough to see that the three of them are colluding, in Kitty's telling of the story, in the marketing of high culture. They are moving into the genre in part to disguise agency, to make their actions inevitable.

Note that when Kitty calls her reward "poetic justice," she is all but admitting to their mutual authorship of a melodramatic tale. Compare her line—"He may have deemed it poetic justice to reward a girl who was unsentimental over him!"—with Joan Fontaine's famous remark in the "woman's" film *Letter from an Unknown Woman* (Max Orphüls, 1948): "I wanted to be the one woman who never asked you for anything." Beyond just identifying the pressures of commerciality, in other words, lie the more difficult and compelling questions: what it means that Kitty, Booth, and Chase are writing melodrama around the marketing of Shakespeare, and what it means that melodrama writes them.

I will argue that melodrama works for this narration because it provides Kitty and Booth with a particularly resonant vocabulary for a profound "behind the scenes" connection between the tragic, isolated artist and the foolish, sentimental girl. In the long, sprawling history of melodramatic cultural production such occulted connections between high and low have figured repeatedly: the discovery of the long-lost heir living in obscurity, the triumph of the orphan girl over her wealthy malefactors, the heart-wrenching maternal virtue of the woman seduced and abandoned by her aristocratic lover. Melodrama's habit of locating audience sympathies in the lowly and forgotten makes it a seemingly natural mode in which to narrate Kitty's strange power over Booth. The typical melodramatic seduction story, in particular, elevates the heroine while emphasizing her position of cultural disadvantage. She is lowly, but the aristocratic seducer is seized by an inexplicable desire for her. She is forgotten and relegated to the seducer's past, but she springs forward with an emotionally compelling declaration of her former importance in the seducer's life. Potentially sullied by her real or apparent vulnerability to seduction, she establishes or restores her virtue by suffering silently through a long period of exile and obscurity. While telling a story of maximum separation between high and low, melodrama simultaneously gives the low not only equal footing but even in some sense moral authority over the high. So, too, Kitty claims authority. In her telling, Kitty's admittedly inferior talents and perceptions are called forth regularly by Booth, who delights in her company, and by Mr. Chase, who delights in her power to influence Booth. The narrative, though it insists on the virtue of both Kitty and Booth, nevertheless depicts the great Shakespearean as a kind of seducer—this will become particularly pronounced in the scenes discussed below—who leaves young Kitty to cherish their former intimacy in silence. Kitty keeps her affection for him as an open secret, only confessing it in later moments of *Unknown Woman*–style melodramatic revelation: in her weeping when they part, and again in the moment of authoring the 1931 memoir.

*   *   *

One of the strengths of melodrama as a vocabulary for this encounter has to do with its emotional capaciousness, in this case its ability to do justice to the tremendous power of the play itself in performance, and specifically as performed by Edwin Booth. This is, after all, the stated object of Kitty's desire, the force to which she will yield weakly: not Booth himself, but Booth's Othello. As Kitty tells it in 1931, Booth needs her desire. On the night of the performance, he calls her to the green room. Kitty will be in the audience that night, not onstage, though in her telling of the story she could scarcely play a more prominent role in the production. Booth has promised to perform the play specifically as a favor to her. He has arranged for her to sit in a private box, and Mr. Chase has provided her with flowers and candy. She is in the rather precarious position of being Othello's date for the evening. Alone with her in the green room, Booth asks her what she thinks of him in his black makeup: "'You are the first Othello I have seen, Mr. Booth, whose skin does not make me shudder at the very thought of Desdemona's marriage.' . . . I did not say another word on his appearance. What was the need? He knew what a thing of masculine beauty he was as Othello." Booth does indeed seem to know: "You are a young girl. Desdemona's psychology is not unlike your own. She is not abnormal. I contend Othello should be attractive enough for Desdemona to fall in love with him. Othello is not a tragedy of abnormal passions. This is your night. I have not forgotten my promise." Then, as the overture begins: "'I shall act to you!'—said in his most professional tones" (208–9). However tempting it may be to question the use of the word "professional" in this context, the conflation of seduction and artistry are clearly essential for this extraordinary description of Booth's greatness as Kitty sees it. In her version of theatrical history, Booth is a towering figure in part because he truly desires her spectatorship and needs to acknowledge an essentially illicit relationship to her virtue.

In her position as privileged spectator that night, Kitty comes to speak as though she were the entire audience: "They each and

every one—one feels it—fall in love with him, even as Desdemona." Again, "Every one settles down as if suppressing a sigh of
bliss. . . . But the plot is so reasonable, all at once! Desdemona's
love unescapably natural" (211). Then, as anticipated, Othello
strangles Desdemona: "The death scene is a blank in my memory. I
do not know what Mr. Booth did in this act. I only know what I felt.
He had reduced me to an unthinking state. I was nothing but feeling" (215). It may well be understood why Kitty calls the next
morning's reviews "an anti-climax." Nevertheless, she continues to
map herself and Desdemona onto the audience: "And the next
morning's papers! Not a writer did here perceive a divided duty;
divided allegiance; divided acceptance; divided opinion. Edwin
Booth was crowned the greatest living Othello" (217). Imagining
now that she, the audience, and the critics have all become enrap-
tured Desdemonas, Kitty undoes the play's violent ending entirely.
Desdemona had, of course, spoken cautiously of her "divided
duty": "You are the lord of all my duty, / I am hitherto your daughter. But here's my husband" (1.3.184–85).[8] Constrained to acknowledge her father's authority even while defying him, and able to defy
him only by vowing obedience to her husband, Desdemona had
skillfully carved out a place for her desires. The scene of her declaration is, in fact, just a momentary pause on the way to her death.
As Susan Snyder has argued, *Othello* begins with a moment of
comic closure, the typical comic ending in which the bride and
groom are brought together, their defiance of the forbidding father
woven neatly into the restored social fabric, and the wedding banquet enjoyed.[9] In *Othello* this apparent resolution, the one Desdemona attempts to effect in the lines above, unravels immediately.
By managing to forget the play's ending and close her reflections
with this moment, Kitty rewrites *Othello* strikingly. It is Shakespeare's play, it is Mr. Chase's marketing triumph, it is Edwin
Booth's performance, but in the end it is Kitty's blissful sighs in
response to all of these master-craftsmen that rule the day. No one
can perceive the divided duty here.

Whether or not "each and every one" of the night's spectators
responded to Booth the way Kitty did, she may not be entirely so-
lipsistic in imagining her own desire as a wider cultural phenomenon.[10] Booth's fame in this period has been intimately linked by
critics to what Ann Douglas calls "the feminization of American
culture," the process through which femininity became accorded
moral authority, a project closely allied to melodrama's embrace of

the suffering victim.[11] Notwithstanding the important critiques to which Douglas's work has been subjected, however, and not forgetting Williams's reminder that melodrama is only a feminized construct in some of its forms, we can nevertheless trace in Kitty's identification of herself and her peers with Desdemona a paradoxical assertion of female agency.[12] More precisely, by using *Othello* as an opportunity to demonstrate "racial sympathy," to speak admiringly about Booth's black makeup and to describe Booth as welcoming Kitty/Desdemona's "not abnormal" desires, the memoir taps into the great source of feminized and racialized melodramatic authority in the period, Stowe's *Uncle Tom's Cabin.* To experience the plot of *Othello* as "so natural," to gloss over the death scene or to reframe it as a mystical moment of consummation, to imagine Booth's audiences as Desdemona not in the tragic moment of her death but in the comic moment of freeing herself from paternal authority by loving Othello, is to claim for the sympathetic spectator of the play some part of what Harriet Beecher Stowe claimed for readers of her novel: that they could be made to "*feel right.*"[13]

Shakespeare's *Othello,* in fact, articulates its own version of a protomelodramatic spectatorship, best described when Othello is called before the Venetian senators to explain his elopement with Desdemona.[14] When Brabantio accuses him of witchcraft, famously, his response in self-defense amounts to a formula much like Stowe's: "She lov'd me for the dangers I had pass'd, / And I lov'd her that she did pity them" (1.3.167–68). Though the play, of course, goes on to punish both Desdemona and Othello severely for this moment of mutual understanding—a punishment Kitty neatly excises from her consciousness by rewriting it as pleasure—the similarity between Stowe's and Othello's sense of audience relations is striking. In both cases, to hear the story of racialized suffering sympathetically is to acquire virtue, to become lovable, and to exercise a potential "civilizing" influence, as promised explicitly by Stowe and implicitly by Othello's speech.[15] It is possible, in fact, to read *Othello* as a play that is intrinsically about purifying feminized spectatorship, however unsuccessfully. Othello himself, as an exoticized Moor on the English stage, is a spectacle seeking a legitimizing spectator in the person of Desdemona. In such a reading the play would be seen to register the fragility of this solution, which is ultimately the fragility of theater's moral and cultural place in early modern England. Though both Desdemona and Othello turn themselves into agonized, self-sacrificing victims, nevertheless in the end they become a tawdry show in which a Moor strangles a white woman in bed. As at least one critic has reminded us, tragedy is simply melodrama seen from another perspective.[16] If Kitty's rewriting of *Othello* borrows the cultural authority of Stowe's novel, the novel itself may have gained some of its power by reconfiguring some of the elements of an incipient "racial sympathy" already present in Shakespeare—or by selectively ignoring Shakespeare's pessimism as Kitty does in favor of a feminized authority that defies the great father of all writers. It is, after all, a bold move both for Stowe and for Kitty to shift the perspective of Shakespeare's race tragedy. In one view Kitty's version is the most radical of all, focusing on Desdemona's pleasure and sympathetic power instead of her sacrificial death—or little Eva's.

Writing in 1931 about her experiences in 1887, then, Kitty testifies to the persistence of certain melodramatic tropes across a crucial period of cultural change, by no means limited to a relationship with *Uncle Tom's Cabin*. It is difficult to avoid hearing early film in her narration; Booth in his makeup attempting to bring high culture and a right understanding of Othello's race to America while nearly seducing an innocent girl is eerily evocative of D. W. Griffith's *Broken Blossoms* (1919), set in London, while perhaps the actual production of *Othello* might more closely resemble the companion piece, *Birth of a Nation* (1915). Moving ahead in time—we are working here with the long tradition of popular melodrama rather than with specific influences upon Goodale—the production of the memoir itself feels like a happier version of *Letter from an Unknown Woman,* as mentioned above, in which a seduced and abandoned woman writes a letter at the end of her life about how she has raised her seducer's son in secret all these years, carefully cherishing the momentary intimacy that has been forgotten utterly by her elite musician lover. Along similar lines, Kitty's memoir pointedly notes that she has never forgotten her intimacy with Booth, that he looms large even in relation to her deceased husband, that she married a nice man as Booth told her to, that even her husband once said that if he could come back to life for just a moment he would want to come watch Booth play Hamlet (not to relive their wedding day or the birth of their children).[17] Such evidence as is available suggests that Booth was not deeply preoccupied with Kitty.[18] By making a big deal about what is finally a slight intimacy with Booth, Kitty aligns herself with a whole line of virtuous heroines and heroes from melodrama, speaking like Joan Fon-

taine for the desire to revivify the past, to expose and celebrate a
hidden history, to establish some equality between what is low and
forgotten and what is elite and forward-looking.[19] It is not hard to
understand why, when she is writing as Katherine Goodale in 1931,
Kitty relishes a loving audience's power to melt Booth back into the
San Francisco Fire Boy, a sentimental figure like her, wearing his
commercially expedient wig and foolishly grateful for all the attention. The emotional language she uses has by 1931 become a way
to telegraph a whole form of consciousness about high and low,
past and present. In melodrama the meek do inherit the earth and
the past is never really past. Booth may appear to sweep Kitty off
her feet and walk away, but the founding premise of that story—a
premise Kitty seems to endorse with great energy—is that Kitty and
her kind will always have the last word. So, too, I want to suggest,
the forces of elite, modernizing theatrical refinement may be surprisingly subject to the returning influence of the popular and the
sentimental.

*   *   *

The melodramatic way of claiming emotional and moral power
over the forces of modernization and elitism is by no means restricted, however, to memoirs by supporting actresses with bad
crushes. In what remains of this essay, I want to outline ways in
which Kitty's paradigm is in the end our own critical paradigm, an
influential and barely acknowledged structure of feeling that helps
to govern what we say about Shakespeare, about the popular, and
about our own place as scholars of theater history. When Lawrence
Levine makes his much-cited argument about the growing division
between high and low Shakespeare, he falls into a kind of difficulty
that proves instructive. Levine notes that he is often accused of
being nostalgic for some lost golden era of American unity, a charge
he disputes:

> If a sense of loss does permeate this book—and I suspect it does—it has
> to do with the loss of what I perceive to have been a rich shared public
> culture that once characterized the United States. . . . I do not mean to
> imply that the Americans of the past were the creators and products of
> a stable, unvarying, undifferentiated culture. . . . What I mean, in refer-
> ring to a shared culture, is that in the nineteenth century, especially in
> the first half, Americans, in addition to whatever specific cultures they
> were part of, shared a public culture less hierarchically organized, less

fragmented into relatively rigid adjectival boxes than their descendants were to experience a century later.[20]

I don't fundamentally disagree with Levine's reading of Shakespeare's cultural place, or with his notions of historical change. I do want to contend, as I have begun to do above, that what looks to Levine like a relatively solid sense of high culture is subject to multiple compromises with the low and the popular that complicate his reading to some extent.

For the purposes of the present argument, however, I am most interested in the disavowal of affect that marks his self-defense: "If a sense of loss does permeate this book—and I suspect it does." It is a near-compulsory humanist gesture, the acknowledgment of some investment in the topic that carefully stops short of hindering objectivity. It may remind us of Booth's wan smile, without the lapse into aggressive tears. But the loss of intimacy described in Levine's book actually sounds like something worth getting choked up about:

> Although in the mid-twentieth century there was no more widely known, respected, or quoted dramatist in our culture than Shakespeare, the nature of his relationship to the American people had changed: he was no longer their familiar, no longer part of their culture, no longer at home in their theaters or on the movie and television screens that had become the twentieth-century equivalents of the stage. If Shakespeare had been an integral part of mainstream culture in the nineteenth century, in the twentieth he had become part of "polite" culture—an essential ingredient in a complex we call, significantly, "legitimate" theater.[21]

It is not the highbrow Shakespeare who has been exiled from our culture, here, but rather the low, popular, intimate Shakespeare who enjoyed a good burlesque. Without at all wishing to trivialize, I want to suggest that the popular Shakespeare in Levine's argument looks a lot like Barbara Stanwyck at the end of the film *Stella Dallas* (King Vidor, 1937)—wistfully surveying the scene of elite culture from which he has been excluded. In the film, it may be remembered, Stanwyck stands alone in the rainy night, staring through the window of an elegant home—trashy, common, and self-excluded—while her daughter marries a respectable man inside. Stanwyck's and Shakespeare's sacrifices are necessary, it seems, to produce a new, more refined generation.

I want to be clear, as Levine is, about why his argument really does have a genuine, if only partially acknowledged, element of pathos: it is not be cause we have lost a chance to experience the American equivalent of Merry Old England with its festival pleasures, nor because we have bid farewell to the ideal of the noble common man. The mourning in Levine's work—should we call it melancholia?—instead has to do with a long trajectory in which enlightenment objectivity has been the province of high culture. Historically accurate Shakespeare productions are opposed to sentimental and anachronistic distortions ("bastardizations" would be the melodramatic term); ideological critique is opposed to the kind of false (lower-class, feminized, or hypermasculine) consciousness that succumbs to the seductions of dominant discourse. It is sad, actually. This is the cultural split that allows elections to be won or lost on the basis of a candidate's moving "life story," the same split that makes "being out of touch" or "not getting it" the number one election-year crime. Leftists in particular—or even mild liberals—are forever on the verge of being "defined" as Louis Jordan, with no way to communicate to anyone outside the "cultural elite." What happened to popular Shakespeare has happened to all of us, and though we may live well enough without Shakespeare, we are paying dearly for the larger social changes.

When as critics we approach high and low cultural forms and their history, I want to argue, we may be bound to the melodramas from which we imagine ourselves to be distanced. The notion of a shared public culture comes back to us again and again like a distant memory of union that is tantalizing and discomfiting. Our own critical paradigm runs parallel to *Letter from an Unknown Woman.* Joan Fontaine writes hauntingly about her abandonment by the elite artist she loves; so too, we critics write hauntingly about a divorce between high and low culture again and again. Again, these iconic moments in film are selected not because I regard them, anachronistically, as influences upon Goodale. It is true that both *Letter from an Unknown Woman* and *Stella Dallas* were novels before they became screenplays, but the deliberately idiosyncratic range of references here is meant to emphasize melodrama's peculiar ability to transcend historical eras and cultural forms, surfacing just when we might expect it to have been supplanted.[22] Indeed, melodrama often surfaces precisely *as* abandoned, as a haunting reminder that what we thought we had left behind is determinedly still present. To focus on the later Hollywood classic "women's pictures," moreover, is to benefit from a robust tradition of film criticism that has explored melodrama's place on the American cultural map.

I began working on this topic because I was so struck by the parallels between the arguments that get made about nineteenth-century America and the ones I was familiar with about early modern England. Both periods are said to begin with a union between high and low and to end with a rigidly enforced cultural hierarchy. Nor are such claims limited to these two eras.[23] I am not suggesting that these arguments are entirely wrong, and of course we are talking about vastly different histories and circumstances. But how many times can a supposedly definitive cultural split like this take place? And how is it that this splitting off of high from low seems inevitably to mark the close of one of our identified historical "periods"?[24] It is just possible that certain tropes of lost intimacy are making us into the scholarly version of Louis Jordan, forgetting who Joan Fontaine is and what she looks like. Like him, we are not quite able to recognize what doesn't fit our paradigm of tortured clitist isolation. Linda Williams has argued that one of melodrama's characteristic gestures is to modernize, to seek out new cultural problems, new unjust exclusions, new forms of suffering as grist for the generic mill: "Part of the excitement of the mode is the genuine turmoil and timeliness of the issues it takes up and the popular debate it can generate when it explores controversies not yet placed on the agenda of liberal humanism."[25] The same could be said of the excitement generated within academic circles in recent decades, as scholars like Levine recover lost cultural forms and detail processes of cultural stratification.

I have been suggesting, however, that some of the impasses our discipline has reached—oddly, academics have never been more preoccupied with popular culture than we are now, precisely at the moment in which we believe we cannot be popular—are connected to our engagement with the tropes of melodrama. The point is not to try to rid our thinking of melodramatic elements, but rather to argue for a reinvigorated study of of such elements, including the evolution of melodrama as genre and melodrama as mode. Though such study engages questions of form, it is by no means, as scholars like Williams have shown, reductively formalist. It is especially ironic that Shakespeareans are nervous about studying form because we think it will compel us to talk about timeless, unchanging, universal truths we reject categorically. On the contrary, we need a deep engagement with literary form—and we need to acknowledge our own cooperation with genre and mode as critics—if we are to read history at all, our own or Shakespeare's. We could start by recognizing that melodrama is neither the thing from which Shakespeare and the objectivity of scholarship have to be rescued nor the heartwarming answer to our modern cultural divides. It is, instead, a shared action through which we, like Kitty and Booth, simultaneously regret and replicate those divides. But what else are we doing when we write literary history as a repressed melodrama? Or in this case, when we write a melodrama about the suppression of melodrama itself? To quote Williams one more time: "The worst thing we can do to melodrama is to condescend to it. The next worst thing we can do is to ignore it."[26]

We could, if there were room within the present context, say much more about the history of melodrama in the development of elite literary culture in America. Peter Brooks has written very influentially on melodrama's central place in the work of Henry James; Thomas Postlewait argues compellingly about how Eugene O'Neill's hatred of his father, who was a star of melodrama, has seeped into and given shape to what he calls "the suspect history of American drama," in which melodrama is definitively supplanted by realism.[27] Williams insightfully identifies what she calls the "American Melodramatic Mode," a persistent set of patterns that come to us from the nineteenth-century stage and from Hollywood, but that are at this point so ubiquitous as to shape everything from coverage of the Olympics to election cycles and the O. J. Simpson trial. In other words, there are plenty of indicators that melodrama is central to what we think of as modern, both elite and popular, not supplanted at all.[28] Melodrama informs both the backbone of American popular culture and our critique of American cultural hierarchies.

In addition to telling the history of the genre, though, we could meditate a little more on the opportunities it gives us for thinking about itself. For this second approach, I want to turn very briefly to the work of Stanley Cavell, who finds in *Stella Dallas* the epitome of a genre he calls "The Hollywood melodrama of the unknown woman." Characteristically, Cavell imagines his melodramatic women to be offering us (if "us" is a history of male skeptical philosophy) the potential for a real conversation with the low and the feminized.[29] In his reading of *Stella Dallas,* Stella is much more than a preposterously dressed, clueless victim of the canons of taste and elite decorum. She is instead a knowing performer who accomplishes both the social successes of her daughter and the possibility of autonomous subjectivity for herself. By walking away, like Ibsen's Nora, from the scene of marriage, Stella implies a form of knowledge hidden from the limited imagination of her wealthy ex-husband. Cavell and Stella Dallas can't tell us exactly what it will mean to think about melodrama from within melodrama, but they do suggest, at least, that we may learn to speak of the progress of cultural history (and thus our own work) as something other than the endless vanquishing of low culture and the triumph of elitism. For Cavell, Stella's walking away from her own marriage and that of her daughter teaches her and us that she has "the right not to share their tastes," the right to be something other than the victim and pupil of an exclusionary esthetic.[30] It offers us, too, what Cavell calls "the promise of return, of unpredictable reincarnation."[31] Stella is perhaps walking into exile at the end of that film, but in the very moment of her departure, the painful pleasure she gives us assures us that she will appear again and again, not vanquished by the future but ready to reappear in any era: on the point of being excluded, powerful because endangered, both forgotten and unforgettable.

I am suggesting then, that along with our interest in the story of exclusion, the story in which high triumphs over low, we remain interested in the power of the low to claim authority, to present itself in new forms, to govern our perceptions of the high. To hear Kitty tell it, she has not only witnessed Booth's greatness from a position of infinite deference, but has also dressed him in a wig, made him perform, kept him sober, and brought him back to life in 1931. This is not to say that we should neglect the forms of searing loss and constraint to which Stella and her kind are subjected, gendered constraints that feminist film criticism has proven itself particularly adept at analyzing. Acknowledging those constraints, however, film scholar Christine Gledhill nevertheless notes that "Stella's image is structured in pathos rather than clear triumph or defeat."[32] Like Stella, and like genres themselves, popular forms may be too elastic simply to give way before the forces of historical change. Though melodrama famously establishes a sense of Manichaean opposition between high and low, good and evil, past and present, it also works in subtler ways to blur those oppositions. Not least because melodrama pops up again and again in new places, always ready to announce itself as a sign of modernity, stories of

its demise tend to be vastly overstated.[33] Perhaps our narratives of
change require a similar elasticity, a similar power to negotiate both
cultural triumph and cultural exclusion.

Such a grappling with the power of the low and the popular, after
all, may be particularly central to Shakespeare studies. For all the
excellence and sophistication that our field has brought to the academic discussion of Shakespeare, finally, our privileged position in
higher education is grounded in public school classrooms, movie
theaters, and the marketplace, in Kitty-style fan culture that gives
Shakespeare at least a residual marketability as the popular face of
elitism.[34] Like Booth, Shakespeare is a figure for greatness who has
an inexplicable need for the silly devotion of people who can never
be like him. As Williams reminds us, breaking with melodrama
would mean breaking with the popular itself.[35] Rather than breaking with the melodramatic love of Shakespeare, we ought to strateg-
ize about our cultural place with full understanding that high and
low—the various imaginings of elite Shakespeareans and of the
culture that supports us, a culture we are so often thought to have
abandoned—are divided by a common story.

Notes

Warm thanks to Elizabeth Bolton, Claire M. Busse, Alice Dailey, Kendall Johnson,
Homay King, Matthew Kozusko, Bakirathi Mani, Steve Newman, Kristen Poole,
Katherine Rowe, Bethany Schneider, Lauren Shohet, Kate Thomas, Julian Yates,
Carina Yervasi, and especially Patricia White for spirited discussion and assis-
tance with this essay, which exceeds the scope of individual citation.

1. Katherine Goodale, *Behind the Scenes with Edwin Booth* (Boston:
Houghton Mifflin, 1931), 179. Further reference to this volume will be given by
page number in the text.

2. Booth was not in fact a local boy, but he spent formative years in Gold
Rush–era San Francisco, developing a solid career as a popular entertainer in
melodramas like the *San Francisco Fire Boy,* as well as in Shakespearean roles.
See Daniel J. Watermeier, "Edwin Booth Goes West: 1852–1856," *Theatre History
Studies* 25 (June 2005): 77–105. Goodale describes *Fire Boy* and recounts Booth's
comic memories of its plot (146–48).

3. Lawrence Levine, *Highbrow/Lowbrow: The Emergence of Cultural Hierarchy in America* (Cambridge, MA: Harvard University Press, 1988).

4. Richard Butsch, *The Making of American Audiences: From Stage to Television, 1750–1990* (Cambridge: Cambridge University Press, 2000).

5. See Charles H. Shattuck, *Shakespeare on the American Stage: From Booth
and Barrett to Sothern and Marlowe* (Washington, DC: Folger Books, 1987), 31–53;
Shattuck, *The Hamlet of Edwin Booth* (Urbana: University of Illinois Press, 1969),

306–9; L. Terry Oggel, *Edwin Booth: A Bio-Bibliography* (New York: Greenwood Press, 1992), 39–45.

6. Goodale's memoir was written in a kind of two-part process. She kept a diary during the 1886–87 tour, returning to that diary and revising it before publication in 1931. While clearly inaccurate in many details, I want to argue, the memoir is pitch-perfect in terms of sensibility. Note that a life of Booth published the year after Goodale's also describes him in terms of melodrama, in this case managing to disparage melodrama itself while still invoking the form to characterize Booth's own larger-than-life suffering: "To raise the curtain on the life of Edwin Booth, tragedian, is to reveal a melodrama of abashing theatricalism. We shall find it preposterously extravagant, and then we must remember that it is a melodrama written by Fate" (Richard Lockridge, *Darling of Misfortune: Edwin Booth, 1833–1893* [New York: Century, 1932], 3). Lockridge's prologue continues for several pages to put forward the notion that Booth's life was excessively tragic; he refers, of course, to the fact that Edwin Booth's brother John Wilkes had assassinated Lincoln, and to the repeated stories of loss, melancholy, and mental illness that marked their family life. "But not even the cinema will have such melodrama, nowadays," he states, somewhat mistakenly (4).

7. See Daniel Watermeier, ed. and annotated, *Edwin Booth's Performances: The Mary Isabella Stone Commentaries* (Ann Arbor, MI: UMI Research Press, 1990). Stone comments emphatically about how she dislikes the long wig and costume he wore in the part of Hamlet in 1883, just a few years before Kitty's encounter with him (13). Shattuck notes that Goodale has apparently confused this episode with another one, for while Barrett did indeed persuade Booth to wear a wig at some point during the tour, the reviews of this particular performance specifically mention that Booth's hair is gray (*Hamlet of Edwin Booth,* 307).

8. All references to *Othello* are taken from the Arden edition, ed. M. R. Ridley (London: Methuen, 1958).

9. Susan Snyder, *The Comic Matrix of Shakespeare's Tragedies: "Romeo and Juliet," "Hamlet," "Othello," and "King Lear"* (Princeton: Princeton University Press, 1979), 70–90.

10. See the more mixed reception documented by Lois Potter in *Othello* (Manchester: Manchester University Press, 2002), 45–46.

11. Ann Douglas, *The Feminization of American Culture* (New York: Doubleday, 1988), 1st ed., 1977. On Booth's fame as a feminized artist, see *Melodramatic Formations: American Theatre and Society, 1820–1870* (Iowa City: University of Iowa Press, 1992), 240–42; and Karl M. Kippola, *Out of the Forrest and Into the Booth: Performance of Masculinity on the American Stage, 1828–1865* (dissertation, University of Maryland, College Park, 2003).

12. For important critiques of Douglas's paradigm, see the edition of the journal *differences,* edited by Philip Gould, and especially his introduction, "Revisiting the 'Feminization' of American Culture" [11 (3): i–xii (1999)]. See Linda Williams, *Playing the Race Card: Melodramas of Black and White from Uncle Tom to O. J. Simpson* (Princeton: Princeton University Press, 2001), 19–20, on feminine melodrama as only one aspect of a much larger mode.

13. Harriet Beecher Stowe, *Uncle Tom's Cabin: Or, Life Among the Lowly* (Boston: John P. Jewett, 1852), 2:817, italics original.

14. On *Othello* and melodrama, see Virginia Mason Vaughan, *Othello: A Contextual History* (Cambridge: Cambridge University Press, 1994), 135.

15. See Vaughan, *Othello*, regarding Booth's presentation of Othello as a comparatively refined and intellectual figure, in opposition to Salvini's more expressive and exoticized performances (172–73); see also Potter, *Othello*, 40–47.

16. Consider, for instance, Ira Hauptman on the subject of melodrama's relation to tragedy: "Think of the melodramatic play in which the hero has become a drunkard, and his desperate, weeping wife comes to the saloon to show him their helpless little baby. And the hero sees the baby and melts and gives up his terrible life. Now consider: from the point of view of the baby this is not melodrama but *The Eumenides.* . . . His needful existence puts a new moral responsibility on his parent-gods and, wondrously, inexplicably, they reconcile themselves to each other to meet it. To an audience of Titans the struggle in *The Eumenides* between gods and furies and the transformation of the furies into benevolent deities is pure melodrama" ("Defending Melodrama," in *Melodrama,* Themes in Drama 14 ed. James Redmond [Cambridge: Cambridge University Press, 1992], 281–90, esp. 288).

17. See, for instance, 316–17. Goodale's husband was George Goodale, hailed at his death as "dean of American theatrical critics." He was dramatic editor for the *Detroit Free Press* from 1865 to 1919 ("George P. Goodale, Critic, Dies at 75," *New York Times,* May 8, 1919).

18. Shattuck quotes Booth on the subject of Goodale: "[S]he is a pretty and good little body; her case [as an actress] is hopeless." Booth did tactfully arrange to drop Kitty from other roles on the basis of technical exigencies (*Hamlet of Edwin Booth,* xxi).

19. It should be noted that Goodale herself is in no way an unsophisticated observer of the American cultural scene, well connected as she is to the theatrical milieu. It is thus all the more interesting that in her adulthood she should choose to write about Edwin Booth from the perspective of a breathless young girl. On the tradition of sentimental women's writing in relation to notions of high culture, see Jane Tompkins, *Sentimental Designs: The Cultural Work of American Fiction 1790–1860* (Oxford: Oxford University Press, 1985).

20. Levine, *Highbrow/Lowbrow,* 9.

21. Ibid., 31.

22. *Letter from an Unknown Woman* is an adaptation of the 1922 novel by Stefan Zweig. *Stella Dallas* was adapted from a 1923 novel by Olive Higgins Prouty. Its consistent appeal is attested by film adaptations, both the King Vidor 1937 version, and the 1925 film by Henry King. It ran as a radio serial from 1938 to 1955 and was remade yet again in a film version starring Bette Midler in 1990, directed by John Erman. See Jennifer Parchesky, "Adapting *Stella Dallas*: Class Boundaries, Consumerism, and Hierarchies of Taste." *Legacy: A Journal of American Women Writers,* vol. 23 no. 2 (2006) 178–79.

23. The compelling argument made in *The Politics and Poetics of Transgression,* for instance, might look different if the flourishing culture of Shakespearean burlesque in eighteenth- and nineteenth-century England were taken into consideration (Peter Stallybrass and Allon White [Ithaca: Cornell University Press, 1986]). See also Thomas Postlewait, "From Melodrama to Realism: The Suspect History of American Drama," in *Melodrama: The Cultural Emergence of a Genre,* ed. Michael Hays and Anastasia Nikolopoulou, 39–60 (New York: St. Martin's Press, 1996); and Stephen Watt, "Modern American Drama," in *The Cambridge*

Companion to American Modernism, ed. Walter B. Kalaidjian, 102–26 (Cambridge: Cambridge University Press, 2005).

24. I am grateful to Elizabeth Bolton for raising this question.

25. Williams, *Race Card,* 18–19.

26. Ibid., 309. Williams has outlined the ways in which this mode teases us with a simultaneous pull forward in time (miraculous intervention "in the nick of time") while simultaneously calling us back to an idealized past (*Race Card,* 30–38); see also Williams "Melodrama Revised," in *Refiguring American Film Genres: Theory and History,* ed. Nick Browne (Berkeley: University of California Press, 1998), 42–88. Bruce McConachie notes that melodrama in the nineteenth-century theater functioned precisely to mark a thin border between elite and popular cultures (*Melodramatic Formations: American Theatre and Society, 1820–1870* [Iowa City: University of Iowa Press, 1992]).

27. Brooks, *The Melodramatic Imagination: Balzac, Henry James, Melodrama, and the Mode of Excess* (New York: Columbia University Press, 1985); see Postlewait above, n. 23.

28. As Christine Gledhill has remarked, "Darwin, Freud and Marx were all products of the melodramatic imagination" ("The Melodramatic Field: An Investigation," in *Home Is Where the Heart Is: Studies in Melodrama and the Woman's Film,* ed. Christine Gledhill [London: British Film Institute, 1987], 5–39, esp. 20).

29. Stanley Cavell, *Contesting Tears: Hollywood's Melodrama of the Unknown Woman* (Chicago: University of Chicago Press, 1996).

30. Ibid., 217.

31. Ibid., 219.

32. "Christine Gledhill on 'Stella Dallas' and Feminist Film Theory," *Cinema Journal* 25, no. 4 (Summer 1986): 44–48, esp. 48; see also "E. Ann Kaplan Replies," 49–53.

33. On the strong continuities between stage melodrama and film, see the pioneering work of A. Nicholas Vardac, *Stage to Screen: Theatrical Method from Garrick to Griffith* (New York: Benjamin Blom, 1968).

34. The many scholars who investigate Shakespeare's uses in popular culture are, of course, too numerous to list here. See, for example, Douglas Lanier, *Shakespeare and Modern Popular Culture* (Oxford: Oxford University Press, 2002); Michael D. Bristol, *Shakespeare's America, America's Shakespeare* (New York: Routledge, 1990) and *Big-Time Shakespeare* (New York: Routledge, 1996); Richard Burt, *Unspeakable ShaXXXespeares: Queer Theory and American Kiddie Culture* (New York: St. Martin's Press, 1998); Kim C. Sturgess, *Shakespeare and the American Nation* (Cambridge: Cambridge University Press, 2004).

35. Williams, *Race Card,* 308–10.

REVIEW ARTICLE

Shakespeare and the Gothic Strain

LINDA CHARNES

IT MAY NOT SEEM IMMEDIATELY OBVIOUS that Shakespearean drama and Gothic literature should share scholarly space. Shakespeare represents the apex of literary culture, while there is still a whiff of something slightly disreputable or "pulpy" about Gothic texts. They are, however, deeply intertwined, and this review essay will explore some of the implications of that interlocutorship through an expanded review of the recent anthology *Gothic Shakespeares*, edited by John Drakakis and Dale Townshend (2008). I make no claims to be an expert on nineteenth-century fiction, but I am a longtime fan of Gothic texts and herewith offer some further reflections on the topic that, hopefully, will add to and complicate the conversation fruitfully begun in *Gothic Shakespeares.*

For many years, in literary studies at least, the term "Gothic" has been associated primarily with the early nineteenth-century novel and particularly with romance or even "ladies'" novels. A hybrid of fairy-tale elements, ghost stories, sagas of families fallen into disrepute and disrepair (madwomen in attics, angry poor relations, and debauched former aristocrats), the Gothic novel developed a trajectory separate from, but parallel to, the more canonically "respectable" later Victorian novel. The Gothic novel's "baptism" in England is often (arguably, as we will see) attributed to Horace Walpole's *The Castle of Otranto: A Gothic Story* (1765); its successive tradition has ventured into terrain as sophisticated as the novels of Edith Wharton and Henry James. Consequently the term "Gothic" is now a magician's hat out of which many rabbits may be pulled.[1] It has been applied to films as well as literary texts, ranging from Murnau's *Nosferatu* to Ridley Scott's *Alien* and *Blade Runner,* from classics such as *The Cabinet of Dr. Caligari* to recent (Japanese-inspired) horror films such as *The Grudge* or *Dark Water;* from melodramatic musicals (Andrew Lloyd Weber's *Phantom of the Opera*) to noir detective stories; and, of course, to the recent explosion of vampire novels, films, and television serials.

To avoid wandering, Melmoth-like, through the 150 years during which Gothic literature has developed, I will concentrate on some key thematics that link these genres, a thread that often includes one or more of the following: a shameful secret of some sort, often intergenerational; an enemy (external or internal) whose outlines are blurry or vague; and a dwelling or location in decay—often an old family estate or even a geographic region, as with HBO's recent Southern Gothic vampire serial *True Blood,* set in post-Katrina Louisiana. Whereas many genres, including science fiction, involve enemy or alien invasions, the Gothic invokes its own special brand of dread: of something or someone already "in the house" as it were (or under the stage, or ground, or lake, or floorboards), issuing audible but indecipherable demands.

Aside from *Hamlet, Macbeth,* and *Richard III,* few of Shakespeare's plays seem especially proto-Gothic. However, *Gothic Shakespeares* brings together a group of British, American and Canadian scholars who attempt to define "the Gothic" in conceptual, aesthetic, historical, and generic terms, and collectively to argue that Shakespeare is not only Gothic in himself but a cause that the Gothic is in others. Speaking to the elasticity of the term in his introduction, John Drakakis points out that even at the most superficial level, a "predilection for spectres, graveyards, the paraphernalia of death," as well as "the emphasis on the 'non-rational' as a category of human experience," renders Shakespeare's plays open to the descriptive term "Gothic" (1). There is, I would add, a difference between rendering Shakespeare "open" to the Gothic charge, and delineating what is singularly Gothic as a genre or aesthetic category. After all, an "investment in the resources of the supernatural" (ibid.) has been a literary feature since the dawn of storytelling and does not alone define the Gothic. As Drakakis points out, the Gothic *movement* in literature begins in the eighteenth century and is well-established as a literary genre by the nineteenth century in both Britain and America. Its historical definitions are open to contestation, falling on a spectrum between a type of architecture associated with "the ghosts of Catholic Europe" (7), a version of the "ancient-modern" debate, and a literature that traffics in the crumbling edifices of decay: a conceptual and emotional aesthetic that may or may not be tied to the buildings of the past or the lingering debates of the Reformation.

There are also multiple literary and geopolitical histories with respect to the Gothic, including gendered histories that may be
bound up with how romance conventions, or supernatural elements, are foregrounded. If one subscribes to a more patriarchalist
geneaology, then Horace Walpole, as mentioned earlier, is usually
regarded as the "father" of the Gothic novel. But Walpole has a pre-
cursor, and many of the elements that come to define the Gothic
can be found in Sarah Fielding's (Henry's sister) earlier novel *The
History of Ophelia,* which was published in 1760 and often goes
unremarked in discussions of the genre. Fielding was, according to
Peter Sabor, who edited the first modern edition, "the second most
popular English woman novelist, behind only Eliza Haywood"
(30).[2] Certainly Fielding's use of Ophelia's name is too significant a
connection to neglect in any discussion of Shakespeare and the
Gothic, despite the critical tendency to do so.

Gothic Shakespeares is no exception in this regard; the essays
here tend on the whole to maintain a Walpolean genealogy, although Ann Radcliffe, writing thirty years after Walpole, is certainly given her due. As the purpose of the volume is to explore
Shakespeare as the preeminent repository for eighteenth- and nineteenth-century writers of melodramas, novels, and plays, as well
as subsequent treatments of the Shakespearean Gothic in films and
contemporary culture, I would like to emphasize that although
Hamlet may be the most immediate candidate for a Gothic facto-
tum, one could argue that the history or "fate" of Ophelia has its
own Gothic trajectory, depending on which valences of the genre
are privileged and with whom one chooses to identify. Feminist
scholarship of the last twenty years has redefined how we might
read the tradition of the novel in general, as well as Gothic fiction
in particular. For Terry Castle, one of the most influential scholars
on Gothic texts, the late eighteenth- and nineteenth-century novel
has a spectral history with an additional component: the uncanny
effects of repression on female experience, including lesbian desire. Departing from Ian Watt's foundational theory of the novel as
the dominant realist literary form, Castle addresses the Gothic as a
specifically counter-Enlightenment sensibility, one that leads directly to psychoanalytic theories of how the human subject experiences hauntings and things "off limits" in spite of (perhaps due to)
the dominance of rationalist epistemology:

> [Freud's] central insight—that it is precisely the historic internalization
> of rationalist protocols that produces the uncanny—not only sheds

light . . . on the peculiar emotional ambivalence the Enlightenment now evokes in us (it has both freed us and cursed us), it also offers a powerful dialectical model for understanding many of the haunting paradoxes of eighteenth-century literature and culture. (15)[3]

Other feminist theorists of Gothic fiction, including Deirdre Lynch, Susan Gubar, and Sandra Gilbert, concentrate on the broader representation of women in this offshoot of the nineteenth-century novel.[4]

Gothic Shakespeares illustrates, without directly addressing, some of the tensions between gendered critical trajectories, which become more pronounced as the essays move toward the postmodern and present-day examples of the Gothic. The essays vary greatly in sensibility and theoretical approach, providing a wide set of lenses onto the Gothic, none of which are complete nor aim to be. However, one area of focus seems to me to be conspicuously lacking: the American Gothic tradition, a species that deserves some attention given the importance of Charles Brockden Brown, whose epistolary novel *Wieland; or, The Transformation* (1798) is considered the first Gothic American novel, and of Edgar Allen Poe, the first master of the Gothic short story form. Although spontaneous combustion (*Wieland; or, The Transformation*) and beating hearts beneath floorboards (*The Tell-tale Heart*) do not seem very Shakespearean, if E. J. Clery is right that "scratch the surface of any gothic fiction and the debt to Shakespeare will be there," then surely that debt is represented in the new republic.[5] In Brockden Brown's *Wieland,* especially, there are many Shakespearean as well as now-"classic" Gothic themes: intergenerational failure, somnambulism, "supernatural" occurences, guilt, and jealousy. Given how much attention is paid in several of the essays in the later half of the anthology to American horror films and American-authored vampire fictions, one cannot help but feel that the American tradition (which was developing simultaneously alongside the British) gets short shrift.

This criticism notwithstanding, there is still much to fascinate Shakespeare scholars in the anthology. Elisabeth Bronfen's essay, which follows the introduction, discusses the Renaissance practice of positing night linguistically, as "Plays were intially staged in daylight" (23). She traces the proto-Gothic use and imagery of night in *The Merchant of Venice, Romeo and Juliet,* and *A Midsummer Night's Dream.* Shakespeare, Bronfen argues, uses the trope of night not only as a cloak for actions unsanctioned by day, but as a counterworld in which "nocturnal scenarios" and "psychic scenarios" are juxtaposed (23), one replete with "dangerous nocturnal enjoyment" (41). While Bronfen's discussion does not directly address the peculiar ethos of "the Gothic," she does skillfully outline the "heterotopic quality of theatre" (23), which often uses darkness and night as a counterrealm that privileges imagination, irrationality, wildness, and disobedience.

Steven Craig's essay gives us what may be the clearest historicist definition of the Gothic in the volume. From Bishop Hurd's eighteenth-century polemic "Letters on Chivalry and Romance," Craig deduces that

> The Gothic, as Shakespeare purportedly conceived it, comprises a set of superstitions and enchantments carried by groups of unspecified migrant barbarians who plunged the civilized world into darkness . . . however, as Hurd's veneration of the Gothic and of Shakespeare has it, this darkness was conducive to the life of the imagination. The Gothic is inherently paradoxical: what is conceived as "barbarian" is also potentially liberating. (43)

Craig's essay links the emergence of Bardolatry to the fascination eighteenth-century writers evinced with Shakespeare as a "dark Genius." Arguing largely against Jonathan Bate's introduction to the Arden edition of *Titus Andronicus,* Craig convincingly outlines the reductiveness of an approach to the Shakespearean Gothic that limits it to "England's break with its dark Catholic past in the middle of the sixteenth century" (49).

Dale Townshend's essay, "Gothic and the Ghost of Shakespeare's *Hamlet,*" analyzes the centrality of Shakespeare, and to a lesser extent, Milton, in eighteenth-century depictions of the Gothic, and traces the twinning of "the Sublime" and the Gothic (the apotheosis of which is Mary Shelley's *Frankenstein*). This is an important linkage and one that is somewhat undertheorized elsewhere in the volume. The Enlightenment constructs man's relationship to the awe-inspiring *spiritus mundi* as that of an appreciative, and properly awed and humbled, audience. The Gothic, one could argue, is the dark underbelly of the Sublime, one in which that same *spiritus mundi* escapes the bounds of the classical aesthetic cage so lovingly assembled by Edmund Burke and threatens to run amok. Elizabeth Montagu, along with Voltaire, asserted that there was "something barbaric about Shakespeare's theatre" (67); but Montagu does not fault Shakespeare for this as much as she does the unenlightened age in which he lived and wrote. As Townshend astutely points out, "It was Shakespeare . . . who introduced, via the interventions of his numerous defenders, a sense of the ghostly to the already overdetermined signifier 'Gothic' during the middle decades of the eighteenth century." Texts such as Matthew Lewis's *The Monk* and Horace Walpole's *The Castle of Otranto* bring together or "suture" aspects of classical romance with supernatural elements, at the heart of which there are "the latent passions of civil rage and discord." Far from being limited to Shakespeare's age, however, such latent passions saturate late eighteenth- and nineteenth-century novels, despite their more genteel patina of manners, morals, and sentiments.

Our modern sense of the Gothic is inaugurated, according to Townshend, by Walpole's addition of "the subtitle 'A Gothic Story' to the second edition of *The Castle of Otranto* in 1765" (73). For this, there is no Shakespeare play more fitting than *Hamlet,* which "serves the writers of Gothic romance and drama as a blueprint or set of dramatic instructions pertaining specifically to the appropriate treatment of the dead" (73). But this blueprint is more one of avoidance, since Shakespeare's *Hamlet* mostly instructed eighteenth-century writers in how to "avert the catastrophes of the fifth act of *Hamlet* through highly conventionalized endings reminiscent more of Shakespearean comedy than tragedy" (73). The tendency to soften the endings of Shakespearean tragedies to render them less barbaric is a bad, if interesting, habit in the two centuries that follow Shakespeare's lifetime. Much like the contrived "comic" endings of *The Merchant of Venice,* or *Twelfth Night,* the Gothic novel's commitment to appropriate treatment of the dead does nothing so much as foreground the *failure* of such treatment to lay things adequately to rest. "Mourning," Townshend argues, may be "the fundamental obligation in Gothic writing" (75); but the anxieties it betrays toward latent passions is always inadequate to the task, despite efforts to bring "the workings of verifiable knowledge and empirical truth" to the process (73).

Here we enter the psychoanalytic lexicon that is required for any understanding of the Gothic, with its harmonics of depression. Townshend's discussion of Radcliffe's *Mysteries of Udolpho* introduces the Kristevan abject: "the putrefying corpse of the mother either consumed in a filthy act of cannibalism or walled up internally within the subject's internal crypt. Psychoanalysis is at its most Gothic when pathologies of mourning are at stake" (93). To which I would add that the Gothic is most Gothic when failures of psychoanalysis are at stake. Particularly as the Gothic sensibility moves toward the twentieth century, it becomes increasingly difficult to see ways in which the usual plot resolutions offered in earlier Gothic novels "cure" the deeper malaise at the heart of the mode. If the (now-discredited) Freudian "death drive" explains some of the Gothic's fixation on decay, it certainly fails to account for what will turn out to be, with the interminable shelf life of vampire fiction, an "undeath drive."

Sue Chaplin's essay, "The Scene of a Crime," seems ideally placed to follow Townshend's, with her stated goal of combining a Derridean analysis of mimesis with a post-psychoanalytic discussion of the juridical implications of the Gothic: "Through Shakespeare, Horace Walpole's *The Castle of Otranto* (1764)—the faked 'Gothic Story' that dubiously imitates Gothicism—exemplifies the operation of a literary and juridical mimesis that simultaneously instantiates and derives its authority from a fiction of authority that essentially fabricates a crime-scene (98)." Unfortunately, this opening sentence instantiates a prose that derives its authority from excessive jargon and confusing, overly Latinate subordinate clauses. Even a reader well versed in the theory she references may find an argument difficult to discern. Since Chaplin has recently published a book on the topic, this conceptual enjambment may result from trying to compress a complex argument into a brief essay.[6] If I understand correctly, Chaplin links both the Gothic and Shakespeare to the Derridean (initially Lacanian) idea of the arbitrary demand that masquerades as Paternal Law or Logos, built on the foundation of a fictitious "event" that stands for a "hidden crime," which then produces "the false appearance of a presence" (99). This false appearance, according to Chaplin, underwrites the literary canon, epitomized by Shakespearean authority: "The Shakespearean precedent produces this exemplary Gothicism in the Derridean sense that the transgression of borders and the problematization of textual-juridical authority has come simultaneously to re-present [*sic*] the 'Gothic' as a genre whilst also complicating and deferring the 'presence' of the gothic within any given text" (109). Chaplin tells us, "I seek here to interrogate, through Derrida, the relation between law, literature and a 'certain interpretation of mimesis' within the Western tradition" (99). The core idea seems to be that

our understanding of Shakespearean authenticity, of his "originality," can no more be substantiated than any claims eighteenth-century authors made about the Gothic as a genre. Both Shakespearean
and Gothic textuality are "re-ordered and re-presented by critics in
the eighteenth century" (ibid.), giving the lie to any claims for textual authenticity. This seems to me a very plausible claim, especially given the prominence of repression as a mechanism in
Gothic literature.

Chaplin is right to suggest that calling the Gothic a "genre" has
become a trap, considering the "extreme flexibility of taxonomy"
required to address its many components. She cites Alexandra War-
wick's claim that "the Gothic is a mode rather than a genre, that it
is a loose tradition . . . its defining characteristics are its mobility
and its continued capacity for reinvention" (100). Chaplin's argument privileges Walpole's "Gothic experiment," which "took
shape in 1764 as a 'Shakespearean' negotiation of juridical and literary traumas" (102). Her incipiently feminist argument would
have been strengthened by reference to less patriarchally inflected
(if critical thereof) theorists than Lacan and Derrida, as well as by
the female literary tradition that contributes equally, if differently,
to that "loose tradition" that is not necessarily "fathered" by Walpole.

Which brings us back to the obvious link between Shakespeare
and the Gothic first made by Sarah Fielding's *History of Ophelia* in
1760. Although the Ophelia of that novel has a last name (Lenox),
she is still an innocent young girl, orphaned, who trusts the overtures of an unscrupulous would-be lover (Rochester), until she is
kidnapped by him and sequestered again in his estate (not exactly
a nunnery, but to her it might as well be). The novel is satirical and
the exaggerated sexual *naïveté* of its heroine is meant to counterpoint Richardson's *Clarissa;* but the choice of names, as we know,
is always significant. The inner experience of Shakespeare's Ophelia is famously underrepresented in the play. If one were to rewrite
it as narrative, however, it would read like a Gothic fiction: a vul-
nerable young woman sequestered in a cold, dark castle by her
domineering father and brother, no mother (and soon, no father),
and misled by overtures of affection from a dashing nobleman who
turns out to be coarse and untrustworthy. In the play we do not see
her going—only gone—mad; prior to her song scenes, one might
imagine fitful nights wondering where her father has disappeared
to, feelings of abandonment and uncertainty, and an overwhelming

sense that things are not what they seem on the surface. Ophelia's psychological experience is condensed into her brief singing scenes, while Prince Hamlet's experience of his own Gothic dilemma spills into extra innings. Here we see the bifurcation—already blueprinted in Shakespeare's play—of the gendered aspects of the Gothic: romance gone horribly wrong on the distaff side, resulting in madness, hysteria, and symptomatic repression; and intergenerational conflict, with all the unfinished business of mysterious corruption expressed through supernatural elements, on the other.

The flip side of the repressive coin of the Gothic is the (sometimes hysterical) *de-repression* of Romance. Angela Wright's essay "In Search of Arden: Ann Radcliffe's William Shakespeare," examines Radcliffe's role as the "Shakspeare [*sic*] of Romance writers." By the late eighteenth century there were critics, such as Nathan Drake writing in 1798, who decried the influence of Romance writers, especially female writers such as Charlotte Smith, Elizabeth Inchbald, and Mary Robinson, who were said to "turn our girls[,] heads wild with impossible adventures" (112). Radcliffe, Wright points out, was exempted from the "charge sheet of female literary subversive" most probably due to her use of Shakespeare in her writing (ibid.). Nathan Drake (1798) referred to Radcliffe as "the Shakspeare [*sic*] of Romance writers" (111), and celebrated Radcliffe's sanitizing of "the horror and superstition that characterized Shakespeare's tragedies," the way she removed the "terrifying aspect of his supernatural characters" (ibid.).

Like Walpole's *Otranto,* Radcliffe's work did "attempt to blend the two kinds of romance, the ancient and the modern," as well as pay homage to the moral concerns of the "mid-eighteenth century novel" (112). But as Wright argues, her novels referenced Shakespeare's work with increasing sophistication, not reductiveness: "With the later novels *The Mysteries of Udolpho* and *The Italian,* Radcliffe reserves her use of Shakespearean tragedy in particular for the moments when her heroines are thrown into crisis" (117). She did not, however, shun the supernatural, and in *Gaston de Blondeville,* Radcliffe resurrects the ghost of Shakespeare's murdered king Hamlet in the form of "a murdered knight who, due to the failures of justice, is forced to confront his own murderer" (126). Wright describes this ghost as less "magisterial" than Shakespeare's: rather, a "silent, shadowy presence that lurks in the margins of the story" (126). To my mind, this "shadowy presence" seems precisely what is Gothic about Radcliffe's ghost, to hearken back to my opening comments about Gothic dread. It may be less impressive than the ghost of King Hamlet, but the fact that it is less *expressive* renders it to my mind creepier and *more* Gothic. Gothic traffics in the apocryphal, not the "magisterial"; one could argue that lurking in margins and keeping silent is more unsettling than, for instance, standing pat (as does the Old Mole in act 1, scene 5) and declaiming one's list of grievances. As a compromise, one might say that Old Hamlet is a Gothic ghost when he first appears to Prince Hamlet's friends, to whom he neither speaks nor seems to see, and a different kind of ghost when he addresses his son.

The essay by Michael Gamer and Robert Miles takes Shakespeare to the Gothic stage "with a single, controversial word: *Vortigern*" (131), the "allegedly lost and recently discovered play by Shakespeare," which was performed on April 2, 1796, and later discovered not to be authored by Shakespeare but by a "twenty-one-year-old law clerk, William Henry Ireland" (ibid.). Ireland, it seems, wanted to take the literary world by storm and not only chose to forge a work by Shakespeare but, as Gamer and Miles point out, "in that writer's most prestigious genre: tragedy (with 'historical' thrown in, for good measure)" (ibid.). His subsequent confession and the calumny it brought upon him for desecrating the Bard's name (his own father disowned him) provides a glimpse into "the oxymoronic position Shakespeare played within the drama of the Romantic period, of being the period's most reproduced original" (133). German Gothic adaptations of Shakespeare came under severe fire from the literary elite for trying to bring Shakespeare and the Gothic together onstage. Both Coleridge and Wordsworth criticized such adapations, Wordsworth "condemning successful adaptations . . . as 'sickly and stupid German Tragedies' bent on driving the invaluable works of our elder writers, I had almost said the works of Shakespeare . . . into neglect'" (133). Stoking fears that Britain's glory days of homegrown playwrights were behind them, the popularity of German dramatists in London paradoxically brought fresh elitist disrespect upon the Gothic, the excesses of which were now commonly associated with "foreign" drama (134). Kotzebue's popularity in particular seemed to trigger ire, at what seemed, in Wordsworth's words, to be a "usurpation on that throne, which SHAKESPEARE [sic], and his compatriot race of dramatists, once filled with equal honour to themselves and to the national character" (135).

It seems that the Gothic was either being improved by association with Shakespeare, or Shakespeare was being degraded by association with the Gothic. Such ambivalence bled across lines of nationalism and aesthetics, as the original "foreignness" of the Gothic, its inheritance of the barbaric strain, could never be stamped out. During a time in the late eighteenth and early nineteenth century when bowdlerized versions and adaptations of Shakespeare's plays were already fueling domestic arguments over the place of the Bard, a "wildly successful play such as that written by the Irish writer Charles Robert Maturin," author of *Bertram* and the "late Gothic masterpiece *Melmoth the Wanderer* (1820)," proved an easy target. Coleridge trashed *Bertram* in a review "unleavened by irony" (135), as Gamer and Miles point out, "Coleridge's review comes, then, at the end of nearly three decades of English ambivalence over German and Gothic drama, in which audiences, reviewers, and literati first embraced this new literature as a true likeness of Shakespeare, and then (as the 1790s and the war with France progressed) rejected it for its perceived immorality and revolutionary principles" (136). This account beautifully sums up the Gothic's oxymoronic status as privileged bastard—privileged insofar as critics such as Coleridge wanted to claim the Gothic for English origin (given its references to Shakespeare and Milton) despite its taint by foreignness; bastard insofar as it still represented an essential "corruption of taste and principles" that could not possibly be native to the "elder writers" (137). Politics (particularly for Coleridge, *Bertram*'s supposed "Jacobinism") was inextricable from aesthetic judgment.

But this alone cannot account for the sheer rococo *weirdness* of the eighteenth-century Gothic's appropriation of Shakespeare. In Walpole's *Otranto,* for instance, this can be found in the way the novel neither fully dispenses with nor indulges in Shakespearean horror, offering instead a kind of mash-up of elements with respect to horror that leaves things feeling unresolved no matter how nicely matters are wrapped up. As Robert Hamm Jr. has argued (elsewhere, not in the anthology under review), the eighteenth century, and Walpole in particular, had a special interest in "expressive bodies" and the challenges of representing them in non-theatrical genres, as evidenced by Walpole's interest in expressive bodies and the way in which the period's preoccupation with a speaker's performance of emotion shaped *Otranto.* The novel marks an important point at which the natural language that governs visible, theatrical bodies is employed to heighten the private experience of the solitary reader.[7]

This may account for the dismemberment of Shakespeare's most overbearing Ghost into multiple specterlike elements in Walpole's narrative, including an animated portrait, the "ghostly appearance" of disarticulated parts (giant helmet, armored foot and leg) seen only in partial glimpses, and an animated skeleton that "stands for" Death itself (Hamm, 677–79). It is as if the emotional trauma Hamlet expresses linguistically in his encounter with the Ghost were somehow inadequate to the requirements of the novel without recourse to "special effects."

One could argue, however, that Walpole's ever-more-complicated tricks and turns, an effort to outdo Shakespeare on the horror front, come perilously close to comedy by virtue of sheer contrivance if not overkill. The Gothic novel is always skirting the edge of melodrama. Part of the problem is that the Gothic novel had aspirations toward the Sublime, as newly articulated by Edmund Burke's *A Philosophical Enquiry into the Origin of Our Ideas of the Sublime and Beautiful* (1757), which was focused primarily on the impact of certain perceptions on the mind of the viewer or reader. The Sublime arises from "[w]hatever is fitted in any sort to excite the ideas of pain, and danger, that is to say, whatever is in any sort terrible, or is conversant about terrible objects, or operates in a manner analogous to terror . . . productive of the strongest emotion which the mind is capable of feeling."[8] This is, after all, also the century in which an excessively Germanic use of capital letters as Transcendentalizing Heuristic afflicted writers ranging from (at the early end) Aphra Behn, to Immanuel Kant, to Ralph Waldo Emerson. Mary Shelley may have been the only author who successfully combined horror and the Sublime without veering into what would shortly come to be called Grand Guignol, a lurid twist on the Gothic mode.[9]

As the Gothic migrates through the nineteenth and twentieth centuries, its geopolitical, as well as aesthetic, implications are to a large extent eclipsed by its horror components, nowhere more apparent than in the emergence of the new medium of film. Peter Hutchings's essay, "Theatres of Blood: Shakespeare and the Horror Film," opens with Universal's 1931 film version of *Dracula,* in which the crazy Renfield quotes from *Hamlet:* "words, words, words." After oddly dismissing the connection between the film and Shakespeare's *Hamlet* as untenable ("The *Hamlet* quotation is sufficiently odd to be noticeable but insufficiently elaborated to be fully meaningful" [155]), Hutchings fails to notice one strikingly meaningful correlation: Renfield has been pressed into service by a dead, or rather, undead, "Father" (vampires are masters—as with Renfield, or "Sires" of those on whom they feed, and one might certainly see Hamlet's ghost as figuratively feeding on his son).

After a few more tentative disclaimers about how neither horror films nor Shakespeare, as "areas of our culture, are in themselves cohesive or in possession of distinctive and commonly agreed identities" (155), Hutchings ventures into Roman Polanski's 1971 *Macbeth,* Kenneth Branagh's 1996 *Hamlet,* and Julie Taymor's 1999 *Titus.* Unfortunately, he continues to make observations that catalog more than unpack connections between Shakespeare and horror films. Polanski, for instance, famously directed *Rosemary's Baby,* and Branagh, *Mary Shelley's Frankenstein* (a misnomer, given his bizarre deviations from Shelley's text). Along the way Hutchings remarks that typical dichotomies between "high-cultural Shakespeare and low-cultural horror" do not hold up with respect to either, since *Titus Andronicus* is often considered one of Shakespeare's clumsier and more "crude" plays (157–58), while some horror directors, such as Roger Corman, have produced films, especially his Poe films, that are "ambitious, intelligent, and cultured" (158).

Agreed. Shakespeare can be crude, and horror films can sometimes be elegant. But what, Hutchings asks, "of those Shakespearean adaptations that seem less restrained and less subtle" (such as Taymor's *Titus*)? Here he ventures into cinematic and film-production techniques that are shared as conventions in horror films as well as in Shakespearean filmic adaptations, techniques such as the "milky contact lenses" worn by the ghost in Branagh's *Hamlet,* which "are also a common device in horror cinema, used for signifying the presence of evil or the monstrous" (158). Once again, granted: filmmakers share props and technical knowledges for producing certain kinds of "special effects." But what does this have to do with things especially Gothic, either in Shakespeare or in horror? The question remains unanswered in the essay, which does, however, provide useful details of filmic adaptations of Shakespeare, both more vulgar (*Throne of Blood*) and more refined (Olivier's *Hamlet*).

The bigger contention I have with Hutchings's discussion is the way it treats the horror genre as somewhat interchangeable with the

Gothic, to the extent that both deploy violent, scary, or gruesome actions or images. There is also little attention paid to the role of gender with respect to horror. After all, if the Walpolean tradition of Gothic studies underplays female subjectivity, surely the evolution of the horror film has foregrounded it, if not exactly in "feminist" ways. As Carol Clover has famously argued, "At the bottom of the horror heap lies the slasher (or splatter or shocker or stalker) film: the immensely generative story of a psychokiller who slashes to death a string of mostly female victims, one by one, until he is subdued or killed, usually by the one girl who has survived." It seems to me that one could profitably view the emergence of horror/slasher films as a grotesque evolution, from female victimization and febrility in Gothic fiction to an admittedly crude way of "staging" Ophelia's revenge, in the form of what Clover calls "the final girl."[10] Imagine Ophelia as final girl: at her best, like *Alien*'s Ellen Ripley, who starts off as just one of a large and arguably more important cast and ends up being the only one to escape the madness alive.

Hutchings concludes by suggesting that Shakespeare and the horror genre "could further develop a cultural relationship based not on simplistic high/low distinctions but instead on productive differences and some rather surprising similarities" (166). This is a good description of what his essay does: it compares and contrasts, lists similarities and differences. There is nothing about what in Shakespearean drama makes it *affectively* pliant to Gothic appropriation. There is little mention of the genre of film noir as a Gothic mode. Gothic horror should not be conflated merely with the horrible, such as the disgust and prurience inspired by Hannibal Lector's cannibalism, for instance, or movies about serial killers, like *Saw* (and *Saws 2–5*). A film such as *The Sixth Sense* may properly be termed Gothic; *The Hills Have Eyes,* however, is just plain horrible.

Perhaps I am taking the Gothic too seriously. Glynnis Byron's essay, "'As one dead': Romeo and Juliet in the Twilight Zone," brings Shakespeare into the phenomenal contemporary rise of the vampiric soap opera; in particular, Stephanie Meyer's vampire romance novel series, *Twilight*. Like that of their predecessor, vampire fiction queen, Anne Rice, Meyer's fan base is largely female; and Byron sets out to understand why someone without a heartbeat (Edward Cullen) has become such a huge heartthrob among female readers. The trope of the brooding young male, destroyed by life, holding a grudge in one hand and carrying a torch in another, owes much, as Byron points out, to Emily Brontë's *Wuthering Heights* (168). But it is the portability of the story of *Romeo and Juliet* that makes it so effective in "its capacity for recontextualization" (172). The same must be said for the "enduring popularity of the vampire" (ibid.); and in recent decades, there has been a confluence of both themes in the massive growth of the "vampire romance industry" (a distinctly American one). Byron's essay engagingly expores this phenomenon in contemporary mass culture and why it has so much traction that there is even a publishing company offering "personalized romances" (172–73).

Byron concedes, rightly in my view, that "there is no trace of anything the least bit Gothic in such works as these," which are "ultimately little more threatening than Count Chocula" (173–74). Nor does Byron attempt to force Shakespeare's *Romeo and Juliet* into the spiked collar of the Gothic: "To apply the term 'Gothic' to Shakespeare's play would be to drain an already threatened term of any meaning whatsoever" (174). This is an important statement. If one of the problems with Hutchings's essay is its conflation of Gothic horror with slasher schlock, Byron skillfully avoids this mistake, while simultaneously acknowledging that the "infection" of popular romances by vampires in the twentieth century almost makes Romeo and Juliet's invitation to the party a foregone conclusion. The problem with such romances is that they sentimentalize both the vampire narrative and the tragic resonance of Shakespearean tragedy by literalizing what it means to be "star-crossed": "Once the vampire had been demystified, humanized, and all too often sentimentalized, rewritten to embody some aspect of our contemporary condition, it was only a small step towards producing him as a tragic romantic hero" (175). Imagine if you will, Romeo and Juliet with seriously different tastes in food and impossibly conflicting sleep schedules. There is also a version of "family feuding" in vampire romances—sometimes between conflicting vampire clans (human-friendly vs. predatory) or between vampires and werewolves, who incessantly conjure poxes on each others' "houses."

Byron does single out Meyer's *Twilight* series as adhering more closely to what the Gothic puts on offer: "the conventional construction of the human through the abjection of the monstrous" (182). Oddly, however, the monstrous-Sublime in these novels is not hideousness (*pace* Frankenstein's creature) but excessive

beauty, a glittering, coldly crystalline perfection that renders the
normal human body abject by comparison. The Gothic, when done
correctly, fundamentally threatens identity categories and thereby
puts subjectivity at risk: "Sites of horror . . . are essential to the construction of subjectivity and otherness" (ibid.). In Romance, subjectivity is ultimately stabilized and usually rendered conventional
again; in vampiric narratives, subjectivity may be permanently altered and estranged: "In the fairy-tale endings of such works as
Ann Radcliffe's *Mysteries of Udolpho* (1794), passions and super-
stitious fears are ultimately rejected. Transgression gives way to re-
instatement of the heroine's position and property, excess is
controlled, and desire is regulated" (184). Meyer's *Twilight* series,
Byron argues, avoids the resolution offered by such endings by deferring its heroine's "transformation" or "turning" (a vampire rebirth), toying simultaneously with mechanisms of control and the
ever-possible threat of loss of standardized subjectivity. Shakespeare's *Romeo and Juliet,* one could argue, does something similar; but the end of the play gives the tragic deathblow to Romance
by entombing, permanently, its dead lovers. Or so we thought. Little did Shakespeare know that his star-crossed lovers would endlessly be dragged out of the grave each night as the Undead,
interminably sentenced to romancing each other over the tomb-
stone.

The final two essays in *Gothic Shakespeares* return us to the European origins of the Gothic. "Gothspeare and the Origins of Cultural Studies," by Fred Botting and Scott Wilson, opens with a
clever fable, based on the plot of *The Tempest,* in which a Tunisian
prince—"Sheikh Zoubeir" (a phonetic double of Shakespeare if
one puts on a silly accent), "head of the Arab resistance to the Ottomans," in 1575 is usurped by his brother and driven to flee by sea
from both said brother and the Turks. Landing on "Morecambe
Bay" (187), bereft and armed only with a contact—"fellow poet . . .
Fernandino, Lord Strange, son of . . . the fourth Earl of Derby"
(ibid.)—Sheikh Zoubeir finds both shelter and employment with a
"talented professionally ambitious group of players . . . Lord
Strange's Men," subsequently anglicizes his name—"Sheikspeare!'
exclaimed the Arab in delight'" (ibid.)—and is reborn as the (Arabian) Swan of Avon.

Botting and Wilson go on to proclaim that "Shakespeare is a
Gothic invention, a fiction. "'He' [*sic*] emerges as an effect of the
modernity for which Gothic becomes fiction's purest modality, a

language to infinity" (188). This statement is true *if* we insert ourselves in the history of Sheikh Zoubeir, which the authors' opening
gambit has set us up to do (imaginatively, one presumes, although
it is not entirely clear): "While he invented nothing—or very little—apart from himself, Shakespeare has become the fictive name
for the limitless horizon of an infinity of fictions that endlessly sus-
tains both the modern myth of culture and its postmodern generalization in and as aestheticized, objectivized and autonomized
medium of exchange that has 'created its own order'" (ibid.). Combining Foucault's death of the author with Jean-Joseph Goux's theory of symbolic economies, Botting and Wilson seem to be
suggesting not that Shakespeare was really an Arab sheikh or that
he did not "exist," but that our understanding of Shakespeare, how
we have received and constructed the corpus, is inextricable from
the post-Gothic history that retroactively structures how we regard
Renaissance literature and culture as falsely "opposed" to mass
culture.

This argument nicely combines points suggested in both
Chaplin's and Hutchings's essays. The eighteenth century generally, and the Romantic movement in particular, "canoni[zed] the
Bard and elevat[ed] Nature and the Imagination the pinnacle of aesthetic value" (188). An elevation was established "on the basis of
a fundamental exclusion of Gothic productions," which "came to
connote all that was low and base, all that could be associated with
an unruly, undiscriminating mob"; in short, all that came to be
identified as mass or popular culture. The repudiation of the legacy
of that "prolific swarm" of "nomadic, fierce, warlike, free Gothic
tribes" that existed outside the Roman classical order (189) was a
denial of the Deleuzian heterogeneity that actually comprised early
Anglo-Saxon England. Through the eighteenth-century embrace of
neoclassical aesthetic values, things Gothic—associated with the
multiple identities in flux: "Goths, Scythians, Scalds, Vandals,
Huns, Saxons"—disrupted the elegant contours of the literary and
cultural makeover. Claimed by the later eighteenth- and nineteenth-century literary "establishment" for the side of the Burkean
Sublime, Shakespeare's Gothic potentiality was sublimated into
his "dark Genius."

This is an interesting argument, and perhaps it might have been
launched with a slightly less distracting—if entertaining—conceit.
For instance, why declare that "[Shakespeare] himself invented
nothing—or very little—apart from himself"? Such a statement as-

sumes a one-dimensional notion of what it means to "invent," and
Botting and Wilson are too sophisticated to actually believe this.
To be sure, Shakespeare did adopt stories, conventions, tropes, and
theatrical effects used by others. But one could argue that "invention" never happens ex nihilo but rather is what happens when
something new arises that is greater, or even just productively different, than the sum of conventional parts (if this were not true, the
entire field of Shakespeare studies could be subject to the same
charge). The essay becomes much stronger as its authors venture
into the rise of Gothic romance novels, particularly Walpole's role
in spawning "an appetite that allowed another swarm to emerge:
the 'new species of romance'," that "disturbing and monstrous hybrid that became known—and vilified—as the Gothic romance"
(192). The field of cultural studies, they declare, "is a creature of
Romanticism" (ibid.).

A rebellious creature. For if Romanticism is founded, as Botting
and Wilson argue, on the constitutive repression of an unruly
Gothic multiplicity, and if cultural studies is a creature of Romanticism, then the Gothic—with its messy, irrational, rude, supernatural, trespassing stampede—its "ill-formed crowd" (193), is cultural
studies' illegitimate father. Popular culture, "for all its bourgeois,
homogenizing intent, remains rife with the tensions and class an-
tagonisms of its historical formations" (195). And the study of such
culture is conducted through the almost inescapable frame of the
eighteenth-century's revision of England's own literally Gothic
past. A history of barbarian, multiple, tribal, Germanic incursions
and settlements, not controlled by Rome, is replaced by a set of
class assumptions about what kinds of people, stories, emotions,
relationships, narrative devices, and products are "proper" (i.e.,
classical, aesthetic, high-culture) and what kinds are not (irrational, "lowbrow," nonexclusive, for the masses). The authors conclude this fascinating essay with a series of "if Shakespeare were
alive today" scenarios, the most pertinent of which is "If Shakespeare were alive today he'd be writing a biography of Shakespeare
entitled *How Shakespeare Became Shakespeare*" (195)—which I
suppose could just as legitimately be entitled *How Sheikh Zoubeir
Became Shakespeare.*

The afterword, written by Jerrold E. Hogle, himself an expert on
the Gothic novel, provides a helpful recap of the preceding essays,
finding links that connect them and offering further reflections that
productively take up some of the volume's unfinished business.

Writing with the aim of "bookend[ing] the pieces between this Afterword and John Drakakis's Introduction" (205), Hogle asks a key question: "Why has this relationship [between Shakespeare and the Gothic] remained so basic both to the genesis of the Post-Renaissance 'Gothic' in Walpole and his many successors and to the development of numerous variations on the Gothic since that never quite silence the echo of Shakespeare in them?" (205). On the surface, "there is a tug-of-war at levels of both ideology and symbology in his plays that the Gothic both repeats and transforms in its own variations on an 'ancient-modern' dialectic" (205–6). Although Hogle acknowledges that the Gothic, with its "genre-crossing nature," develops "the manifestations in Shakespeare of the most pervasive conflicts between divergent ideological claims" (211) (especially the Catholic-Protestant agon epitomized in *Hamlet* and played out within the Anglican Church throughout the eighteenth and nineteenth centuries), he knows that the answer is not reducible to a conflict between competing ideologies. There is still a strangeness that radiates from the Gothic (at its best, for instance, in Wilkie Collins's *The Woman in White* or *The Moonstone,* or Henry James's *The Turn of the Screw*), something left over after it has been picked apart by ideology critique.

This leftover constitutes what Hogle correctly calls "the psychological side of this conundrum" (213), or, citing Joel Fineman's work, "this otherness from the self *in* the self" (214; italics in original). The exploration of self-estrangement, in dramatic as well as poetic form, is arguably Shakespeare's greatest "invention" and contribution to literature and culture. The "self-division in haunted Gothic characters beginning with Walpole's is unquestionably founded" (ibid.) in Shakespearean language, with its presciently modern awareness of the "separation of the signifier from the signified" (215). Such a separation means that all representation is by definition haunted, except that in the Gothic, the ghosts that Shakespeare parades front and center inhabit the dark corners of the stage, the Gothic's stock in trade. Gothic dread enters through peripheral vision, and what makes it so effective is the way that the Gothic manipulates anxieties provoked when reason is *withheld.* Another way to put this would be to say that the Gothic gives aesthetic form to the passive-aggressive *repression* of violence. Whereas open violence gives us horror (as in *Titus Andronicus* or *King Lear*), passive aggression generates dread by making us *doubt* our own perceptions of threat (as in *Othello* and *Hamlet*).

Perhaps this is why Ophelia's experience in *Hamlet* is truly Gothic after all. Reasons—for Hamlet's rejection and her father's murder—are withheld from her, and her passive-aggressive *reaction* is formalized in her "gone-mad" scenes, in which she hands out verbal barbs along with flowers. So uncomfortable are these scenes to watch that Gertrude's bizarre blazon of Ophelia's subsequent drowning comes almost as a relief: an aesthetic *stabilization* that neutralizes some of the accusations implied by Ophelia's earlier words. This is why neither Laertes nor Claudius ask Gertrude the obvious question: if someone were close enough to see and hear Ophelia float and chant lays, why didn't they fish her out? One could argue that Gertrude's beautiful story of Ophelia's death is an effort to cure the discomfort provoked by an implicitly Gothic situation. So powerful is its anodyne force that the verbal blazon in the play gives rise to a visual one beyond it, in which Ophelia's tortured and undecipherable grief are further aestheticized and frozen in time, famously by Pre-Raphaelite painters such as Arthur Hughes, Dante Gabriel Rossetti, John Waterhouse, and, of course, John Everett Millais.

Perhaps if "classical" values in art are underwritten by a Lacanian symbolic order in which the mirror-stage of unmediated identification is superseded by the triangulating force of the Paternal Logos, then Gothic values—that Gothicky "feel" within the various forms—have their own symbolic order, one in which the mirror-stage is not superseded at all but rather superimposed upon gestures of order and control; and where the identifiable (alien/foreign) barbarism of the past meets up with the more diffuse barbarism of an eternal present. After all, as I said at the beginning of this essay, Gothic dread involves a feeling of vague threat, of indirect haunting, a sense that danger comes not from outside or over "there" but here in the house, literal or figurative. No matter how hard the Age of Reason and the "Augustan" period worked to eliminate the secret dramas of dark corners, whether in adapted "editions" of Shakespeare or in novels of manners and sentiment, they did not succeed, as is evident in the extraordinary rebirth of the Gothic as a cultural ethos in the twentieth century. The Gothic may be the bastard offspring of generic inbreeding, unsure of its commitment to proper aesthetic values, but it is strident in its ambitions for representational acknowledgment. The authors in *Gothic Shakespeares,* along with other scholars who write about Gothic literature (with or without Shakespeare in mind), are largely in agreement that the Gothic must be recognized as a legitimate companion literature in the march toward and through Enlightenment progress. Given the fresh surge of critical and cultural interest in all things Gothic, *Gothic Shakespeares* is indispensable reading for anyone interested in Shakespeare's eerie and enduring influence on eighteenth- and nineteenth-century Gothic literature, as well as its more contemporary apparitions.

Notes

1. Like scholarship on Shakespeare, scholarship on eighteenth- and nineteenth-century British and American Gothic literature is vast. Ranging from Brockden Brown, Poe, Melville, and Hawthorne to Walpole, Radcliffe, Shelley, and even Walter Scott, from Sarah Fielding and Jane Austen to Dickens, Conrad, and Henry James, critical claims on and for the Gothic involve multiple nationalities and literary trajectories. Further reading on the Gothic might include, in no particular order, Eve Kosofsky Sedgwick, *The Coherence of Gothic Conventions* (New York: Arno, 1980); Jacqueline Howard, *Reading Gothic Fiction: A Bakhtinian Approach* (New York: Oxford University Press, 1994); Robert Hamm Jr., "Hamlet and Horace Walpole's *The Castle of Otranto*," *Studies in English Literature 49, no. 3* (Summer 2009): 667–92); Terry Castle, *The Female Thermometer: Eighteenth-Century Culture and the Invention of the Uncanny* (New York: Oxford University Press, 1995); E. J. Clery, *The Rise of Supernatural Fiction, 1760–1800* (Cambridge: Cambridge University Press, 1995); Marshall Brown, *The Gothic Text* (Stanford, CA: Stanford University Press, 2005); Fred Botting, *Gothic* (New York: Routledge, 1996); James Watt, *Contesting the Gothic* (Cambridge: Cambridge University Press, 1999); Frederick Frank, *Guide to the Gothic II: An Annotated Bibliography of Criticism, 1983–1993* (Lanham, MD: Rowman and Littlefield, 1995); Jerrold E. Hogle, ed., *The Cambridge Companion to Gothic Fiction* (New York: Cambridge University Press, 2002); Susan Wolstenholme, *Gothic (Re)Visions: Writing Women as Readers* (New York: State University of New York Press, 1993); Ian Duncan, *Modern Romance and Transformations in the Novel: The Gothic, Scott, Dickens* (New York: Cambridge University Press, 1992); and Donya Samara, "Gothic Criticism(s)," in *Novel: A Forum on Fiction* 29, no. 2 (Winter 1996): 243–47.

2. Cf. *The History of Ophelia*, ed. Peter Sabor (Peterborough: Broadview Press, 2004).

3. Terry Castle, *The Apparitional Lesbian: Female Homosexuality and Modern Culture* (1993). Also of interest is Scott J. Juengel's review of Castle's book *The Female Thermometer*, in *Criticism* (Summer 1997); cf. Ian Watt, *The Rise of the Novel: Studies in Defoe, Richardson and Fielding* (Berkeley and Los Angeles: University of California Press, 1957). As well as Castle, Nina Auerbach has produced a veritable mountain of scholarship on women and "the strange" in Victorian literature. See especially *Our Vampires, Ourselves* (Chicago: University of Chicago Press, 1997); and *Woman and the Demon: The Life of a Victorian Myth* (Cambridge, MA: Harvard University Press, 1984).

4. See Sandra Gilbert and Susan Gubar's magisterial study *The Madwoman in*

the Attic: The Woman Writer and the Nineteenth-Century Literary Imagination
(New HAVEN: Yale University Press, 1979); and Deirdre Lynch, The Economy of
Character: Novels, Market Culture and the Business of Inner Meaning (Chicago:
Chicago University Press, 1998).

5. In fairness, there is brief mention of Poe, in the context of Roger Corman
movies, in Peter Hutchings's essay "Shakespeare and the Horror Film," 157–58.
The Clery quotation is taken from the introduction to the forthcoming anthology
The Shakespearean Gothic, ed. Christy Desmet and Anne Williams (Cardiff: University of Wales Press, 2009). For an interesting recent discussion of Wieland in
the context of Enlightenment history, see Anthony Galluzzo, "Charles Brockden
Brown's Wieland and the Aesthetics of Terror: Revolution, Reaction, and the Radical Enlightenment in Early American Letters," in Eighteenth-Century Studies 42,
no. 2 (Winter 2009): 255–71.

6. See Sue Chaplin, Gothic and the Rule of Law, 1764–1820 (New York: Palgrave Macmillan, 2007).

7. See Robert Hamm Jr., "Hamlet and Horace Walpole's The Castle of Otranto,
668.

8. Quoted in Hamm Jr., "Hamlet," 681.

9. Jane Austen's Northanger Abbey, published in the same year as Shelley's
Frankenstein (1818), is a famous parody of Gothic novels and their conventions;
evidently even at the apex of their emergence, such conventions were seen as potentially melodramatic and risible.

10. Cf. Carol Clover's now-classic study, Men, Women and Chainsaws: Gender
in the Modern Horror Film (Princeton: Princeton University Press, 1993), 1.

REVIEWS

Global Traffic: Discourses and Practices of Trade in English Literature and Culture
from 1550 to 1700
Edited by Stephen Deng and Barbara Sebek
New York: Palgrave Macmillan, 2008

Reviewer: Brinda Charry

Global Traffic: Discourses and Practices of Trade in English Litera-ture and Culture from 1550 to 1700 is possibly among the most noteworthy edited collections in early modern studies in recent years. It is certainly a significant contribution to early modern "new economic criticism" in general, and to studies in literature of the period in relation to global trade in particular. The essays in the collection effectively demonstrate the theoretical premise laid out in the introduction by coeditor Barbara Sebek: "early processes of globalization must be viewed as intertwined economic and cultural phenomena" (3). Many of the contributions engage with work in related disciplines, most notably economic history, in thoughtful ways, even as they provoke interesting questions on the purpose and scope of interdisciplinary analysis. The introduction also suc-cinctly lays out issues in the field of "materialist criticism," and how much work described as such evades Marxist categories of analysis and focuses on fetishizing tangible objects. While not all essays in *Global Traffic* overtly deploy Marxist methodologies, many of them deal with issues of labor, class, and race, and most of them most certainly "go beyond a mere thematics of trade" and focus on trade as real economic activity (5). While the focus of the collection is clearly England of the period, the essays are interested in how the macronarrative of early modern globalization occurred in specific sociopolitical situations.

The essays in the first section of the collection, titled "The Emerging Epistemologies of Trade," purport to examine the conceptual shifts ushered in by international trade. Daniel Vitkus's opening chapter is a fine example of sophisticated interdisciplinary work. Vitkus's essay encompasses economic history (mainly England's trade with the Mediterranean), economic theory (including global systems theory), and literature. Other chapters in this section are Ian MacInnes's study ("'Ill Luck, Ill Luck'? Risk and Hazard in *The Merchant of Venice"*), which examines the "epistemology of risk" in the period. MacInnes provides a rare account of insurance in the period and how the concept of risk became gradually detached from the idea of Providence. This lays the ground for a smart, effective reading of the Shakespearean text in which MacInnes argues "risk, both financial and emotional, becomes the real economic subject of the play" (52). While much of the criticism on the economic themes of *The Merchant* are included in the chapter's list of works cited, it would have been useful to briefly consider Walter Cohen's much-anthologized essay, "*The Merchant of Venice* and the Possibilities of Historical Criticism" (first appeared *English Literary History* 49, no. 2 [1982]: 765–89), which many students of *Merchant* know as among the earlier and most effective economic readings of the play. Bradley Ryner's chapter, "The Panoramic View of Mercantile Thought: or, A Merchant's Map of *Cymbeline"* reads *Cymbeline* in the light of seventeenth-century debates regarding economic worth that appear in mercantile treatises. Ideas regarding the value of goods and commodities were based on notions of trade as either abstract and systemic or as a network of personal relationships. In contrast to the models put forward by the treatises, Ryner argues, the play rejects the idea of a uniform, universal assessment of value "by emphasizing the limited perspective of individual characters and the retrospective nature of all knowledge" (78). The chapter's "literary" concerns include an interesting discussion of mercantile mapping as a representation of the nature of metaphor and linguistic representation itself.

Together, the essays in the collection consider both canonical texts (three chapters centering on Shakespeare's plays and others on Jonson and Marlowe), as well as less well-known ones. David Morrow's chapter, also in section 1, uses a rarely examined text titled *The Tryall of Travell* (1630) to discuss the ways in which the merchant class deployed the discourse of travail, pilgrimage, and redemption to establish its moral and social worth. The chapter makes an important supplement to earlier work that suggests that the emerging middle class simply appropriated chivalry and other aristocratic discourses, and Morrow's findings would be very useful to those interested in examining plays with merchant-heroes, as well as pilgrim narratives. While the language of Christianity (notions of travail, redemption, etc.) is well considered in this chapter, the study could perhaps have been supplemented by a brief analysis of the clergy's various (and often conflicting) views on the new mercantilism, as laid out in sermons and other tracts issued by the religious establishment. Further, as Morrow himself admits, the chapter does not map the material basis of this emerging middle-class ideology, and the study remains more discursive than materialist in its focus. While this is inevitable in a work of this nature, a brief section outlining the so-called "rise of the merchant classes" would have been useful. Similarly, Lea Knudsen Allen's otherwise fine chapter on how foreign origins and travel made objects desirable is also "not interested in the 'true' economic value generated by high costs involved in long-distance trade but, rather, in the symbolic value objects gain as they travel from one site to another" (96). However, Allen's study could also have, perhaps, benefited from a brief discussion of "true economic value" and how it corresponds/contrasts to the symbolic value these goods accrue. In short, the discourse analyses could have been strengthened further if performed in the context of the particularities of material/economic histories in a more in-depth way.

Part 2, titled "Transforming Home Through Trade," includes essays that demonstrate how domestic spaces were transformed by early globalization. Three of the four chapters in this section make specific goods their focus: Amy Tigner's essay is on imported plants, Kristen Brookes's on tobacco, and Gitanjali Shahani's on Indian cloth. Anxiety and fear of the foreign object is the running theme in these chapters, putting them in interesting conversation with Allen's chapter in the preceding section, which argues largely for the fascination held by the exotic. Tigner's very informative chapter "The Flowers of Paradise: Botanical Trade in Sixteenth- and Seventeenth-Century England" is on the "ecological and cultural impact" (137) of foreign plants on England (though the study clearly focuses on cultural, rather than ecological, effects). The essay also demonstrates that the import of exotic plants into England contributed to the discourse of England as the new Garden of Eden. The subsequent growth of these plants led to the naturalization of international trade, and perhaps colonialism, because if "the seeds from around the globe could be brought into England and cultivated with success, England could, in essence, if not, in fact, possess the entire world . . ." (154). While the chapter mentions a few flowers and includes an interesting section on the tomato, a brief listing (that needs by no means be comprehensive) of the various exotics that were brought into England would better satisfy the curious reader. There is also no mention of the New World potato that reached England and Ireland via Spain in the 1590s. Kristen Brookes's chapter on another plant product, tobacco, follows Tigner's. This chapter demonstrates that smoking was viewed as the "incorporation of the alien into the English body" and was associated with anxiety about racial transformation (157). Smoking, Brookes argues, was perceived as even more threatening than drinking or eating foreign foods because "the oddity of seeing smoke coming out of the body . . . brought to early modern English minds the notion of a foreign substance traversing the body . . ." (159). However, the brief discussion of anticoffee discourse that is included in the chapter largely makes the same point: that coffee was also associated with "internal blackening." Discourse analysis is clearly the focus of this chapter, but, once again, at least a passing mention of the magnitude of the tobacco trade would have been beneficial.

Gitanjali Shahani's chapter on the import of Indian fabrics examines a range of documents to demonstrate that fear and antagonism, as well as desire, characterized early modern responses to this prized commodity. The essay does not lack data on the volume and growth of the foreign cloth trade. Further, Shahani makes important connections to our own contemporary economic scenario and the current discourse around foreign-made goods, and also gestures toward the role that cloth went on to play in English imperialism in India and to Indian anticolonial struggles. Both this essay and Ann Christensen's "'Absent, Weak or Unserviceable': The East India Company and the Domestic Economy in *The Launching of the Mary, or The Seaman's Honest Wife*," also include gender issues in their analyses. While Shahani briefly examines the widespread perception of women as consumers of foreign objects, Christensen's focus is gender. She effectively puts into dialogue texts that support the influential East India Company with other texts that represent the Company and its activities as a disruption of domesticity and as contributing to the suffering of women whose men were at sea.

The essays in section 3, titled "Trade and the Interests of State," look at how long-distance trade was increasingly identified with the state as "economically based conceptions of the state emerged" in the period (10). While no single chapter focuses on the complex (and not always amicable) relationship between the Crown and the major trading companies of the period, a brief account of this aspect of economic history would have strengthened the argument being put forward in this section. The first chapter, Edward Test's, is a reading of *The Tempest* in the context of Newfoundland salt-cod fishery and exploitation of vast bodies of mobile, temporary workers. Newfoundland was an "unsettled settlement" in a new economy characterized by trade without settlement (202). This history provides the context for Test's original reading of Shakespeare's play in which the island is not a colony but "a liminal space temporarily occupied for the exchange of daughters and kingdoms" (212).

The penultimate chapter by Matthew Day brings together early modern text studies, travel literature, and globalization in significant ways. Day considers how travel literature of the time was subject to censorship by both the trade and trading companies through various means, and for multiple reasons (some of which were peculiar to texts of this variety), including the need to protect commercial interests. The final chapter by Stephen Deng, "Global Œconomy: Ben Jonson's *The Staple of News* and the Ethics of Mercantilism," looks at how the Aristotelian ideal of moderation was echoed in mercantilist author Thomas Mun's writing and in Ben Jonson's 1626 play. The household economy is represented as a microcosm of the national economy: one is dependent on the other. Furthermore, both represent moderation, the Aristotelian idea of the "golden mean," as "consistent with 'capitalist', or at least 'protocapitalist' goals within a moral economy offering a challenge to the stereotype of amoral capitalist excess" (259), an idea that resonates in a world experiencing the consequence of corporate greed and excess.

In fact, the most significant contribution of *Global Traffic* is that the themes and issues it deals with insistently remind us of the early modern as the *early modern,* that is, as a period in which our own world—globalized, altered by international trade and capitalism, and pondering the value and meaning of these transformations—incubated. While some contributors (prominently Shahani and Morrow) remark on connections to the present, or on how early

modern trading activity already held the seeds of later developments, notably imperialism, one cannot but wish that such links,
which could have been made without succumbing either to pres-
entism or to claiming that the age saw the birth of full-fledged
imperialism or capitalism, were more prevalent through the collection.

The afterword by Jean Howard reemphasizes that "When we tell
the story of the enormous changes that global traffic and early capitalism wrought, we need to make cultural productions central to
that story . . ." (271). The cultural production the essays in the collections deal with is English drama. Together the chapters provoke
interesting questions regarding our understanding of the meaning,
nature, and place of literary texts when read against the context of
early modern mercantilism and globalization. The economic realities of the period are manifested in a variety of literary and other
narratives that are at the center of the dozen or so studies included
here. But what of the literary narrative itself? In certain cases it is
not made quite clear how analyzing a literary production adds significantly to our understanding of early modern mercantilism (or of
early modern literature) other than to underscore the fact that the
literary text appears to reflect and echo, or sometimes differ from,
certain nonliterary/nondramatic narratives. It would be interesting
to explore how economic issues (and the moral issues and conflicts
that arose from them), when taken up by dramatists and poets,
sometimes became conflicts of a peculiarly "literary" nature. All
critical methodologies need not, of course, insist on such questions. But Howard's piece too presses the issue when she reminds
us that the ideology of cultural productions is a complex one. The
theater was clearly a space that participated in the effort to accomo-
date the changes in the new economic climate, but the theater's responses are marked by "contradictions and occlusions," and
"sometimes of most interest are the instances where the edges are
rough, the work of ideological resolution most strained" (267).
Howard's own brief analysis of William Rowley's play *A New Wonder; or A Woman Never Vext* demonstrates this tension. A few other
chapters in the collection, while putting literary and nonliterary
texts in dialogue with each other, demonstrate that the literary engagement with the "real" is often, and quite obviously, different because of its status and role as literature. In Ryner's essay on
Cymbeline, for example, the play, because it is written for a purpose
and audience different from that of mercantile treatises, engages

with economic debates and realities to arrive at conclusions distinct from those treatises.

   Global Traffic certainly succeeds in raising valuable questions regarding the role of English literature in relation to "discourses and
practices of trade." This alone makes it a worthwhile contribution
to early modern cultural studies. The focus of the anthology is clear
and precise without being restrictive, and the essays are to be com-
mended for the originality of the topics examined and the depth of
the research involved. Moreover, the collection comes at an important point in the critical engagement of literary critics with early
modern trade and globalization, exploring hitherto unexamined aspects of this phenomenon or revisiting older questions in significant and useful ways.

Frame, Glass, Verse: The Technology of Poetic Invention in the English Renaissance
By Rayna Kalas
Ithaca: Cornell University Press, 2007

Reviewer: William H. Sherman

Like other contributions to what has come to be known as the New
Materialism in Renaissance studies, Rayna Kalas's *Frame, Glass,
Verse* sets out to explore the physical materials that underwrite our
imaginative and cognitive activities—the beehives and gardens behind selective reading, say, or the clocks behind new forms of narration. This approach is strongly associated with the University of
Pennsylvania English Department, where Kalas wrote the doctoral
dissertation on which this book is based; and its twin catchphrases,
one tying *subjects* to *objects* and the other linking *matter* and
meaning, are peppered throughout the text. In the extended reading of John Donne's "A Valediction of my name, in the window,"
which closes the book, indeed, they are found in the same sentence: the poet's name etched on glass becomes a "sign that is both

material and transparent, a sign that holds in balance lover and be-loved, writer and reader, subject and object, and finally matter and meaning" (199–200). Not every critic has what it takes to make this method sing, and at its most reductive it can take the life out of both things and texts. But in the hands of a scholar like Kalas, who combines a command of history and theory with a gift for close reading, it is capable of transforming our understanding of materi-als and metaphors alike—in this case, the frames, mirrors, looking glasses, and windows that gave light and form to the Renaissance poetic imagination.

These objects have so often supplied the images of choice for ar-tistic, critical, and philosophical projects that they are bound to strike us as transhistorical and even universal. *Frame, Glass, Verse* may be best approached, then, as a critique of the projection of two distinctly modern ways of seeing into early modern culture. The first concerns the "pictorial logic of the modern frame," the "alien-able quadrilateral" that divides artistic substance from its technical support. The second involves the visual logic of the modern (look-ing) glass that makes art reflective and imitative rather than consti-tutive and drives a geometrical and psychological wedge between reality and representation. To help us undo these constructions—or at least to put them in their proper perspective—Kalas gives us beautifully illustrated histories of frames, reliquaries, mirrors, and perspective glasses and nuanced interpretations of texts by Shake-speare, Spenser, Gascoigne, Lyly, Puttenham, Nashe, Harvey, and Bacon. In doing so, she recovers "an English Renaissance that rec-ognized poesy as *techne* rather than aesthetics, and figurative lan-guage as framed or tempered matter, rather than verbalized concepts" (xi). While Kalas is primarily interested in poetry proper—leaving us to extend her readings to dramatic, theological, or cosmographical texts—her analysis of *poesis* is far wider than the title's narrow emphasis on "verse" suggests.

When Renaissance writers described the composition of words, minds, pictures, and selves, they habitually turned to the language of framing. And to understand why and how they did so, Kalas re-minds us that the "frame" referred not to the border around pic-tures but rather to the essential acts of embodying, orchestrating, and tempering. And Renaissance writers' pervasive use of glass—reflective and transparent, steel and crystal, convex and flat—also points to a specific moment in its status as a tempered substance: during the fifteenth and sixteenth centuries, as Kalas explains, in-novations in verse-making and glassmaking went hand in hand.

The book falls fairly neatly into two sections, though they are not signaled as such. The preface, introduction ("The Renaissance and Its Period Frames"), chapter 1 ("The Frame before the Work of Art"), chapter 2 ("The Craft of Poesy and the Framing of Verse"), and chapter 3 ("The Tempered Frame") are almost entirely devoted to frames. In chapter 4 ("Poetic Offices and the Conceit of the Mirror"), chapter 5 ("Poesy, Progress, and the Perspective Glass"), chapter 6 ("'Shakes-speare's Sonnets' and the Properties of Glass"), and the coda ("The Material Sign and the Transparency of Language"), the focus shifts almost completely to glass. The two parts tell stories that are more different than Kalas admits, and more might have been done to draw them together; as it stands, the book offers more of a diptych than a single panel or canvas. And while frames and glass give Kalas more than enough to work with, I found myself wondering about their relationship to other recent object lessons in Renaissance poetics that favor the ear, mouth, heart, or stomach rather than the eye.

For all her focus on the visual and the material, Kalas is finely tuned to the work that words do. Throughout the book, Kalas unpacks poetic conceits, spins out elaborate etymologies, and follows Raymond Williams and Reinhart Koselleck in considering the ways in which key words can teach us about social and conceptual structures. If I am ever asked to edit Shakespeare's sonnets, I will reread chapter 6 before I even think about glossing the poems' exquisite play on "frame," "perspective," "steel/stell," and "glass." But *Frame, Glass, Verse* will appeal to more than editors and critics: a contribution to the history of optics and philosophy as well as literature, this lucid and wide-ranging book has much to teach scholars who are interested in all aspects of Renaissance word- and world-making.

Shakespeare and the Problem of Adaptation
By Margaret Jane Kidnie
New York: Routledge, 2008

Reviewer: Thomas Cartelli

In the domain of Shakespeare studies, where most books seek no greater distinction than to become the next link on the latest fashionable scholarly chain, M. J. Kidnie's *Shakespeare and the Problem of Adaptation* stands out from the pack as vividly as its richly colored Joan Mitchell–inspired cover. Kidnie's book distinguishes itself not only in terms of its level of address, the clarity and precision of its writing, but in terms of the honesty, imagination, and intellectual daring with which she pursues her objectives. Although her book's title indicates that adaptation will be her primary subject, Kidnie will resist applying that term to almost every "instance" or reproduction of a Shakespeare play (or, as she prefers, "work") she describes and discusses. Why? Because, as she writes in her space-clearing introduction, her book is less about the *practice* of adaptation "than it is about the identity of Shakespeare's works and the intimately related *problem* of adaptation" (7). On Kidnie's terms, one can only *adapt*—in the sense of displace, translate, or transform—a work that is, or is said to be, moored in a specific place and time, "sealed off in/as the past" (69), and for her, there is no fixed, determinate, authoritative text or production of Shakespeare's that can be confidently identified as the "authentic" point or moment of origin on which all later texts and productions are founded and evolve. A scholar who has already contributed much to the recent revolutions in both textual editing and performance-oriented criticism, Kidnie proposes "a more flexible account of the criteria by which one distinguishes one work from another, locating them not *prior* to the work's instances of production, for example, in the mind of the artist, but *subsequent* to production in users' perception of sameness and difference among the many variants found in distinct production instances" (29).

Die-hard traditionalists might consider such an approach altogether too "presentist" or theoretical. Though it may occasionally seem both these things, Kidnie's methodology is, actually, as she herself remarks, "constructionist and pragmatic" throughout, showing "points of contact with the theoretical positions of Stanley Fish and Richard Rorty" (7) as well as with those of Richard Wollheim and Joseph Grigely, among others. From Fish, Kidnie takes the idea of the authorizing power and function of "interpretive communities," which negotiate, chart, and record the shifts and permutations of a given literary work's textual status and range of available meanings. From Grigely's "vision of radical textual democracy, exemplified [in his] theory of textualterity," she takes the claim that "every text in its uniqueness is . . . no more or less an instance of the work than another," but pointedly qualifies it by affirming "one's ability in a present moment to draw distinctions and resemblances among instances" (29). Kidnie's preference for a terminology of "work/instance" as opposed to "play/performance" or "text/edition" is rooted in variations she works on Richard Wollheim's "type-token thesis" (17–19), which she subjects to painstaking analysis in the process of developing her own model of pragmatic adaptation.

With and without qualification, "instances" becomes a keyword for Kidnie and often does double duty to cover both the reproduction of a work in the form of a new edition and its reproduction on stage, screen, or television, effectively taking the place of the more familiar terminology of adaptation and appropriation. In a related terminological move, Kidnie resists using the "slippery" all-purpose term "play" on the grounds that "[i]t sidesteps entirely debates in textual studies about versions and works, it can embrace either edition(s) or performance(s), or both, and does not sound particularly theorized, yet remains available to theoretically inflected analysis" (28–29). She also takes this step "to redeem a term that is in danger of being entirely surrendered to Idealist criticism" (29), though Kidnie courts Idealist risks of her own making by choosing to have the word "work" substitute for "play" or "play text" whenever she chooses to refer to the "aura," essence, or prevailing understanding of a given Shakespearean play at a specific moment in history.

Kidnie lays most of this argument out in her first chapter, aptly titled "Surviving performance: Shakespeare's contested works," but enriches and elaborates on it in her four succeeding chapters of applications, each notably different from the other. The first of these—chapter 2, "Defining the work through production, or what

adaptation is not"—directly targets the authorizing practices of established interpretive communities in a sustained comparative
analysis of the construction and reception of two very different
Royal Shakespeare Company productions produced within five
years of each other (1997 and 2003) in Stratford and London: one
often found too radical to be recognizably *Hamlet,* the other seemingly rendered authoritative mainly because it featured Judi Dench
enlarging a role usually delegated to lesser luminaries in *All's Well
That Ends Well.* Kidnie offers an astute, largely favorable reading of
the former—Matthew Warchus's controversially "mediatized" production of *Hamlet*—while delivering a considerably more critical
assessment of the institutional politics that rendered the latter both
a critical and commercial success, concluding that "in this particular case what was recognized as authentic Shakespeare resulted in
part from what could be recognized at this moment in the company's fortunes as an authentic Royal Shakespeare Company" (46).

The book's very differently focused third chapter—"Entangled in
the present: Shakespeare and the politics of production"—turns
"from anxieties about the work's transmission in text and performance to explore cases that openly declare an adaptive distance from
Shakespeare's works" (65), the cases in question being Djanet
Sears's *Harlem Duet* and Robert Lepage's *Elsinore.* Kidnie attempts
to demonstrate here, in her discussion of *Harlem Duet,* how an "instance" that is mainly designed to "write back" to its fixed Shakespearean target or objective, in this case *Othello,* manages to trigger
"a complicated process of reciprocal exchange, one not fully in
control of the modern deviser" (89). In this process, "one marks
Shakespeare's work continuing to take shape in response to, at the
same time as it seems to ground, adaptation" (85), and, she concludes, "In such a model of recurrence, writing back to Shakespeare is always writing *with* Shakespeare, . . . *Othello* is less
countered than *en*countered" (87). This conclusion is itself an exemplary "instance" of Kidnie putting her own theory into practice
insofar as it turns on the notion of an unmoored and "continually
evolving work" escaping "a past to which it has been at least rhe-
torically consigned to intrude on and potentially redirect current
production" (89). Particularly crucial for Kidnie is how this process
troubles and renders porous and uncertain "the boundaries separating [the work] from adaptation," making it seem as if "the work
is always itself undergoing something like an adaptive process"
(89). By contrast, in her account of *Elsinore,* the "work," in this

case "Shakespeare's *Hamlet*," is unmoored from its material posting in one or the other "authentic" texts to serve in place of those
texts as the still-evolving medium and shape-shifting mirror of another also-evolving production.

As good as her treatments of these two staged "instances" are,
they pale by comparison with the freshness, daring, and thorough-
ness of Kidnie's takes on the BBC's effort to make Shakespeare
available to new audiences in its recent four-part series, *ShakespeaRe-Told*. Kidnie's belief in the project's goals not only encourages her to find cutting-edge virtues in one of the series'
comparatively lesser achievements—its version of *Much Ado
About Nothing*—but to allow these modern-language "adaptations," which are authored under their "original" titles by contemporary screenwriters, to stand as "authentic" instancings of the
works they nominally represent. Though Kidnie claims, in strict
constructionist terms, that seeking "to determine in any absolute
sense the series' status as either interpretation or adaptation is to
ask the wrong question of production since there is no fixed original the essence of which can be repeated or captured through performance," her concurrent claim that "the point is rather to look
beyond the instance at hand to the surrounding contextual circumstances to determine how, at this moment and for a particular community of users, the work is being defined (and redefined) as a
conceptual tool" (134) may unduly privilege the aims of the producing institution at the expense of its viewers. Kidnie clearly
wants to make a case for the films' standing as instancings or interpretations (as opposed to adaptations), and manages to do so by
having "the surrounding contextual circumstances"—which include the BBC's attempt to fulfill its government-mandated responsibility of "Building Digital Britain" (131)—effectively underwrite
their function and authorize the unusually prosaic mainstream
forms at least two of them take. Kidnie especially admires the experiment in digital technology that, at the end of each program, invited viewers with digital capability "to press the red button" on
their remotes, thereby giving them access to a number of interactive
options, and getting them "to use their television in an unaccus-
tomed way, gaining a greater comprehension of what digital offers
and how to use it, and so prompting among analogue and digital
viewers alike a reconception of the medium of television" (131).

This is, of course, not the only virtue Kidnie finds in the series.
Indeed, she offers a compelling audience-centered defense of the

many manifest liberties the series' creators take in adapting each of the four plays in question, which include *Macbeth, A Midsummer Night's Dream,* and *The Taming of the Shrew* in addition to *Much Ado:*

> The work cannot remain exactly what it was four hundred years ago, or even twenty years ago, in part because the audiences who must discursively apprehend it by means of instances have been conditioned to "see" differently. For this reason, it is not self-evidently the case that *ShakespeaRe-Told* "translates" the works to television (a choice of words that presupposes an innately adaptive and alien medium). On the contrary, the series integrates into its formal strategies of story-telling modern communication technologies that—to the extent one has come to take them for granted as ordinary parts of daily existence— *already* inform in fundamental ways one's perception of the legitimate boundaries of Shakespeare's works. (126)

Much that Kidnie has to say here is persuasive, though her wording at times is more wishful than evidential, and at odds with some of her more rigorous distinctions. I specifically wonder who exactly the one is that takes for granted the effects of "modern communication technologies" and how these technologies really inform that same "one's perception of the legitimate boundaries of Shakespeare's works." If what she is trying to say is that "one" takes for granted the genre-conventions of mainstream British television, that is another thing entirely, though very different from what she means to imply by "modern communication technologies." For it seems indisputable that both the *ShakespeaRe-Told Much Ado* and *Dream* play directly to the designated lower middle of what I take to be the series' target audience, and do so with very little in the way of wit or wonder, respectively. In this respect, they don't so much accord with "one's perception of the legitimate boundaries of Shakespeare's works," as seek to extend those boundaries to embrace the preemptively downgraded viewing habits of that audience.

Other readers' objections are apt to echo those of Trevor Nunn, whom Kidnie quotes to the effect that "Ultimately for me, it's the language that matters—no language, no Shakespeare" (114). Kidnie finesses Nunn's objection by demonstrating how arguably the best of the series' productions, its *Macbeth* scripted by Peter Moffat, compensates for the loss of Shakespeare's language by "writing what at times registers as strange television dialogue." She goes on to claim that Moffat "authors Shakespeare for a new medium and a new millennium by projecting a distinctive authorial *effect* that is consistent with modern perceptions of the canon as high art" and that "[p]aradoxically, it is this slanting proximity to the work, one's ability to hear the 'Shakespeare' in Moffat's *Macbeth,* that makes an interpretation 'based on the play by William Shakespeare,' as the title credits put it, less self-evidently adaptation" (119). Kidnie is entirely right here, but her being right undercuts some of what she is trying to claim for the other productions in the series. If it's hearing the "Shakespeare" in Moffat's *Macbeth* that makes *Macbeth* Moffat's, then what's the effect of *not* hearing the Shakespeare, but instead *seeing* a Shakespeare-derived plot literally flattened and overrun by the romantic and comedic genre conventions of British commercial television in *Dream* and *Much Ado?* If Shakespeare cannot continue to exist in language that has become largely incomprehensible to most audiences, can his plots and characters alone continue to register as or warrant what is construed to be quintessentially Shakespearean?

In her provocative final chapter, "Textual origins," Kidnie addresses "issues of adaptation as they bear on the production of Shakespeare's works as reading texts" (144), and takes her argument about the redefining role played by interpretive communities to what some may consider its breaking point, but which I would identify as its proper pragmatic and constructionist conclusion: "Because the work does not exist somewhere (not even in the First Folio), but always 'survives' somewhere else, it remains susceptible . . . to the ways scholars conduct and write textual histories. Inevitably, as conceptions of the work continue to alter over time, so will assessments of what will or should count as either an authentic or an adapted textual production, along with the criteria or terms by which it is recognized" (153). Offering informed commentaries on how the Reduced Shakespeare Company plays not only "the works but the one-volume *book* in which those works are now commonly circulated" (142), on the "criticisms of modern editorial practice mounted by performance and theater history scholars such as Alan C. Dessen and Don Weingust," among others (144–45), and on the editorial theories and practice of John Jowett and Gary Taylor on the one hand and Barbara Mowat and Paul Werstine on the other, Kidnie supplies both a panoramic and site-specific study of the current state of the art. In so doing, she stresses the shaping effects of prevailing practices of textual and theatrical production in resistance to "the dominant inclination to regard past histories as foundational" (164) to either.

In the end, "the problem of adaptation" is, for Kidnie, a "condition of uncertainty [that] is always inherent to work production" (161), founded as it is on the provisional basis of all designated sites of origin. But it is not for all that inimical to the rites of distinction-making or judgment: "The work is the conceptual construction, pragmatically known and always located somewhere other than at the site of production, that makes it possible to regulate a work's identity and what will count as adaptation. It allows one to assess existing textual instances as more or less genuine, and to generate criteria of error sufficient to justify various forms of editorial emendation; without it, judgment is disabled" (161). One may detect here a bit of hedging or backtracking in Kidnie's language— for example, "what will count," "more or less genuine," "criteria of error"—as she seeks to balance the abstract implications of her argument with its specific application to textual production. What, after all, can be considered "genuine" if every designated site of origin or point of departure is provisional? Also at issue here is Kidnie's occasional failure to resist what she earlier terms the "potentially misleading" impulse "to conceive of the work as a single or unified thing" (8) in whatever specific slice of time or space it prevails, as if only one interpretive community at a time can dictate what a work is and what it signifies. Never at issue is how relentlessly lucid, penetrating, and risk-taking Kidnie's writing and thinking are, how many inroads into established ideas about textual origins and editing she makes, and how many doors of theatrical and televisual perception she opens. *Shakespeare and the Problem of Adaptation* should prove a wondrous, necessary book to anyone interested in the best-case future of Shakespeare studies Kidnie both models and presents in its pages.

A Politics of the Scene
By Paul Kottman
Stanford: Stanford University Press, 2007

Reviewer: William N. West

All the world, observes Paul Kottman in his ambitious, exciting book *A Politics of the Scene,* is a stage. Working with rigor, tact, and scrupulous care in the fields of political philosophy and literary study, Kottman explains how Jaques' observation in *As You Like It* is more than the easy chestnut it has been taken to be. In Kottman's original and welcome reading, the emergence of the concept of the world as a stage is a crucial moment in the history of human activity in general, and therefore also of the sciences that seek to grasp the complexity of the kinds of human interactivity that are called political. But whereas political theatricalists like Shakespeare or political theorists like Hannah Arendt insist on the truth of the figure of the *theatrum mundi*—all the world really is the stage upon which human action and life take place, become visible, and answer to other human life—Kottman shows how the discourse of political theory, here represented by Plato as its founding father and Thomas Hobbes as its revolutionary secularizer, has insisted that the *theatrum mundi* is no more than a figure, one that tells us what politics is like, but not what it is (206). Political theory, Kottman persuasively argues, has for the strand of its history running from Plato and Aristotle through Hobbes to Carl Schmitt and Jürgen Habermas, been constructed to exclude the theatrical scene—the worldly face-to-face of the here and now—in favor of transcending it for avowedly higher otherworldly principles. Theatricality is thus foundational to a dominant tradition of political science, and of human action more broadly, but only insofar as the experience it provides can be overcome by theory, a move that sets politics in a realm that "has nothing to do with the sharing of words and deeds between singular people" (5) rather than in a here and now where one human being encounters another.

As Kottman notes, the scene has not been given nearly as much attention as have other shared terms in the lexicons of politics and theater, such as action, representation, person, and so on. But for Kottman, this recurrent oversight has been crucial in the distancing of political theory from political theaters; it is the scene, Kottman avows, that marks a time and place in which individuals come together, address one another, and establish real, singular relationships through their words and deeds. Such scenes of everyday life—and they are countless—are addressed toward an anticipated future here and now when the participants of the scene may possibly resume those relationships, and reform, extend, or abrogate them, by their further actions or words. This, in a word, is real politics—a consequential here and now encounter that imagines itself being taken up in a future scene. Not every encounter, of course, is political, especially in a modern world in which the opportunities and demands to interact with others have become nearly overwhelming. For Kottman, this makes theater all the more important, as a staging that has the particular task of recalling its onlookers to the particularity of every other of their encounters outside the immediacy of the theater.

Kottman is influenced not only by Arendt's notion that what can be called politics is interaction that establishes relations among people, but by her sense that fully political interaction acknowledges the absolute uniqueness of each of its makers, who therefore come together in ways that can never be entirely codified, predicted, or even fully known. The theatrical scene, then, offers a particular selective representation of the actions such a worldly scene might allow, and can thus provide another scene for an encounter among the individuals who participate in it by watching. This book is all the more welcome because of how it suggests that the study of Shakespeare, or even better, the ongoing performances of the plays of Shakespeare and others, actually contribute to the arguments of political science rather than merely reflecting or exemplifying them. Indeed, more than just giving political life a language and a shape, theatrical performances are here shown to be a real part of that life.

Kottman's first two chapters discuss how the proposition that the world is a theater is reified in classical political treatises: rather than properly scenic, singular, face-to-face interaction between individuals being understood as establishing relationships with an eye to possible futures for those relationships, interaction is reconceived as an agent working on a passive receiver. In Plato's *Republic,* the idea of mimesis as an action that might bring forth anything in the world is replaced by a concept that mimesis is a production of something, so that its outcome is an artifact rather than shared event. What this means is that mimesis for Plato is always directing its makers and beholders beyond the here and now to something elsewhere, such as the realm of forms. Beholding is the sine qua non of mimesis, since even if one makes an imitation as a craftsperson does, the first step is observing the form that one will copy. This conception, Kottman argues, becomes a peculiar problem when it is transferred to the realm of human interactivity. For the craftsperson-lawgiver-philosopher of the Platonic state, the mimetic act of making begins not from the unique histories of its elements, in this case the people of the state, nor from their future-oriented actions; it can only recognize in them passive raw materials. In a similar mode, Aristotle privileges the life of contemplation over the active life. In either case, the idea that human interactivity is its own goal is converted into a sense that it is no more than one step toward something else.

The next two chapters move to a fascinating discussion of Hobbes's *Leviathan,* which Kottman argues follows Plato in rendering "Politics without a Scene" by imposing a fictional state of nature onto people and an equally fictional moment of contract that creates the state of Leviathan. From these universal fictions Hobbes moves to bind unique individuals to particular kinds of behavior under a sovereign. Kottman sees in this a further distancing of politics from the contingency and partiality of the scene and an embrace of the stance of the mathematical sciences that were also developing in the mid-seventeenth century. By reducing human life to a merely physical "motion of limbs," Hobbes can predict its course—really, the general range of its future possibilities—with all the certainty of a Galilean physicist describing the motion of a planetary body. Leviathan is thus presented as an inevitability. Here Kottman distinguishes the spectacular constitution of Leviathan from the theatricality of the scene. The here and now interaction of the scene requires an encounter of unique individuals and the possibility of their remembering and reshaping the encounter in a shared history. But Hobbes's analysis renders any action that such a scene might precipitate moot, since it can only lead to other inconsequential actions or to the formation of Leviathan; sovereignty is in more ways than one the only way out of the violent state of nature. Leviathan is not the image of something else, but "the accomplishment of representations as such" (83); it is not pri-

marily a show of force to awe its subject-constituters, but a totalitar-
ian saturation of the visual field (here I think Kottman means this
both literally and figuratively, for the field of thought) that excludes
every other thing, so that no alternative to it, or even difference or
dissent within it, seems possible (85).

The next four chapters turn to Shakespeare, as well as returning
to Arendt and other political philosophers, especially Adriana Cavarero, to flesh out an alternative to the undifferentiated anthropo-
morphism of Hobbes's Leviathan in the form of the scene. In the
first two of these, Kottman argues that the scene goes further than
notions of embodiment can in illuminating political activity, because a theatrical scene presumes embodiment in the actors, but
also goes beyond to depict interactions or their misfires; its subject
is not just motion or embodiment, but relations between unique elements. Taking on some long-standing poststructural truisms, Kottman sketches the scene as a method of analysis that foregoes
epistemological mastery in an effort to preserve the particularity of
the person and their relations to other singular people (106). What
is most important in the scene is not what is accomplished, but
who speaks in accomplishing it, who is thereby involved in the future it proposes, and how that future transforms its partakers (109).
The ontologically nonhierarchical precession of scenes that make
up political life provide no Archimedean point from which to lever
a state into existence; its production is an ongoing work of all those
involved, composed of all their relations and interactions that extend for however brief a period across time. Memory proves to be as
important as anticipation to the imperfect stability of such polities,
including the way scenes of remembering become in turn new
scenes that can be remembered subsequently by a polity, providing
continuity without excluding change. Most important, then, a play
is caught by the scene of its performance—that is, the situation in
which it is offered and the ways in which it is taken up, accepted,
or contested as the representation of an interaction and an exemplary opportunity for new interactions—rather than by what it represents (127, 134).

A chapter on *Hamlet* follows, in which Kottman focuses ever
more sharply on what is essential to the scene by paring away still
more from its complex of connotations. Closely following arguments of Adriana Cavarero, whose work he has translated, Kottman
distinguishes between speech as a vehicle for meaning and the
nonsemantic voice as an individuating quality that picks one per-

son from another and enables each to "make a scene" in their irreducible uniqueness (154). Kottman sees this at work in *Hamlet*'s first and last scenes, which he describes as the gathering of a group of individual witnessing voices to the many events of the play, made the more singular in their web of interrelations from the appearance of old Hamlet's ghost to young Hamlet's death. The answer to the question of what happens in *Hamlet* is transformed from an accounting of actions and appearances into the weaving of a unique set of relations that form around them, assembling the actors into configurations that potentially endure and could be resumed in their imagined futures. The next chapter, on the balcony scene in *Romeo and Juliet,* shows how attempts to name such relations fail to grasp their uniqueness, and how any attempts to make a claim about some state of affairs fail to reach what is expressed in the act of saying something. As Romeo and Juliet exchange words in the darkness, their voices exceed their words irreproducibly; aside from whatever they say, they are bound to each other as shar ers of this unprecedented scene. Kottman does not neglect the framing of *Romeo and Juliet,* and how carefully the play both predicts and recapitulates its action. But he argues that within the boundaries of the play and of the theater—boundaries that the name "Shakespeare" has singularly exemplified and policed—the balcony scene, with its willingness to step beyond the fixity of names into the flow of relations that are always open to renegotiation, reveals something of the "pretheatrical" sense of the scene of politics. An epilogue returns to the history of the figure of the *theatrum mundi* and the declamation of Jaques.

A book of this density invites argument. Even considering the brevity of the work, *A Politics of the Scene* can be sometimes curiously emblematic in what it looks to: Plato stands in for the discourse of political theory, Hobbes for its break into modernity, and about three scenes from two of Shakespeare's plays for early modern theater. It is fuller on the political theorists it treats than on the plays, and I found myself wondering how central to Kottman's striking arguments were notions like concrete history, periods like early modernity, and plays like *Hamlet.* The book reaches dauntingly wide, but can these moments really speak for so many others in outlining a tradition and an alternative to it? Kottman's project is an unashamedly presentist one, but I wonder where a survey like this displaces the here and now about which he writes so powerfully. The book is at risk of dissolving its history of moments of en-

counter and its poignant handling of the crucial moment of the
voice into the timeless, illusorily shared present of a Great Conversation. What would then be left is a suggestive gesture toward another conception of politics and theater, but hardly different from
the form that, for Kottman, it takes in Hobbes.

Kottman seems to me to overlook moments in *Leviathan* that suggest a greater proximity between his own and Hobbes's handling of
the political scene, moments in Hobbes's universal history that
seem deeply invested in Kottman's question of the unique relations
that are grounded in a particular here and now of the scene, and
that resist Kottman's reading of Hobbes' totalitarianism as essential
and formal rather than rhetorical and contingent. To give just one
example, Hobbes says that "a very small company of souldiers, sur-
prised by an army" may justly renounce their covenant to their sovereign, since they undertook it only to preserve their lives and their
sovereign can no longer fulfill his part (chapter 20). Though
sketched in a few lines, this seems to me no less a scene in Kottman's sense than anything Shakespeare can offer; it springs from
an encounter as particular as a balcony scene or a ghostly battle-
ment, and it requires that we consider the soldiers as individuals
who reaffirm, reject, or modify the covenant that they are under.
With this one instance, the single-mindedness of the Leviathan
seems called into question almost throughout, for if these soldiers
may justly renounce their covenant because they fear death at the
hands of those from whom their sovereign cannot protect them,
what hinders other individuals from recalculating their own advantage and relation to their sovereign, its enemies, and their supposed fellow subjects? In addition, Hobbes is always concerned
with the many vicissitudes that mediacy brings to representation,
and its essential unavoidability; *Leviathan*'s well-known chapter
16, "Of Persons, Authors, and Things Personated," discussed by
Kottman, takes as its central problem the ways in which authority
is transferred, or fails to transfer, between positions. Arendt's sense
of the singular natality of the person, taken up by Kottman, is probably irreconcilable with Hobbes's views, but even in a speculative
work like this, it seems that more could have been done to weigh
them against each other. Kottman rightly notes that Shakespeare
has come to stand for a certain discretely bounded way of looking
at theater (181); he might think how a reconsideration of Hobbes
could correct the distortions that have stuck to both writers.

Finally, I was confused by Kottman's emphasis on the importance of the witness to the scene and the uniqueness of who is speaking. A critical generation ago, this might have been dismissed out of hand as merest metaphysics; thankfully, though, academic discourse has recovered grounds for talking about individuality and singularity again. Nevertheless, Kottman shows a tendency to mystify the moment of the encounter into something of surpassing excellence, to my mind giving short shrift to the complex interactions that develop as an encounter is recalled and taken up by others. Kottman says, for instance, that when there are no longer two witnesses to an event, that moment has died to politics. On the other hand, according to Kottman, the performance of a scene in a theater seems to be able to reanimate that moment, literally call it back to liveliness and open it to new witnesses. Finally, Kottman's own argument requires that we see the witnesses as free to reconfigure their relations, to each other and to what they seen, in any subsequent meeting. It is hard for me to see how any claim to a more authentic witnessing can be maintained without recourse to some extrapolitical scheme of verification; like any other relation, that of witnessing might well be, and empirically is, open to dispute. When it comes to the performance of the theatrical scene, Kottman argues convincingly that its own situation is more important than what it represents, yet his readings of scenes of Shakespeare neglect any actual situation (and what would this be? performers to their audience? reader to a book?), and look instead at the representation of a scene. This strikes me as akin to what Kottman quite rightly critiques in Hobbes as a stance that is more theoretical than theatrical, but it raises the question of whether or not any discourse can really include the hic et nunc. If Hobbes's rich analysis of personation, authorization, and action is not to be used, this seems to call out for some fuller consideration of mediation and representation.

As this conclusion suggests, a book like this does not end easily—like the scenes Kottman describes, it throws itself into a future of discussions and relations with its readers and rewriters. I like to imagine that Kottman would be happier not to find easy acquiescence to his challenging arguments. He has written a book that demands engagement and that repays it. Above all, he calls readers to the possibility that literature might speak on its own behalf to other fields like politics and philosophy. That is a voice well worth listening to and answering.

Shakespeare in the Worlds of Communism and Socialism
Edited by Irena R. Makaryk and Joseph G. Price
Toronto: University of Toronto Press, 2006

Reviewer: Alexander C. Y. Huang

What kind of conversations would one have with Shakespeare in times of political crisis, in times of revolution and wars? Much ink has been spilled over Marxist approaches to literature, but little is known in the English-speaking world about Shakespeare's fortunes in the communist and socialist worlds except for, perhaps, Jan Kott's Poland (*Shakespeare Our Contemporary* [*Szkice o Szekspirze*[, 1964). For those who know—or think they know—Shakespeare, a foray into this global cultural history is a triple experience of the Shakespearean text, of rewritings with their attendant ideologies, and of the Marxist critical tradition (our own or "theirs"). Over a decade in the making, *Shakespeare in the Worlds of Communism and Socialism,* a collection of eighteen well-illustrated, wide-ranging articles, is a sophisticated contribution to the scholarship on Shakespeare in the modern world. The book takes readers on a kaleidoscopic tour to Ukraine, Latvia, the USSR, East Germany, Hungary, Poland, Cuba, China, and back to North American academic circles. The coeditors rightly note that of all these countries, "China has had the strongest, and longest, history of Shakespeare reception" (10). On the other hand, North Korea, "with its closed society and rejection of anything Western," and Vietnam as "an emergent Communist state," are not covered for lack of "evidence of Shakespeare's role in the adaptation of Marx" (9). While this may be true of North Korea, there are plenty of interesting works in Vietnam, including stage productions in *tuong* "operatic" style and *A Dream in Hanoi* (2002), a controversial documentary directed by Tom Weidlinger that chronicles an English-Vietnamese bilingual coproduction of *A Midsummer Night's Dream* in Hanoi by the Central Dramatic Company of Vietnam and the Artists Repertory Theater of Portland, Oregon. Likewise, Cambodia and Laos would have provided fruitful contrasts and parallels to the unpredictable relations among communist and socialist ideologies and Shakespeare that the volume aims to address.[1]

One of the pitfalls of intercultural scholarship is the alluring evolutionary model that promulgates teleological history, which is addressed at the opening of the book. To their credit, coeditors Irena Makaryk and Joseph Price are quick to direct readers' attention to "the deeply ambivalent nature of Communist Shakespeare"— serving and subverting at once the official ideologies (5). Indeed, as most essays demonstrate, there is no single, fixed template for the appropriation of Shakespeare in these countries despite the dominance of the Soviet experience of revolution (6). The succinct but informative introduction steers readers away from any assumption about evolutionary trajectories of the uses of Shakespeare.

The volume is divided into four parts, the first two arranged chronologically and the next two thematically. Short, section-specific introductions by Makaryk precede the essays in each part. Part 1, "Shakespeare in Flux: 1917 to the 1930s," contains essays by Irena Makaryk, Laura Raidonis Bates, Arkady Ostrovsky, Laurence Senelick, and Alexey Bartoshevitch on the process of making Shakespeare available, for purposes of "unifying cross-cultural interests" and "homogeniz[ing] readership," in the twenty-eight languages of Ukraine, Latvia, and Stalin's Russia. As in communist China, Shakespeare was appropriated as a "founding father" of socialist realism in these locations. Among the surprising stories told in this section are one of an intellectualized production of *Macbeth* for peasants in 1920s Urkaine and another about the perceived social functions of comedy in Russian theater. A specialist of Shakespeare reception, especially in the USSR, who is proficient in Russian and Ukrainian, Makaryk delves into a 1924 experimental modernist production of *Macbeth* by Les Kurbas, one of the most important Ukrainian directors, that came under attack by party officials who believed that "the foundational role of theatre should not lie in aesthetic delight but in its social significance" (30). Through the case study of Kurbas and analysis of the impact of the ideologies of socialist realism, this chapter delineates the larger picture of how the party leaders scrambled to create a coherent theory in the process of "the homogenization of theatrical art and cultural life" (34). Opening with a discussion of an enthusiastically received production of *Much Ado About Nothing* in Moscow in 1936, Bartoshevitch's chapter asks why so many classical comedies, including those by Molière and Shakespeare, were produced in the thirties and forties, an unprecedented phenomenon in the history of the Russian theater. The answer lies in the advent of "historical optimism," which made Shakespeare a spokesperson of the rising "winning" class of the proletariats. Comedies provided salutary illusions and satisfied a "craving for harmony" (109). Interestingly, *Much Ado About Nothing* and Stalin's 1935 proclamation that "comrades, life has become more joyful" (106) also found a ready home outside of the context discussed by this essay, and the Soviet dramaturgy lived on. As Marxism moved eastward from Europe, it increasingly took on utopian purposes. Soviet directors working in Maoist China under the Soviet-Chinese collaboration scheme, such as Yevgeniya Lipkovskaya, similarly favored comedies (e.g., her production of *Much Ado About Nothing* in Chinese) and propagated Stalin's negative view of Hamlet as an intellectual. They appropriated comedy's utopian vocabulary and idyllic and pastoral elements to project a bright communist future.[2]

The situation changed with Stalin's death in 1953, and *Hamlet* took center stage, as amply demonstrated by Makaryk's second essay in the volume. For good reasons, part 2 turns to various uses of *Hamlet* during World War II, with an emphasis on the German experience. Essays by Werner Habicht, Lawrence Guntner, and Maik Hamburger unpack the political and literary meanings of Shakespeare and *Hamlet,* which were intensified by East-West polarization in Germany. Hamburger discusses Piet Drescher's *Hamlet* in Potsdam in 1983, which he calls "the bluntest exposition of dictatorship known to GDR theatre" (208). The history of Shakespeare in East Germany reveals the permeability of the physical and intellectual boundaries established by official ideologies and the Berlin Wall. An in-depth study of the "flagship" production of *Hamlet* in Moscow (1954) by Nikolay Okhlopkov, Laurence Senelick's essay presents valuable new documentation on the work by one of the most important directors in Soviet theater history.

With essays by Martin Hilský, Krystyna Kujawínska-Courtney, Zoltán Márkus, Xiao Yang Zhang, and Shuhua Wang, part 3 ventures beyond the familiar circuits of the USSR and Germany to translations of and artistic experimentations with Shakespeare in China, Hungary, and Czechoslovakia after 1949, when those countries signed up for the idea of Shakespeare as a "Soviet-sanctioned humanist writer of the people" (213). Márkus traces the developments of the "thematic duality of love and war" of *Troilus and Cressida* from the 1960s to the early 1980s in Hungary. Hilský extracts, through delicious details, multiple layers of intended and unintended meanings when his 1986 translation of *Love's Labor's Lost* was staged in Prague with a curtain made of iron on the set. Among many other examples, act 5, scene 2, in which the king of Navarre and his lords are disguised as Russians, resonated with the Russian occupation of Czechoslovakia (215–20). In the shadow of the political discourse of the normalization and the Prague Spring reformers, Costard's remark, "Walk aside the true folk, and let the traitors stay" (4.3.210), took on different meanings each night as Hilský sat through the performances, hinging upon who is perceived to be the "traitor" and who the "true folk" (223). Courtney's account of Shakespeare in Poland strikes a similar chord by noting the ironic turn his plays take as the country moved from oppression to liberation. Director Krystyna Skuszanka reminisced during an interview with Courtney that under the communist regime, attendance of politicized theater was at once sponsored and encouraged by official policy and seen by the populace as "a meaningful defiance against totalitarianism," an attractive community event to achieve a collective catharsis (242). A liberated Poland no longer provided the stimulus for artistic experimentation and enticement for audiences to attend theater performances.

The last section, "Theorizing Marxist Shakespeares," takes up the questions of critics' and artists' positionality when approaching Shakespeare and literary criticism in Cuba (article by Maria Clara Versiani Galery), East Germany (Robert Weimann), and North America (Sharon O'Dair). In his article on the productive tensions that always exist between academic criticism and the unpredictable energy of theatrical performances in East Germany, Weimann lays bare the limitations of two approaches that tend to yield predictable conclusions: the approach that pursues "a salvaging operation"—recovering certain positions at a particular point in a play's reception history in order to serve today's ideology—and a "muckraking" approach that focuses on past liabilities and accuses communist Shakespeares of being nothing more than a "deplorable aberration from the true standards of Western culture" (329). He suggests, with solid evidence, that "Shakespeare in East German post-war theatre and criticism constituted a public site on which cultural communications inhabited an ambivalent space . . . between ideological dogma and a search for a forceful, irrepressible performative" (346). O'Dair's closing piece examines the tension between poststructuralism and Marxism in the Canadian and U.S.

academies and the unique challenges of democratization in elite higher education. She posits that it is precisely because of scholars' acute awareness of the fact that they cannot turn class analysis on themselves and achieve political transformation from within their institutions that Marxism remains "a site of desire" for North American Shakespeareans (366).

The 402-page book builds upon and supplements such works as *Shakespeare in the New Europe,* edited by Michael Hattaway, Boika Sokolova, and Derek Roper (1994); *Redefining Shakespeare: Literary Theory and Theater Practice in the German Democratic Republic* (1997), edited by J. Lawrence Guntner and Andrew M. McLean; Zdenek Stribrny's *Shakespeare and Eastern Europe* (2000); and *Painting Shakespeare Red: An East-European Appropriation* by Alexander Shurbanov and Boika Sokolova (2001). Shurbanov and Sokolova's book deals exclusively with Bulgaria, while others focus on Eastern Europe. Makaryk and Price's book brings the conversation beyond the Eastern bloc to a global level.

It would be useful to have more interconnected essays on the trajectories of Marxism as it moves from its European homeland to locations discussed in the volume and beyond.[3] It is important to recognize that the strength of the book lies in its capacity to compel readers to consider the unique perils and rewards of engaging cultural events that, for lack of historical distance (such as the collapse of the Soviet Union), may expose our biases for the better. As the introduction and O'Dair's essay cogently argue, the study of ideological Shakespeare is "itself not a neutral act" but rather an exercise preoccupied with pressing issues of our present moment (7).

Notes

1. The reception history of Shakespeare in Southeast Asia is substantial. *Shakespeare in Hollywood, Asia, and Cyberspace,* ed. Alexander C. Y. Huang and Charles S. Ross (West Lafayette, IN: Purdue University Press, 2009); and Alexander C. Y. Huang, "Shakespeare in Southeast Asia," in *The Shakespeare Encyclopedia: Life, Works, World, and Legacy,* 5 vols., ed. Patricia Parker (Westport, CT: Greenwood Press, forthcoming).

2. Alexander C. Y. Huang, *Chinese Shakespeares: Two Centuries of Cultural Exchange* (New York: Columbia University Press, 2009), 142–60.

3. Cf. Daryl Glaser and David M. Walker, eds., *Twentieth Century Marxism: A Global Introduction* (New York: Routledge, 2007).

Performing Maternity in Early Modern England
Edited by Kathryn M. Moncrief and
Kathryn R. McPherson
Aldershot: Ashgate, 2007; and
Shakespearean Maternities: Crises of Conception
in Early Modern England
By Chris Laoutaris
Edinburgh: Edinburgh University Press, 2008

Reviewer: Harriette Andreadis

These books both take as their subject the ideological milieu surrounding early modern maternity, and each makes a welcome contribution to our understanding of this subject. Coming as it does on the heels of feminist and gender analyses of early modern culture, particularly its literary productions, the growing interest in early modern maternity provides an important and fresh perspective, with newly examined materials, on a well-studied literary canon.[1]

The wide-ranging studies in Moncrief and McPherson's *Performing Maternity in Early Modern England* call attention to a substantial body of overlooked materials that are rich with implications for our understanding of the discourse about maternity, and in particular, the relationship of this discourse to the theater. The essays are grouped into four general sections: the performance of pregnancy, the performance of maternal authority, the performance of maternal suffering, and the performance of maternal erasure. What follows is a summary of each of these sections, with an emphasis on the new materials under scrutiny.

In the opening essay of section 1, " 'So troubled with the mother': The Politics of Pregnancy in *The Duchess of Malfi*," Sid Ray concludes that Webster exploits the rhetoric of the King's Two Bodies in order "to naturalize and legitimize female rule" by suggesting "that the female body is well-equipped for authority described as double-bodied," that is, the Duchess's body is double insofar as she is pregnant with child, she is a twin, and she is a wife (one half of her husband). Further, through the figure of the Duchess, "Webster extends the boundaries of conventional thinking, rendering the pregnant woman visible, intricate, redeemed, and above all unfixed and heterogeneous—pregnant with possibilities of female sovereignty, participatory government and merit-based inheritance" (28). In the second essay, "'Show me a child begotten of thy body that I am father to': Pregnancy, Paternity and the Problem of Evidence in *All's Well That Ends Well*," Kathryn Moncrief surveys some of the literature of midwifery, as well as several contemporary instances of staged pregnancy, to offer a new way of looking at Bertram. Seen against the backdrop of early modern pregnancy literature, Moncrief argues, Bertram's skepticism does not come across "as an individual failing or—as he is frequently read—as a product of his simply being 'a cad'"; instead, Bertram appears as "a wary observer of indeterminate evidence who looks more prudent than heartless" (40). For Moncrief, the ending of the play recapitulates the uncertainties and ambiguities of pregnancy as well as those of chastity.

Michelle Ephraim's essay, "Hermione's Suspicious Body: Adultery and Superfetation in *The Winter's Tale*," takes up the issue of ambiguity as it connects to the pregnant woman's ability to deceive her husband about illicit sexual desires. Ephraim contends that the patriarchal order is affirmed, paradoxically, through the "doubling" of Hermione with her statue, the "twinning" of Leontes and Polixenes, and the two-seed theory of superfetation. Deception in connection with pregnancy is also the focus of Robert Bell's analysis of Middleton's experiment with comic form ("False Fruit: Deceptive Maternities and the Failure of New Comedy in Middleton's *A Mad World My Masters*"). Bell demonstrates "that the deceptive personae of Middleton's characters, and in particular the false pregnancy of Frank Gullman, become [Webster's] primary means of interrogating the limitations of New Comedy" (61–62). Concluding the book's first section, Lisa Hopkins explores the ways in which what appears to be a surprising moment in Heywood's *A Woman Killed with Kindness*, Frankford's sudden reference to his children, is, on the contrary, unexceptional and even conventional insofar as motherhood was often under erasure in early modern culture ("Maternity in *A Woman Killed with Kindness*").

Part 2, "The Performance of Maternal Authority," is made up of three essays. Janelle Jenstad's "'Smock-secrets': Birth and Women's Mysteries on the Early Modern Stage" "aims to qualify Gail Kern Paster's thesis that women in Renaissance drama are leaky vessels" insofar as "most plays represent childbirth as empowering rather than embarrassing, as contained and enclosed rather than shamefully leaky and open, whether the birth reproduces the patrilineal order or not" (88). Moreover, Jenstad argues, in *The Magnetic Lady* Jonson as playwright generates the catastrophe of the play by taking on the authoritative female role of midwife and himself revealing women's secrets. In "Disciplining the Mother in Seventeenth-Century English Puritanism," Christina Luckyj brings a fresh perspective to two anonymous prose treatises usually considered as different editions of a single text. Luckyj focuses on their disparities, which, she argues, reveal a conflict between different strains of Puritanism that is played out in "a *struggle* [sic] over the construction of motherhood" (102) and the representation of the mother. Suzanne Penuel concludes this section with an oddly untitled, "Male Mothering and *The Tempest*." Penuel contends that Shakespeare's play "eventually resuscitates the discourse of the mother *within* [sic] the figure of the father" (116) via an early modern transgendered rhetoric. Her speculative and (surely overly) optimistic conclusion invites full quotation: "Blurring the distinctions between motherhood and fatherhood, between feminine witchcraft and masculine sorcery, the maternal patriarch of *The Tempest* perhaps anticipates the appearance of real women on the English stage five decades later—and the eventual fading of the border between maternal and paternal identities in Western cultures" (127).

Section 3 of the collection, "The Performance of Maternal Suffering," opens with an essay by Kathryn McPherson on the churching of Englishwomen ("Dramatizing Deliverance and Devotion: Churching in Early Modern England"). McPherson calls our attention to the shift in emphasis that took place with respect to churching, the "liturgical ceremony that dramatized women's recovery from childbirth" (132), as a result of the influence of Puritanism. McPherson demonstrates how "Early modern discourse about churching . . . refutes a good deal of [David] Cressy's claim that churching was not 'a patriarchal or misogynist instrument for the subjugation of women'" (134). By examining two private texts by women, Alice Thornton (fl. 1625?) and Elizabeth Cavendish Egerton (1625–63), she shows how women reconfigured the churching ceremony to dramatize a maternal suffering that could not have been articulated in the context of a public ceremony governed by a well-established liturgical tradition (141). "Speaking Stones: Memory and Maternity in Shakespeare's *Antony and Cleopatra*," which appears in expanded form as a chapter in Chris Laoutaris's book, imaginatively explores "a feminized language of death, [that] circulated through the unique postures of the maternal body" (155) in funerary monuments. According to Laoutaris, the emergence of this new language in stone countered the conventions of traditional heraldic funerals. Finally, in "Maternity and Child Loss in Stuart Women's Diaries," Avra Kouffman reviews the writing of ten Stuart diarists about their "precarious experiences of maternity" (179). Kouffman concludes that "sect [whether Puritan or Anglican] was the single most important factor that determined . . . range and mode of self-expression" (177), and that the writings of these diarists also reflect "the conventions and attitudes [postures of piety and self-denigration] modeled for them by the clerical community" (179).

The final section of the collection, "The Performance of Maternal Erasure," returns to the earlier emphasis on the theater while focusing on threats to male supremacy. It opens with Donna C. Woodford's perceptive "Nursing and Influence in *Pandosto* and *The Winter's Tale*," an account of how Shakespeare provides "a fantasy of male control over reproduction and nurture" (188) to counter the fear of maternal agency that pervades the play. In "Murder as Birth in *Macbeth*," Gloria Olchowy demonstrates how the elimination of the maternal in Shakespeare's tragedy has implications for patrilineality in Jacobean England, allowing the construction of a new masculine order with "murder as an alternative means of 'being born' into the succession" (203). For Olchowy, "it is the absence rather than the presence of the feminine in that masculinist order . . . that is conducive to the greatest instability and most excessive violence" (209). Mary Stripling, also concerned with masculine instabilities, offers Tamburlaine as a model of "how even a tyrant must wrest control of his family away from his children's mother"; the play would warn fathers "to be especially vigilant in maintaining dominion over the domestic sphere" (223) ("Tamburlaine's Domestic Threat"). Finally, in " 'I'll mar the young clerk's pen': Sodomy, Paternity and Circumcision in *The Merchant of Venice*," the late Douglas Brooks offers a lively account of the play's metaphoric conflation of maternity with the printing press as a mode of expressing anxieties about paternity.

It should be noted that while the often illuminating studies in this volume make noteworthy contributions to early modern scholarship, it is not entirely clear that they live up to the promise of performativity in the volume's title, nor that they take as much advantage of a true interdisciplinarity as that title might suggest. In their introduction, and taking their cue from Judith Butler, the editors describe the volume as arguing "that maternity—both public and private, physically embodied and enacted—must be considered performative and that the maternal body, as a result, functions as a potent space for cultural conflict, a site of imagination and context"; further, the collection features "essays that share a common concern with exploring maternity's cultural representation, performative aspects and practical consequences in the period from 1540 to 1690" (1–2). The introduction also promises "sustained attention to the nuances of social construction in . . . numerous dramatic, medical, autobiographical, polemical and literary texts," while claiming that the "freshness" of the collection's approach "lies in [its] consideration of maternity as explicitly performative" (3).

Although the essays certainly attend to the editors' broad cultural definition of "performative," they are curiously lacking in attention to the specifically theatrical senses of this term, that is, the difficulties of performing gender, not to mention maternity, within a cross-dressing tradition, and to the effects of early modern stage practices on conceptual models of maternity. Further, notwithstanding the fact that several of the essays make use of new archival materials, there is little engagement with some key medical texts, such as the discourse on midwifery, though there are references to well-known gynecological treatises. However, while these may be notable omissions, they don't seriously detract from the accomplishments of the collection as a whole.

A final caveat: in her review of the book, Mary Beth Rose cautioned that several of the essays perpetuate the misconception that Elizabeth I characterized herself as a mother.[2] As Rose notes, Elizabeth would have had little to gain from appropriating this title, given the anxieties and hazards associated with motherhood, particularly in the public arena.

Like the essays in the Moncrief and McPherson collection, Chris Laoutaris's copiously illustrated, erudite, and imaginative study, *Shakespearean Maternities,* introduces us to a rich variety—in fact, to a sizable range—of contemporary artifacts that informed the early modern discourse about maternity. These include anatomical reproductions, cabinets of curiosity, architectural follies, grottoes, archaeological finds, articles associated with witchcraft and superstition, natural historical specimens, "monsters," ceramics, portraits, and funerary statuary and monuments. Laoutaris explores four Shakespeare plays (in corresponding chapters) in conjunction with these materials: *Hamlet, The Tempest, Macbeth,* and *Antony and Cleopatra.*

He begins by asking how female reproductive biology was observed in a premodern culture that lacked the medicalized technologies of the male gaze that we have come to take for granted, concluding that the female reproductive body was encountered—or actually seen—only in crisis: that is, only when either a fetus was recovered or a maternal body was dissected could the womb be made available to direct male scrutiny. Most important, "The triumph of the biomedicalized body . . . has obscured the significance of those other disciplines which fostered alternative ways of knowing the maternal" (11); and it is those other ways of knowing that undergird this study and provide fascinating insights not only into Shakespeare's plays, but also into the larger cultural milieu.

Chapter 1, "Flesh and Stone: Dissecting Maternity in the Theater of Anatomy," explores the cultural connections between anatomical discovery and the "largely unacknowledged *satiric* [*sic*] impulse of early modern anatomy" (29), as seen in the works of Vesalius, Aretino, Titian, and others. Beginning in the early sixteenth century, the new anatomical knowledge, disseminated to a wider audience by the culture and epistemologies of dissection, was part of a broader insistence on verification by direct experience. As Laoutaris reads *Hamlet,* Shakespeare exploits the legacy of Aretino and Vesalius, particularly in its satiric emphasis, in portraying his protagonist's failure to find authoritative knowledge in the maternal body.

Chapter 2, "The Cabinet of Wonders: Monstrous Conceptions of the Theatre of Nature," argues that the language of wonder that informed descriptions of constructed grotto-spaces and cabinets of curiosity serves as a window into the treatment of the maternal body in *The Tempest.* The chapter opens with a lively and informative analysis of the Ovidian-inspired visual language of grottoes.

The appropriation of this language can be seen in descriptions of Somerset House, Woburn Abbey, Skipton Castle, and Hatfield House (among others), in observations about cabinets of curiosities, and in the emerging discourse of *scientia*. As one of the preeminent voices of the new epistemology, Bacon adapts this language to his own purposes, representing the earth as a nurturing mother whose secrets may be gainfully extracted by human means. Such a maternalized nature has monstrous capabilities; thus, in Bacon's rewriting of wonder, all reproductive processes, by implication, have a potentially monstrous outcome. Laoutaris concludes this chapter with a fresh look at Caliban through "the demands of primogeniture and the mechanisms which undergird the exploitation of natural resources in the New-World" (141).

Chapter 3, "Strange Labours: Maternity and *Maleficium* in the Theatre of Justice," offers an enlightening survey of the contemporary materials of magic and of countermagical measures, such as concealed magical artifacts like shoes and mummified cats found walled up in early modern houses. Most suspected witches in England were women, making it easy to associate witchcraft with maternity; thus, Laoutaris argues, witchcraft came to be seen as "an inverted or corrupted form of maternal nurture . . . Indeed English accounts of such devilish practices [i.e., practices that incorporate household objects and other elements of domestic culture] in particular dwell upon the near-maternal relation between the witch and her familiar" (163). Laoutaris traces further the "unique conjunction of demonology and skepticism" (199) to show how, in *Macbeth,* Macduff exemplifies "a parthenogenic mythos which defines itself against [the] . . . demonized maternity" (197) of Lady Macbeth and the three witches.

The final chapter, "Speaking Stones: Memory and Maternity in the Theatre of Death," takes up the opposition between entrenched and emerging modes of memorialization and the role of women in the changes taking place in commemorative practices. Laoutaris here examines more intimate rituals and monuments associated with women in contrast to the customary heraldic funeral procession and funerary display, focusing on the ways in which the vocabulary of maternal commemoration and a feminized discourse of mourning began to encroach on the traditional endorsement of primogeniture by the heraldic funeral. In Cleopatra's "nurturing" death—specifically, in her final "fantasy of blissful maternal embrace" (259) of the breast-feeding serpent-baby—Laoutaris sees a perhaps buried rejection of the heraldic tradition, and a "recapitulation" of the "good death" of the Renaissance mother, as illustrated in contemporary funerary monuments. The chapter—indeed, the entire book—is richly fleshed out with contemporary illustrations that provide a striking window into early modern experience and understanding.

Although *Shakespearean Maternities* offers genuinely fresh insights into early modern material culture, the connections that Laoutaris would make between material evidence and Shakespeare's plays are not, in some instances, altogether convincing. Still, this book, like the Moncrief/McPherson collection, is an important contribution to an emerging subfield in cultural criticism, directing the reader to a plethora of new primary sources and positioning the phenomenon of early modern maternity in a richly informed contemporary landscape.

Notes

1. See the earlier studies of Janet Adelman *Suffocating Mothers: Fantasies of Maternal Origin in Shakespeare's Plays; "Hamlet" to "The Tempest"* (New York: Routledge, 1992); Theresa M. Krier, *Birth Passages: Maternity and Nostalgia; Antiquity to Shakespeare* (Ithaca: Cornell University Press, 2001); Caroline Bicks, *Midwiving Subjects in Shakespeare's England* (Aldershot: Ashgate, 2003); and Laura Gowing, *Common Bodies: Women, Touch and Power in Seventeenth-Century England* (New Haven: Yale University Press, 2003), among others.

2. *Shakespeare Quarterly* 60, no. 2 (Summer 2009): 233–35.

Kenneth Burke, *Kenneth Burke on Shakespeare*
Edited by Scott L. Newstok
West Lafayette, Indiana: Parlor Press, 2008

Reviewer: David Mikics

Scott Newstok's *Kenneth Burke on Shakespeare* provides an extraordinary service. This volume collects all of Burke's known discussions of Shakespeare, from his peculiar and at times wonderful essays on *Othello, Julius Caesar, Coriolanus, Timon of Athens,* and *Antony and Cleopatra* to stray remarks made en passant in Burke's various books (Newstok has deftly assembled these passages in an appendix). *Kenneth Burke on Shakespeare* enables us to take a panoptic view of a significant critic. The book's blurbs by Harold Bloom, Stanley Cavell, Paul Alpers, Stephen Greenblatt, Patricia Parker, and William Pritchard—attest to Burke's influence among Shakespeareans.

What, then, did Burke contribute to Shakespeare studies? In contrast to Wilson Knight, who brilliantly explored the Shakespearean mythos, but at the expense of narrative structure, Burke joined mythos and structure, and attempted to show how they work together. In this he resembled Northrop Frye, a largely unacknowledged influence on Burke. But in contrast to Frye, Burke underlined the fact that Shakespeare's drama is an advanced instrument of persuasion, committed to addressing different segments of the audience in much the way that a politician addresses a crowd (thus the iconoclastic punch of Burke's deservedly famous "Antony in Behalf of the Play," first published in 1935).

The main presence in Burke's criticism is Aristotle, and Burke often wrestles with the Aristotelian question of the priority of plot over character. Like Aristotle (in the Chicago school reading), Burke argues that tragic plot functions by way of the audience's judgments about right and wrong action. But unlike Aristotle, he is also anthropologically oriented, and so emphasizes the audience's identification with the sacrificial victim. For the identification to work, the victim (the tragic hero) needs to be a fascinating character who recognizes and incorporates different aspects of the audience.

In order to explain this process, Burke turns to the study of rhetoric, with its overt appeal to the crowd. Often he finds a kinship between political manipulation and aesthetic response; though he sometimes acknowledges the difference between the two, he fails to grapple with the task of defining this difference.

Burke's double focus on plot and character leads to an interesting dilemma. Newstok reproduces Burke's comments on a Washington University graduate student's paper on *Troilus and Cressida* (a good example of how far this ingenious editor has dug): Burke tells the student, "You are tending to write glosses from the standpoint of sheer portraiture, thereby losing somewhat the stress upon dramaturgic function. The two realms of observation overlap considerably, hence all this is to the good" (169). The waffling here is deeply telling. From time to time Burke assails A. C. Bradley for being a character critic and thus neglecting the play's persuasive functioning or (in Aristotelian-Burkean jargon) "entelechy." (Bradley still stands pretty much untouched, as one might expect.) But Burke's own comments occasionally display a confusion about how character portrayal and dramatic logic intersect. In his stimulating essay on *Othello,* from 1951, Burke argues that Shakespeare (in a notoriously unconvincing move) makes Iago jealous of Emilia so that he can play off Iago against Othello: the latter's jealousy is noble, Iago's is ignoble. So Iago's jealousy functions structurally, rather than as an insight into his character. (Shakespeare, and Iago too, have barred the way to such insight, Burke implies—following Coleridge.) Yet in the course of this discussion, Burke concedes that "in our novel-minded age at least, the actor is helped in building up his role by such portraiture as Bradley aims at" (86). So Burke waffles again on the question of character and structure. Iago may only seem to be a limit-case in this respect: the actor's job could be to indicate how Shakespeare's Venetian villain, ever wily, slips out of the motives that he plays at having. But this, too, is a form of portraiture, and the audience studies the portrait.

In order to unravel this a bit further, we might consider an example not discussed by Burke: does Hamlet delay because he identifies with Claudius (Ernest Jones's argument, perhaps best refined by William Kerrigan in his *Hamlet's Perfection*), or is the identification demanded by the structure, and the symbolic logic, of the play? I suspect that Burke would have said that Shakespeare constructs a parallel between Hamlet and Claudius for symbolic reasons, and that Hamlet's identification, assuming that it is there, exists in order to make the parallel work, not to offer us knowledge about Hamlet's psyche. But this line of argument begs the question. Hamlet doesn't identify with his uncle just because Shakespeare makes him do so; his identification inevitably tempts us, driven toward the heart of his mystery, to psychoanalyze him. Add to this the fact that Hamlet, like Iago, is a character dedicated to shaping the play itself, and the mutual implication of plot and hero thickens still further. There is, to be sure, a kind of character criticism that fails to account for the structural dynamics of the play—but (as Burke seems to admit in his *Troilus and Cressida* remarks), when a critic does the job well, there's no reason why these two aspects need be in opposition.

In his ambivalence about portraiture and dramatic function, Burke seems to acknowledge that Aristotle can be turned on his head: structure also has its roots in character. In a superb essay on *Antony and Cleopatra,* Burke sensitively traces the dialogue between the imperial and the everyday that is at the heart of the play. The poor worm, Cleopatra murmurs, is the "baby at my breast / That sucks the nurse asleep" (5.2.300–301)—and, Burke sublimely remarks, "Here all the Mediterranean grandeurs are swept away in a flash" (119). But, as Burke seems to grant, the play's opposition (and then paradoxical equation) between world-claiming grandeur and ordinary existence would mean little if it were not incarnated in the triumphant beings we see onstage. In a case like this, how is it possible to decide between the hero and the play?

Burke frequently tempts us to think we can choose structural myth over character, so that we won't be tricked by our sympathy for Shakespeare's heroes, but instead remain alert to how Shakespeare uses them to manipulate us. The tragic protagonist becomes a sacrifice brought forward to appease us; we can renounce and embrace him at once, and therefore go away reinforced in our biases (until the critic steps forward to instruct us in the hidden Shakespearean mechanisms that control our responses). The ostensible hardheadedness of this line bears a resemblance to the ideological decoding fashionable in the 1930s and '40s, and again today; but Burke wears a more genial face than the Marxist or Foucauldian one. He seems uncertain as to whether the tragic process just described is an exhilarating or a sinister phenomenon—and this uncertainty suggests the generosity of his critical spirit. Burke loves these plays, and he wants us to love them too; but he remains touched by a suspicion that Shakespeare's greatness required him to dominate the minds and emotions of his audience. This ambivalence, too, can be fruitful, like so much else in Burke. Yet his aggressively demystifying turns sometimes raise the reader's eyebrow, rather than her interest (eloquence, he writes at one point, is "the result of that desire in the artist to make a work perfect by adapting it in every minute detail to the racial appetites" [30]).

When Burke ventriloquizes Shakespeare's characters, he once or twice spins off the path altogether. In a 1933 reading of *Twelfth Night* that seems determined to outdo Empson (the latest sensation), Burke makes Orsino say, in his opening speech, "You cannot take my gloom to mean that I am, in that which concerns me, without a future, as there is not one single member of this entire audience that is without a future (without an image of something like that which is, in the sixteenth century, vaguely deemed available in America)" (35). Throughout his career, Burke was capable of such unconvincing large-scale gestures, but he seems to have been particularly reckless early on. Two years later, in the essay on *Julius Caesar,* Burke is much more persuasive, though this too has its odd moments (Brutus, we are told, "takes on the nobility that comes of being good for private enterprise" [42]).

Burke is at his best in his most familiar essays: "*Coriolanus*—and the Delights of Faction," "*Othello:* An Essay to Illustrate a Method," and "Antony in Behalf of the Play." "Shakespearean Persuasion: *Antony and Cleopatra,*" which I have also mentioned, is less famous, but equally worthwhile. Other parts of the book present something of a problem. The earliest essays seem tentative and rather wobbly to me; and the ones from the 1970s on give evidence of an unfortunate period of decline, no doubt connected to Burke's increasing ill health. The two latest essays in the book, on *Midsummer Night's Dream* and *Macbeth,* do not make for pleasant reading. When Burke begins, unprompted and at some length, to rant against "our current vulgarians" in his *Macbeth* essay (206), the reader feels like looking away from the disturbing spectacle of an eloquence turned bitter and unbalanced. (In a fine essay from the sixties on *Timon of Athens,* Burke speaks for the worth of invective, as he does in his *Coriolanus* discussion; but invective tended to be a mark of weakness, rather than strength, in Burke himself.) We return with appreciation, and relief, to Burke's central essays on Shakespeare, presented by Newstok with such great scholarly care.

Locating Privacy in Tudor London
By Lena Cowen Orlin
Oxford: Oxford University Press, 2007

Reviewer: Catherine Belsey

Lena Cowen Orlin has written a truly remarkable book. In the first place, the rich, dense scholarship of *Locating Privacy in Tudor London* radically alters our understanding of social relations in the early modern period; and in the second, the case is elegantly and enticingly made. How, Orlin asks, can we recover the nature of everyday life in the early modern period, not least if we are to do this without effacing differences of class and gender? More specifically, what can we tell about the value placed on privacy at this time? In answer, she brilliantly interweaves the story of Alice Barnham, wife of a mid-sixteenth-century London merchant and a businesswoman in her own right, with legal and municipal records, surviving buildings and ground plans, as well as contemporary images, all analyzed in detail to tell a brand-new story—or two. A portrait of Alice Barnham, reproduced in this generously illustrated book, constitutes the enigma that the volume as a whole gradually deciphers, perfectly uniting instruction with pleasure.

The argument itself delivers a radical challenge to current assumptions about the rise of privacy as a social value. Starting from the personal records, a handful of diaries, autobiographical writings, and commonplace books, social and cultural historians have hitherto concurred in assuming that the extensive domestic rebuilding undertaken in Elizabethan England was designed to provide an increase in the space allotted to the private life of the individual. The widespread move out of the shared area of the medieval hall and into a range of chambers, parlors, and studies, permitted, so the story went, a corresponding multiplication of places to develop the consciousness of self. Drawing on quite different resources, *Locating Privacy,* by contrast, demonstrates—and the evidence Orlin produces seems to me irrefutable—that the expansion of domestic spaces was driven far more by the increasing consumption of luxuries. The life of the "middling sort," as of the aristocracy, was conducted to a high degree in public, and these new rooms were first and foremost places of display. Studies or "closets" were designed in the first instance not so much for solitary reflection and the cultivation of interiority as to secure valuable possessions under lock and key.

Personal privacy, in other words, was not yet nearly as highly valued as we have supposed. Indeed, it was more commonly suspect. Ironically, it was the corporations that retreated into ever-diminishing spaces, as their governance grew more oligarchic and more secretive, to the despair of their members. At home it was hard to find a place to be alone. This was a world of eavesdropping, voyeurism, and surveillance, conducted in the name of social order. The records of the courts show that the most intimate domestic relations were open to observation, deliberate or accidental, by neighbors, whether well intentioned or malicious. The difficulty was to find a place for confidential exchanges. In grand households, long galleries designed for walking in bad weather turned out to have the additional advantage that sound did not carry from one end to another, and auditors would be visible before they could overhear. In consequence, long galleries came to be distrusted as much as they were desired.

The story of Alice Barnham, meanwhile, confutes any easy assumption that women were as subjugated in practice as official culture longed to suppose and some well-meaning feminist criticism has led us to believe. Alice Barnham is effectively Orlin's discovery, renamed on the basis of the evidence from a painting traditionally and inaccurately known as *Lady Ingram and Her Two Boys*. She was the wife of an upwardly mobile merchant whose story offers a window onto the life and times of the city fathers and their families. Financial success went hand in hand with civic eminence. Francis Barnham rose to be master of the Drapers' Company and then sheriff of London. He held a range of positions in the city as hospital governor and alderman, offices he seems to have executed with a view to making power serve the profit motive. Such was his entrepreneurial success that his two surviving sons became country gentlemen. This was not achieved single-handed, however. Alice herself made her own contribution to the family's wealth. Not only was she an active partner in her husband's business activities, holding the fort in his frequent absences, but she also had commercial interests of her own, dealing in silk trimmings, such as ribbons, fringes, and tassels. Alice Barnham was probably one of the last of the silkwomen in a profession that at the time was increasingly dominated by men. As a retailer in her own right, she was able to play an independent part in her husband's deals when the couple shifted resources between one enterprise and another. After Francis died, his apprentices worked out their term with Alice, and she went on to bind apprentices in her own name thereafter. Samples of her wares appear in her portrait, which shows, Orlin points out, a woman thinking as she looks up from her writing. The moment is apparently educational for her two sons; the legible words on the paper are devotional; her reflections, however, remain her own.

Locating Privacy is historicist in the best sense. Although this is primarily a work of cultural history, not polemic, there is no joy here for residual proponents of universal human nature or eternal individualism. While there were continuities with our own values—this was an inaugural moment for immense fortunes built on merchandise, not to mention doubtful financial deals and speculation in property—early modern culture was different from ours with regard to the book's central theme. Although we can never know their thoughts, the documentary and material evidence indicates that these people looked out at the world first, apparently more concerned with the face they presented to others, and perhaps to God, than with the inner recesses of personal consciousness.

If there is plenty of "thick description," Orlin's practice of history is a long way from the prevailing New Historicist orthodoxy. Not for her the eccentric anecdote made to stand as the metonym of a whole society's values. On the contrary, she has sifted great volumes of material in order to uncover lives that reveal much about the common attitudes and practices of London citizens at this time. Sadly, however, I doubt whether she will found a school: acolytes would have to be unusually diligent and exceptionally rigorous, as well as highly intelligent and ready to think for themselves. In any case, the sheer amount of inquiry and organization involved is sure to deter facile imitation. But the detailed case Orlin makes and her patient, meticulous work in the archive guarantee that this book will change the existing paradigm, modifying our sense of the period in ways future historians of culture will be obliged to take into account.

Staging Shakespeare: Essays in Honor of Alan C. Dessen
Edited by Lena Cowen Orlin and Miranda Johnson-Haddad
Newark: University of Delaware Press, 2007

Reviewer: Virginia Mason Vaughan

Festschrifts are not as common as they used to be, partly because of the expense involved but also because magisterial status—marked by innovative yet enduring scholarship, not simply longevity—is more difficult to attain in the burgeoning field of Shakespeare studies. The scholar honored in *Staging Shakespeare* is very much alive and kicking, so it is an even greater tribute to him to receive a festschrift at this stage of his career. The anthology pays tribute to the pioneering work of Alan C. Dessen, whose insights into the theatrical vocabulary of early modern play scripts have influenced the work of an entire generation. Like the scholar they honor, the contributors to this anthology share a broad interest in theatrical practices; their essays range from the interpretation of early modern stage directions, to analysis of recent filmic representations, to studies of contemporary intercultural and intermedial appropriations of Shakespeare's plays. As the editors explain, the fourteen contributors participated in a yearlong National Endowment for the Humanities (NEH) seminar that Dessen directed with theater practitioner Audrey Stanley at the Folger Shakespeare Library in 1995–96 on "Shakespeare Examined through Performance." That seminar bridged the usual divide between theater professionals and literary critics, bringing both sides together for an exploration of the dynamics of performance. Most of the essays reference specific ideas or terminology taken from the Dessen opus, particularly his low-key insistence that we recognize the limitations on what we can know and what we can't know. That *Staging Shakespeare* opens with a tribute from actor Patrick Stewart demonstrates that Dessen's work has influenced actors and directors, not just academics. Taken as a whole, *Staging Shakespeare* is an impressive testimonial to a beloved teacher and scholar.

But, as often happens with anthologies, the whole is greater than the sum of the parts. While the essays collected here raise some intriguing questions, their focus perforce is specific, geared to each writer's idiosyncratic interests. The editors have attempted to provide coherence by dividing the essays into four categories that serve much like grocery bags—vegetables here, cereals here, and so on. It is up to the reader to make connections between the essays and put together a meal from the ingredients provided.

After a short introduction that pays tribute to Dessen's oeuvre and career, the collection begins with a section called "Acts of Recovery," which includes three essays that probe specific aspects of early modern staging. Dessen's collaborator on *A Dictionary of Stage Directions in English Drama, 1580–1642,* Leslie Thomson, begins with a trenchant rebuttal of Allardyce Nicoll's explanation of the stage direction, *"Pass over the stage."* Nicoll posited that this cryptic line indicated that the actors were to enter from the yard, ascend to the stage and walk over it, then descend and walk out again through the yard. As Thomson notes, up to a quarter of extant plays employ such a stage direction, so this is no small matter. She then demolishes Nicoll's analysis step-by-step. Combining historical evidence with the sort of common sense that tells us sometimes a cigar is just a cigar, Thomson concludes that the stage direction means what it says: the actors entered, "moved across the stage, and exited" (35). Thomson's no-nonsense approach is just what we would expect of someone who worked at Dessen's side on a major project.

The second essay, Daniel L. Colvin's "Rediscovering the Self: Hal and the Psychology of Disguise," relates Hal's dress, particularly during the Gadshill robbery, to the popular tradition of morality plays where a change of costume signified a shift in moral character. He concludes that attention to the play's roots in the morality tradition mitigates the seeming contradiction between providentialism and Machiavellianism in Hal's "I know you all" soliloquy. Ellen Summers follows with a study of Shakespeare's doubling practices, arguing forcefully that the employment of the same actor in two different roles was guided by a conceptual framework as well as by practical considerations. She also poses a series of questions to use when trying to determine what roles might have been doubled in any particular play.

Section 2, "Performing the Moment," seems indistinct from section 1 because it also focuses on the interpretation of early modern staging. Like Summers, Eric Binnie is concerned with pedagogy: he offers blocking exercises that will help theater students understand how the primary text maps its own performance as he considers the practical challenges of "Getting Richard Down" in *Richard II*'s Flint Castle scene. Edward Isser defends the performance choice he made when he directed *The Tempest* at the College of the Holy Cross in 2002. I attended that production and remember the consternation many of us felt at the play's finale when Caliban exited to join the Europeans on a ship, ostensibly headed back to Italy. Isser explains that the Folio's stage direction *Exeunt omnes* before the epilogue is, to use Dessen's term, permissive. Isser wanted to underscore the play's magical and romantic qualities, and one way to do this was to include Caliban in the newly formed society. Given the Folio's vagueness, Isser's choice is not a matter of right or wrong, but simply choice.

Cary M. Mazer's "The Intentional-Fallacy Fallacy," the collection's most theoretical essay, reminds us that despite Dessen's and others' efforts to bring together those who work in the theater with those who teach and write about it, literary and theatrical approaches to early modern texts can differ profoundly. Mazer observes that since the ascent of New Criticism, literary critics have designated the attempt to discern the author's original intention as the "intentional fallacy." In contrast, stage-centered scholars want to understand what the dramatist envisioned. Mazer works his way around this contradiction by citing a difference between dramatic content and theatrical materials; while the contents of the dramatist's intentions can't be known, his craftsmanship in working with theatrical materials can be discerned. One might add that while the extensive study of stage directions and promptbooks can suggest some standard practices, it is much more difficult to discover if and when a dramatist innovated.

Section 3, "Recordings," hangs together better as a section because each of its three essays discusses a major filmic adaptation. Edward L. Rocklin begins with a comprehensive examination of Richard Burton's Hamlet in a production directed by John Gielgud in 1964. This *Hamlet* is uniquely postmodern in its many iterations, first as a stage play (with variations throughout the run), then later as a film, as an audio recording by the actors from the stage play, and finally as reconstructed in Richard L. Sterne's 1967 book, *John Gielgud Directs Richard Burton in "Hamlet."* Although Rocklin doesn't address the issue, his detailed analysis raises the question as to whether reviewers and theater historians can ever really capture the quixotic dynamics of performance, especially one by an actor as volatile as Burton.

Michael D. Friedman turns to Julie Taymor's *Titus,* particularly her use of young Lucius as a framing device throughout the film. He argues that although she never acknowledged it, Taymor was influenced by Jane Howell's 1985 BBC TV production of *Titus Andronicus,* as well as Adrian Noble's 1994 Royal Shakespeare Company production of *A Midsummer Night's Dream* (released on film in 1996). Both films, he argues, inspired Taymor to use Osheen Jones's young Lucius as a framing device that guided the audience toward a particular emotional response to the action. Caroline Mc-Manus's analysis of the relationship between the female characters and the fool in Trevor Nunn's 1996 film of *Twelfth Night* offers similar insights into the use of Ben Kingsley's Feste as a framing device. Visible from Viola's arrival in Illyria to the final credits, Feste knows Viola's true identity and serves in some ways as a surrogate author, casting the film's entire narrative as his fiction (194). Put together, Friedman's and McManus's essays suggest questions about the impact of filmic Shakespeare, which so often imposes a point of view on the audience rather than allowing the viewer's gaze to fall where it may—as stage productions must.

Staging Shakespeare's final section, "Extensions and Explorations," takes the discussion from traditional stage performances to alternative media. Lisa J. McDonnell suggests the complicated dynamics of intercultural Shakespeare in her description of Hsing-lin Chung's production of Shakespeare's *Taming of the Shrew* in the mode of Jingju, known popularly as Beijing opera. Sheila Cavanaugh moves to intermedial Shakespeare in her discussion of two puppet-show versions of *Macbeth,* which, she contends, proffer insights into the popular impact of Shakespeare's original by highlighting the underlying comic elements usually ignored in straight theatrical productions. Then, in a return to the kind of astute historical analysis that opens this collection, Lois Potter teases out the relationship between early modern oratory and dramatic representation in *Julius Caesar.* Potter shows that treatises on elocution and oratory from the early modern period to the nineteenth century can suggest how the funeral orations would have been staged. The anthology's final essay is Audrey Stanley's "Postscript for Alan Dessen," which recalls their work together conducting the NEH Institute.

Although one wishes that some greater effort had been made to consider these essays in relationship to each other and to underscore their common themes and challenges, *Staging Shakespeare* offers multiple perspectives on the ways early modern plays, particularly Shakespeare's, work in performance from the early modern period to the present. The contributors and editors are to be congratulated for producing a wide-ranging and lively contribution to Shakespeare studies that is also a moving tribute to Alan Dessen.

Engines of the Imagination: Renaissance Culture and the Rise of the Machine
By Jonathan Sawday
New York: Routledge, 2007

Reviewer: Henry S. Turner

Jonathan Sawday has written a sweeping and engaging book about machines in the early modern period, approaching the topic as an exercise in cultural history and addressing a broad audience of both specialists and nonspecialists. The topic is welcome and overdue. Despite a growing interest in the history of science among literary scholars, on the one hand, and the explosion of innovative scholarship among historians of science themselves over the last two decades, on the other—the recent early modern volume in the Cambridge History of Science series, edited by Katherine Park and Lorraine Daston (2006) is a garden of eloquence on the topic, crowded with fascinating specimens of current work—there are surprisingly few books squarely on the problem of machines from the fifteenth to the seventeenth centuries. One of the best treatments, Horst Bredekamp's *The Lure of Antiquity and the Cult of the Machine* (1993; English trans., 1995), focuses primarily on changing notions of history and natural history in the Kunstkammer, locating the machine within a spectrum of collected objects that facilitated a newly empirical approach to the production of natural knowledge and that troubled distinctions between art and nature. As in Bredekamp's earlier work, one of the virtues of Sawday's study is to show that the distinction between art and nature was never quite as categorical as we are sometimes taught. From the classical period through medieval Scholasticism to the work of a figure such as Bacon and beyond, art "imitates" nature, corrects and remedies nature, serves as a "shortcut" to the inefficiencies of nature (as John of Salisbury put it in his twelfth-century *Metalogicon*). The fascination of the machine lies in no small measure in its hybrid quality, in its analytic, revelatory capacity to model natural processes, to intervene in them at the same time that it also departs from them or supersedes them. Despite the obvious differences between Sawday's book and Bredekamp's—in audience, in scope, in disciplinary affiliation—*Engines of the Imagination* is very much in the spirit of *The Lure of Antiquity* and will inevitably be compared with it.

Over the course of eight chapters, supplemented by thirty illustrations, Sawday's aim is to examine machines partly as a distinct intellectual preoccupation for writers across early modern Europe and partly as a newly common physical apparatus that populated the landscape of everyday life. As he conducts the reader through a network of fascinating examples, Sawday shows how the machine was a profoundly overdetermined object for early moderns: a sign of human prowess over nature but also an indication of nature's own cycles and order; an allusion to ancient wisdom as well as an echo of biblical slavery (18). The machine was a bridge between remote sacred time and contemporary, everyday experience, reminding the viewer that the ingenuity he saw around him was a "promise of restitution" (15) as much as a sign of his fallen state. Sawday handles these types of large narratives well; he has an impressive ability to synthesize his material and shifts easily across the many scales of his argument. As it moves from sixteenth-century Renaissance painting to the obelisk at St. Peter's, from the early modern theater to the laboratories of Robert Hooke, from Chaucer's Miller to Milton's Pandemonium, *Engines of the Imagination* vividly renders the peculiar, nonmodern aspects of machines: their theological associations, the sense of wonder they provoked, the ingenuity necessary to compose them, their "formalism," their prestige and complexity—their copiousness, in a word, as well as their sometime utility. In this sense, Sawday takes a valuable cue from Jessica Wolfe's *Humanism, Machinery and Renais-*

sance Literature (2004), which locates the machine in a humanist culture that was discovering the virtues and pitfalls of instrumentality in its many varieties. And his account is similar in many respects to Hélène Vérin's masterful *La gloire des ingénieurs* (Albin Michel, 1993), perhaps the best recent study of the mechanical arts in the period and a regrettable absence here. But Sawday has canvassed the field widely and provides a very full set of citations; if these are sometimes idiosyncratically chosen, with a slight emphasis on the history of technology, they are useful and often accompanied by brief and welcome contextualization—Sawday uses the endnote more effectively than many writers do. His chapters are studded with valuable historical and biographical information, and he has a keen eye for the telling detail. This makes for an exciting reading experience; the book wears its considerable learning lightly and constantly offers up penetrating insights.

Marx's writing about the machine and the history of industrialization has exerted a strong influence on the way that Sawday has conceptualized his topic, so that the nature of labor and its transformation by mechanical devices becomes one of the book's main guiding threads. The problem is an important one, but in places it pulls too strongly toward categories and phenomena that are typical of a later period, and it can sometimes lead Sawday to force his evidence. In one of the book's most interesting and original sections, he describes Agricola's *De Re Metallica* as a "technical instruction 'manual' or 'handbook'" (88), but Agricola's book famously isn't a blueprint for construction or even really a guide to use. Many of the devices are difficult to analyze in mechanical terms and may not even have functioned as pictured (as Sawday himself points out). There were many handbooks for the practical arts during the period, but they had very different formats and exposition. I would myself describe Agricola's book as a demonstration piece, an "oration" about mechanisms in visual form: the part is more significant than the whole, and the book engages simultaneously in a spectacular display of both *inventio* and *dispositio* by composing new assemblages of parts suitable to different hypothetical situations. In pointing to the human figures that populate Agricola's images, Sawday makes an intriguing and legitimate point: something *is* happening in the way productive human activity is represented in comparison to mechanized devices. I was glad to be reminded of the intricacy of Agricola's descriptions, his quasi-realism, his almost stroboscopic analysis of mechanical action as a human-machine assemblage—Latour would find in Agricola a fascinating example of "translation." But the Marxist framework drew a somewhat predictable interpretative horizon around the material; Sawday is an alert and very informed reader of this strange genre, and the more he distanced himself from the Marxist premise, the less restricted he seemed to me to become in his inventiveness and originality, qualities that are abundantly on display throughout *Engines of the Imagination* as a whole.

The benefit of *Engines of the Imagination* is clear, therefore: a multitude of evidence, gathered in one place and often illuminated by highly original commentary, across many different varieties, from tiny devices to theological accounts of the Fall, from public waterworks in Italy to mechanical splendor at the Stuart court, from mechanical insects to *Leviathan*. Sawday moves easily from canonical to quotidian examples; he has readings or brief discussions of all the major English authors of the period and many others besides: Shakespeare, Spenser, Milton, Donne, Bacon, Dekker, Greene, and Jonson, not to mention major sections on Leonardo, Montaigne, the Italian engineer Domenico Fontana, and Robert Hooke. Within the broad umbrella of his topic, Sawday has a number of smaller problems he wants to cover: the importance of anatomy, printing and book history, the centrality of water as a resource, Freud's theory of the machine as compensatory device, seventeenth-century instrumentation and calculating devices, and transformations in the philosophy of mechanics, among many others. This diversity produces a certain tension in the book's organizational schema. *Engines of the Imagination* originated as a BBC Radio feature, and its structure reflects this: section headings don't always contribute substantially to the conceptual architecture of the book but punctuate what is a more-or-less continuous presentation that likes to follow its own nose. On the page, the pace of exposition can be dizzying and the shifts in direction abrupt. Chapter 4, on gender and machines, for instance, opens with an extended analysis of Rosie the Riveter, moves to seventeenth-century paintings of women's work—Rockwell's iconic image is presented as the modern equivalent of spinning scenes by Velásquez—touches on the myth of Aracne as it appears in Spenser, returns to Freud, meditates on the symbol of the wheel, shifts to the legend of St. Catherine, martyred on a "Catherine wheel" studded with saws and nails, then invokes Boethius's Wheel of Fortune before shifting to *King Lear*, the TV game show "Wheel of Fortune," and *Coriolanus*. Overall the chapter seems somewhat dutiful and out-of-place, interrupting a continuous exposition from books of machines (chapter 3) to the larger problems surrounding artifice in the period (chapter 5), where Sawday gathers an especially rich array of literary examples.

The final effect of all this profusion will depend on the reader. Undergraduates will love the enthusiasm, eclecticism, and witty juxtapositions of the book. Graduate students will be grateful for all the work that Sawday has done to collect the important evidence and bibliography, and some will be relieved by the inventiveness and freedom of his style. Sawday may even help them leap into their own enthusiasms, which would be a very good thing indeed. That mythical creature fabled by all publishers—the educated general reader—will remember the colorful details and the broad strokes of the argument; attentive ones will never look at a machine in the same way again.

So far, something for everyone. But specialists are liable to come away feeling a little unsatisfied. Here, too, much depends on temperament: I like the boldly conceived, propulsive energy of the book, even if it comes at the expense of precision and density. I admire the wide range of reading that Sawday has undertaken and the massive act of synthesis that was necessary to consolidate it. I was brought up short a few times by generalizations that arrive without enough discussion of evidence and that glossed over distinctions that seemed important. The quick survey of sixteenth-century paintings of mines and miners in chapter 1, for instance, is welcome—I didn't realize the subject was so established—but leaves me wondering just how, exactly, the paintings show an "optimistic" affirmation of machines and human labor (the reading of Brueghel's *Hunters in the Snow* seems especially underdeveloped, a first idea rather than a real conclusion). Is it really accurate to call Herri met de Bles's *The Copper Mine* (ca. 1540) "the aesthetic equivalent of a more obviously technological work" (7) such as Agricola's *De Re Metallica?* Aren't the differences between these two works an important part of the story Sawday wants to tell? Why not supply the passage from Montaigne's "Of the Education of Children," which seems to recall hydraulic machines? Without these types of careful links, the evocative, textured evidence of Montaigne's travel diary risks becoming extraneous, as diverting as the machines he enjoyed watching but not as useful. Echoes of Lucretius in aphorisms about movement aren't necessarily related to ideas about machines; arguments about links between technologi-

cal change and social and religious change (as on 55), are too broad
to be helpful.

At other points, Sawday's claims can feel a little too speculative
or ruminative, as though the associative style of the lecture hall had
momentarily spilled into the book. Very occasionally this produces
distortion. Sawday alights on the moment in *As You Like It,* when
Jaques mocks the clown Touchstone for consulting a "dial" to tell
the time and then segues into an engaging discussion of watches
and precise time-telling as a marker of social prestige in Shakespeare's period. This may be a perfectly true generalization—it is
hard to evaluate in context—and the imagery of time in the play is
certainly notable. But it isn't entirely accurate to define the "dial"
as a watch, specifically: Touchstone probably doesn't pull an intricate mechanical timepiece from his pocket but rather a sundial or
rudimentary navigational instrument. These types of practical devices did have a rich set of associations, partly social and partly
astrological—like their cousin the almanac   that seem more pertinent to Shakespeare's characterization of a rustic clown than the
broad notion of "owning" time and urban sophistication that Sawday proposes.

For me, the most successful aspect of *Engines of the Imagination*
is its tactfulness regarding the problem of *defining* machines: Sawday explicitly resists offering a normative definition, and in the end
he seems very right to have done so. For the machine is, in the Renaissance as today, perhaps undefinable according to normal conceptual parameters. Writers like Latour or Deleuze would find in
the machine an example par excellence of the inevitable poverty of
definitions, of their severe constriction and inevitable mutation.
Over the course of his book, Sawday does a terrific job of letting a
rich, composite, often contradictory picture of machines emerge
out of the period. He isn't afraid to think conceptually and to har-
ness the essential creativity of interpretation to poke and prod at
big ideas. He can be a very good close reader; at the same time, he
can turn around gracefully and succinctly locate a familiar work in
the unfamiliar tradition he's describing—the discussion of *Paradise Lost* in chapter 7 is a good example, where the (shorter) chapter benefits from a stronger extrinsic organizing principle
(discussion of a major work by a major author). To my mind, chapters 3 and 5 are the most satisfying, since here Sawday achieves an
unusual balance between speculative thinking and concrete argument, a mixture of density in material leavened by abstraction.

Those of us who like to write and to *think* about machines in the early modern period owe him a significant debt for having written his book.

Used Books: Marking Readers in Renaissance England
By William Sherman
Philadelphia: University of Pennsylvania Press, 2008

Reviewer: Marcy L. North

In this eloquent contribution to the history of reading, William Sherman situates the practice of marking in books within the larger field of book history, and he utilizes the handwritten marginalia and annotations in early print editions to discuss broadly the conditions, habits, and perceptions of book use in early modern England. The breadth Sherman achieves in *Used Books* comes with its own challenges. Early modern readers studied books with objectives that are mostly lost to modern scholars. Their active and goal-oriented reading, the selecting, gathering, synthesizing, and responding that characterized it, and the civic contributions that it produced do not have ready equivalents today. Sherman works to bridge the difference between early and modern readers and to show us that, for the most part, the active readers of Tudor-Stuart England who filled their margins with glosses and notation embraced a surprisingly conventional set of reading practices.

The anonymity of most early readers and the idiosyncrasies of the few who have been identified also make generalizations about early reading difficult. Sherman overcomes this challenge by assembling an impressive amount of data on book use, against which he analyzes some of the more prolific markers of books, among them, John Dee and Sir Julius Caesar. He moves deftly from the articulation of large patterns to colorful anecdotes that reveal the agency of known readers. The exceptional readers he discusses prove to be apt examples of larger reading patterns, even when they perform in excess what the average reader was doing in moderation. If, as Sherman has determined, more than 20 percent of the Huntington Library's collection of early modern editions contain substantial marginal annotation (5), and if many well-used books have been used to death, leaving us with a false sample of pristine copies, then the practice of writing and marking in books must have been widespread and, to some extent, conventionalized. By no means was marking in books a marginal activity.

Sherman's preface leads us into the world of the early reader and provides us with a method for finding patterns in the particulars. His introduction, then, sketches out the variety of marginalia that appear in early printed books (from recipes and accounts to learned commentary) and the terminology scholars have used to describe the handwritten marks on the printed page. These two short sections reveal that the subfield of reader history that focuses on marginal annotation is still inchoate. The very material being studied and the terms used to describe it remain subjects of debate. Sherman's book brings some much-needed coherence to this subfield, but at the same time embraces the variety and peculiarity of marginal marks.

The central chapters of *Used Books* are divided into four sections, exploring, first, the practices and methods employed by early readers to organize and record information; second, the reading of religious texts; third, two exceptional scholars whose marginal annotations signaled their active participation in civic life; and fourth, the treatment of "used" books in the recent histories of the rare book trade and library archiving. These four sections together offer modern readers a very rich picture of early reading practices, though Sherman does not always articulate the connections between the sections.

After the introduction, in chapter 2 Sherman turns to traditions of symbolic annotation in books, particularly the use of the manicule, a fist with a pointed index finger that calls attention to important passages, indexes, selects, and takes control of the text. A brief history of the pointing hand reveals that, in the first two centuries of print, hand-drawn manicules could be quite distinctive and playful. Sherman sees the manicule not simply as a pointing device, but as a reminder that early modern learning, reading, and information management involved the body and especially the hand

(48). The manicule is a gesture more than a marker, and it maintains a distinctiveness that even early handwriting does not, thus helping the reader to personalize the printed page and make it his own.

In chapter 3, "Reading the Matriarchive," Sherman observes that the traditional organization of the archives has obscured the contributions of women readers and book owners. To demonstrate early women's active participation in textual culture, he examines several printed books in which the margins and blank leaves serve as domestic archives for women. He then turns to some of the women known as readers and book owners to assess their accomplishments as archivists, with special attention to Lady Ann Clifford.

Chapters 4 and 5 detail the early modern uses of religious texts and the signs of that use—the annotations, family records, and scribbles in Bibles, and the remaking and personalizing of a common liturgy. Sherman demonstrates in chapter 4 that the active reading of scripture, with pen in hand, was not forbidden but encouraged in early modern England. Didactic literature was full of advice on how to make use of the margins in printed Bibles. In chapter 5, Sherman turns from ordinary to extraordinary reading practices to discuss the unusual production of a handwritten, ornate copy of the Book of Common Prayer, dating from the middle of the sixteenth century and now housed in the Huntington Library. This manuscript is unusual, not only because someone put an exceptional amount of work into copying a text that was available in print, but also because the act of copying it made unique and personal what was intended to be a common and public text. Sherman also uses it as an example of the way early modern reading practices integrated manuscript and print; the copyist imitates many print conventions, including woodcuts, in decorating the text, and he recycles ornate medieval initials, pasting them into the Book of Common Prayer. Sherman speculates that this book may have been produced for a woman reader.

Chapters 6 and 7 examine closely the reading practices of two prolific and learned early modern scholars, John Dee and Sir Julius Caesar. In Dee's extensive annotation of travel and navigational literature, in particular a text on Columbus's life and voyages, Sherman finds Dee reading for the practical application of this knowledge; Dee was an advisor to explorer Martin Frobisher (114). The marginalia in the *Life of Columbus* depict Dee as a more pragmatic and less esoteric scholar. Sir Julius Caesar adopts for his own use the commonplace book that John Foxe devised and printed in 1572, and he turns it into an encyclopedia of incredible breadth. Caesar's additions overwhelm Foxe's blank pages and commonplace headings, and the resulting artifact, now at the British Library, is neither manuscript nor printed book. Caesar's legal training is visible in his reading and glossing practices, and his note taking comes to exemplify, for Sherman, a type of discontinuous reading that resulted, interestingly, in the interconnection of ideas.

The final section of the book poses explicitly a question that other chapters have touched on: should the marks in a book be read as the valuable traces of early readership or as the defacement of an archival treasure? The answer often depends on the identity of the reader who has made the marks, the dating of the marks, and the uses to which the book is now put. A famous owner's signature adds worth in a way that an unknown student's underlining does not, especially if the student is a late reader. Although books in mint condition continue to be prized by many book dealers and collectors, certain collectors have come to appreciate the information scrawled in the margins, especially when they are trying to assemble a historically important library such as Francis Bacon's. Still, rare book librarians are unlikely to allow pens in reading rooms anytime soon, and Sherman's final chapter is a stark reminder of how much book use has changed since the early modern period.

These chapter summaries do not do justice to the fascinating paradoxes of early modern book use that Sherman puzzles over and, in some cases, embraces. In chapter 8 on "dirty books" and throughout the study, Sherman acknowledges the fine line between the use and abuse of a book. It is the unused and unread book that has the best chance of surviving the centuries and that, today, is worth the most to rare book dealers. Conversely, some of the best-loved and used books have not survived at all (6). Sherman likewise grapples with the irony that it is the uncommon, the prolific, and the distinctive marks in books that catch our eye and that have earned scholarly attention, even though the less conspicuous marks might come closer to representing common reading practices. One paradox pulls together all of the chapters in this invaluable study, however. Sherman's book addresses a modern generation of more passive, hurried, and often careless readers and introduces them to the active, physically demanding, and civically applicable reading practices of the sixteenth- and seventeenth-centuries. Sherman does not present these paradoxes as interesting asides; they are at the core of his study, and these paradoxes, even more than the intriguing anecdotes and the impressive evidentiary base of this study, will bring the modern reader back to this book for a more active second read.

At the beginning of chapter 7, Sherman articulates the complexity and the value of his own project with a compelling metaphor: "To study readers' notes is to work at the fringe of the tapestries that weave together books, lives, and events. Most of the threads now come away as single strands, providing us with glimpses of color or texture and the agents who produced them but with little sense of the larger patterns and bigger picture to which they once belonged" (127). I would argue that *Used Books* succeeds in showing us some of the larger patterns and pictures that these threads once created. The pictures in the tapestries are far from complete, but the figure of the early modern active reader and marker of texts is beginning to take shape within them.

Remapping the Mediterranean World in Early Modern English Writings
Edited by Goran V. Stanivukovic
New York: Palgrave Macmillan, 2007
and
Speaking of the Moor: From Alcazar *to* Othello
By Emily C. Bartels
Philadelphia: University of
Pennsylvania Press, 2008

Reviewer: Ania Loomba

These two volumes seek to comment on early modern English culture, as well as global relations of this period, by examining English representations of the Mediterranean and Africa. By assessing English "encounters" with these parts of the non-European world, and especially the impact of such encounters upon literature and culture, and by thus extending a field which had once been dominated by accounts of English interaction with the New and Atlantic worlds, both books aim to revise our understanding of early modern global relations.

Remapping the Mediterranean World in Early Modern English Writings consists of thirteen essays by literary scholars working in the United States and the United Kingdom, including some whose earlier work has helped to establish "the Mediterranean" as an object of inquiry within early modern English studies. It also includes an afterword by Daniel Goffman, a historian of the Ottoman Empire, which raises important issues of method and discipline. The editor Goran V. Stanivukovic explains that the volume seeks to expand Fernand Braudel's influential notion of the Mediterranean as a key unit of the world economy by focusing on "the Ottoman Med iterranean" in preference to Greece, Italy, and Spain—a move that he claims shifts "the dividing line" from "the West-East border" to "the new 'forgotten' geopolitical frontier between the north and the south, where 'the north' stands for the European Mediterranean and 'south' for its African, mostly Ottoman coast" (5). The volume also invites a reconsideration of Braudel's views by looking at the *effects* of the Mediterranean world beyond its borders, especially those that resulted from cross-cultural encounters, and were defined by ideologies and practices within northern Europe. Ultimately, a challenging question haunts this book, even when it is not explicitly raised by each essay: what light can such "remapping" shed on the global desires and practices of the English, and how can it help us evaluate the importance of the Mediterranean to the genesis and development of European colonialist practices and ideologies?

As Goffman's afterword points out, the essays emphasize the degree to which "the Ottoman Empire rises above its neighbors to haunt the consciousness of the English." Not surprisingly, it is Turkey itself, especially Constantinople, and other bitterly contested locales like Malta, Rhodes, and El-Ksar el Kabir ("Alcazar" in English writings) that emerge as recurrent sites of English literary representation. Emily Bartels's and Leeds Barroll's essays on Peele's *The Battle of Alcazar*, Richard Wilson's on Marlowe's *The Jew of Malta*, Matthew Birchwood's on Davenant's *The Siege of Rhodes*,

Adam R. Beach's on Samuel Pepys's *Tangier Papers,* and Bernadette Andrea's on "Mapping Malta" do attend, in varying degrees,
to places on or near the "African" coast of the Mediterranean. Others look at territories that have been a more conventional part of
the "Mediterranean," including Spain, as well as areas that are the
subject of older European literature. Thus Stanivukovic illuminates
the homoeroticism that underpins prose romances of the period
featuring Asia Minor, and Elizabeth Sauer cogently shows that the
imperial theme of Milton's epics was articulated by fusing classical
geography and theology with the contemporary vocabularies of
travel writing, maps, and global politics. Edmund Campos's essay
traces the English borrowing and theft of *words* from Spanish in
the creation of its own "imperial lexicon," and offers a trenchant
analysis of "the cultural work of Renaissance English-Spanish dic-
tionaries" in the wake of the Armada victory. Alan Stewart urges
us to rethink the literary uses of spatial distance by arguing that
Robert Wilson's play *The Three Ladies of London* features a Jew in
Turkey in order to comment on the nature of commerce in London.
In a complementary vein, Richard Wilson reconsiders the contested figure of the Marrano Jew in the context of "the boundless
world of negotiable paper" or the new forms of finance that prolif-
erated alongside global capital: he suggests that Marlowe's Barabas
can be seen as a figure lovingly created by the author as an "image
of himself." This idea of mirroring is extended in Daniel Vitkus's
succinctly argued essay, which shows that debates about travel il-
luminate English national aspirations and anxieties, and in Constance C. Reihlan's piece, which suggests that in the work of
Barnabe Riche, the image of the Turk is shaped by attitudes to the
Irish.

Together, these essays show the extent to which the *meaning* of
individual places was reworked in the early modern English imaginary because of European global expansion, England's own changing place in the world, and, especially, the exchanges and
challenges offered by the Ottoman Empire. The "Mediterranean" is
invoked in this book as a revisionary analytic unit which facilitates
such geographical and imaginative reworking. Although the invocation of the Mediterranean as a unit in some essays seems
strained, as a whole the volume sheds light on the way in which
this area was a dynamic and important center of the rapidly changing early modern globe and a crucial index of English literary practices and their ideological investments.

In his afterword, Daniel Goffman complains that places outside of England remain "amorphous" in these essays, as they do in the materials they analyze. For him, this fact "*hinders* analysis of the English *mentalité;* he points out that "recent contemplations on postcolonial theory, especially in its application to the Americas and India, urge us to examine the object as well as the subject of proto-imperialism, colonialism and imperialism. This object, whether it is the Mediterranean, the Moor, the Turk, the Muslim, or the Ottoman, remains absent, or at least silent, in most of these pieces" (274). Whereas Goffman regards postcolonial scholarship as facilitating a turn away from the colonizer to the colonized, European to non-European, both volumes see themselves as offering *correctives* to postcolonial perspectives, which they represent as constraining our understanding of early modern global relations, a point to which I will return shortly. For the moment I want to pursue Goffman's point about who is being represented in such work on travel and exchange, an idea which remains an ongoing problem for those critics who wish to examine the question of global relations from within the discipline of English literature.

The essays that bookend *Remapping the Mediterranean* offer some welcome thoughts on this question. Bernadette Andrea's concluding exploration of "native" identities in Malta raises the issue very subtly from "within" the field of English studies. Andrea writes that critics who read only European sources often invoke a "multinationalism" in Malta as leveling differences between different nationalities and religions, but this "potentially occludes the deeper native claims encrypted in early modern European accounts" (246). She rightly criticizes the way in which Fernand Braudel "follows the celebrationist tendency of his entirely Christian sources" in assessing the 1565 siege of the island and the conflict between the Ottomans and the Knights of St. John. (Of course, "sources" do not always solve the problem of perspective. In the volume under review, Leeds Barroll uncritically invokes Bernard Lewis's notoriously slanted assessments of the Muslim-Christian conflict and Lewis, like other well-schooled Orientalists, is far from ignorant about "native" perspectives or non-European archival sources. Lewis consults non-European and non-Christian materials as well, just as Orientalists were not always ignorant of "native" perspectives and were often highly schooled in them.) Andrea, instead of relying on a simplistic "Christian" versus "Muslim" scenario, or its opposite—an equally simplistic "all are multicultural and hybrid" argument—shows how Maltese indigenes were *differently* occluded and represented in English writings spanning more than a century; particularly fascinating is her account of two Quaker women, Katherine Evans and Sarah Chevers, whose "silencing" of the Maltese is further muted by their male editors. The process, as Andrea shows, disaggregates and illuminates diverse English subjectivities but also underscores the necessity to treat the natives of Malta with equal nuance.

Jonathan Burton's opening article explicitly considers how we can rethink our analytical tools. He outlines the problems we face in depending on a one-sided archive while examining the question of "exchange," and considers how "we can avoid in our own histories reproducing the problem of emplotment that we find in early modern accounts of exchange" (23). One solution he suggests is that we try to overcome our own linguistic and disciplinary training by seeking narratives from the "other side," however sparse these may be—we may recall that Edward Said attempted to rethink the shortcomings of *Orientalism*'s archive by suggesting, in *Culture and Imperialism,* a method of "contrapuntal analysis" which uses diverse perspectives embedded within individual texts, as well as those provided by dialogues between texts, to provide a fuller picture of colonial relations, as well as of metropolitan culture itself.

Goffman acknowledges the importance of Burton's attempt to juxtapose English and Ottoman sources, although he uncharitably, and in my opinion erroneously, claims that this is "what every historian tries to do," and that this is "basic historical methodology (dressed perhaps, in literary clothing)" (276). If this were the case, then there would have been no need to radically rethink historical method, as well as the nature of the "archive," projects that have been prompted by feminist and postcolonial historians (including work on India and Africa that Goffman himself praises).

Those of us who seek, while working within English literary studies, to comment on the nature of global contact within English literary studies are not simply emulating something called "basic historical methodology." Indeed, neither conventional historiography nor conventional literary studies have concerned themselves with questions of cross-cultural contact. Rather, scholarship across the disciplines that is not invested in disciplinary parochialism but in particular intellectual issues has opened up these questions over the past several decades. Many literary critics have illuminated those aspects of culture, writing, and *mentalité* that were ignored by world systems theorists, and that have not interested most historians, especially the question of the complex subjectivities spawned by increasing contact across borders. Our training as literary critics does allow us to think about rhetoric, literary form, writing practices, words, and performance and therefore not only to access a different archive, but read all archives differently (a claim that has been made by radical historians as well). My point here is not to defend the disciplinary practices of literary criticism, which I hardly need to do in the pages of this journal, but to urge a serious consideration of the question raised by Burton about the appropriate methodology for understanding "exchange" and cross-cultural encounters.

The two books under review claim to offer revisions of these subjects by considering literary and cultural texts. But both also make it obvious (although not always self-consciously in the case of the essays in the edited collection) that "exchange" cannot be examined in isolation from the vexed historical issues of colonialism and racism. The authors included in *Remapping the Mediterranean World* are divided on this question, some treating the early modern world as protocolonialist, and others, like Emily Bartels, both in her essay for the volume and in *Speaking of the Moor*, emphasizing the dangers of treating England as already colonial. Such variety is understandably missing in *Speaking of the Moor*, where Bartels seeks to establish the "notorious indeterminacy" of the term "Moor" (a phrase she quotes from Michael Neill). Her aim to show that "within early modern representations, . . . the Moor is first and foremost a figure of uncodified and uncodifiable diversity. . . . In fact, the early modern Moor uniquely represents the intersection of European and non-European cultures" (5). Thus, like the essays in *Remapping the Mediterranean World,* her book is also interested in the creation of new identities and the remapping of global relations through intercultural contact and exchange. Most of the plays she considers—*The Battle of Alcazar, Titus Andronicus, Lust's Dominion,* and *Othello*—take place on the same geographical terrain of the southern Mediterranean. Like Stanivukovic in his introduction to *Remapping the Mediterranean World,* Bartels faults a "postcolonial" critical approach for offering too polarized a version of early modern European attitudes; the implication (for there is no extended analysis on the subject) is that such an approach emphasizes polarization instead of exchange between Europeans and non-

Europeans, and tends to emphasize the protoimperial position of early modern England. *Speaking of the Moor* extends Bartels's earlier work in urging a reconsideration of English attitudes to Africa and blackness: "the uncodified diversity that *is* the Moor's story constantly demands negotiation and so draws attention inevitably—in early modern plays quite consciously—on how and where we draw the line on difference" (7).

This "line on difference" (racial, cultural, ethnic, or religious) has also become one marker of critical difference. As early modernists began to look at English contact with the "old" worlds of Asia, Africa, and the Levant, they began to complicate the model of global relations offered by New World–centered scholarship, which tended to emphasize the asymmetry between Europeans and its "others," the silencing of native inhabitants, and the sheer power of European technology and civilization. As I have argued elsewhere, it is remarkable that most revisionist work faults not New Historicist work on the New World (where it is assumed such polarities of power and representation are accurate), but Edward Said's suggestion that an opposition between the West and the Orient has animated "European imaginative geography" from the Greek times till the present. Such an opposition, as has been pointed out by numerous critics, does not accommodate the complicated relations between European Christians and a variety of Eastern (especially Muslim) societies in the sixteenth and seventeenth centuries when, instead of dominating the East, Europe feared the mighty Turkish empire, but also desired to trade with it and with other Muslim powers, such as Morocco and India.

As Burton remarks in his essay in *Remapping,* these debates are no longer new. However, critical positions are still shaped by this history: some early modernists emphasize the evolving ideologies of racism and protoimperialism in this period, others a more open English attitude to many non-Europeans. Of course, most of us don't take an either/or position, but our relative emphasis shapes our responses to important questions such as these: What was the nature of early modern English commerce and diplomacy? How was commerce related to empire and emerging racial ideologies? Do early modern global relations hint at what was to come in the imperial age, or do they point to a radical difference from our own world today? Bartels's position is clear—drawing upon David Armitage's assessment that England did not at this time have an "imperialist agenda," she declares that "England's overseas interventions

had no established terminologies, ideologies, or geographies. . . .
England had not yet found its colonial footing." Moreover, this was
"a historical moment when globalization is still somewhat embry-
onic." In relation to Africa, she argues that for the English it was
simply a place to go through, and (somewhat contradictorily) that
the English did not set out with "a scheme" to colonize the continent but were following "the unpredictable, economically oriented
lead of the Portuguese" (47). Even the Portuguese, she declares,
"instead of conquering the local people . . . relied on the natives for
provisions, water rights, and aid" (48).

Accordingly, Bartels's interpretations of many well-known texts
and historical events challenge established readings of them. She
argues that Hakluyt's narratives show "traces of uncertainty and
ambivalence within the cross-cultural mission, of mutuality and
mimicry within exchange relations, or of hybridity, intermixing, or
the blurring of boundaries between or within the encountered
cultures . . ." (16). For her, George Best's notorious document on
blackness, actually counters the climate theory of color, and Best's
"representational priority, which colors Africa's features" is first
and foremost the West. Even Elizabeth I's orders on deporting
blacks and infidels, which she concedes are racist in tone, tell us
"more" about the queen's relations with her own subjects than they
do about her racial attitudes and reflect "practical" concerns rather
than "ideological ones." She concludes that "What is particularly
striking is the improvisational nature, the political and ideological
openness and uncertainty of these early approaches, which had no
scheme for colonial domination or for economic development behind them" (51).

Bartels argues that the "hybrid" and "indeterminate" Moor of literature is part of this cultural landscape, "one crux of an open,
evolving, and heterogeneous world picture" (16). Thus, whereas
other critics have argued that the early modern figure of the Moor
can represent a wide spectrum of peoples—including sub-Saharan
Africans, North African Muslims, and Muslims from Asia, as well
as various amalgams of these—for Bartels *all* stage Moors of the period offer a "unique emphasis" on "cultural crossings which significantly involve Europe." While she (rightly in my view) does not
want to separate Moors in moral terms—villains from nonvil-
lains—more controversial is her claim that each of them indicates
a "hybridity" that is radical in unsettling cultural boundaries. Accordingly, *The Battle of Alcazar* does not dramatize the difference

between blacks and Muslims, but "presses its spectators to look beyond the bounds of race, religion, and nation, to see a Mediterranean 'world' improvised from the unpredictable intersections of
Europeans and non-Europeans, of Moors, Arabians and Turks, Portuguese, Spanish, Italians, and at least one Englishman" (43). The
problems with seeing these intersections as producing a level playing field have been remarked upon by Bernadette Andrea's essay
on Malta, as noted above, and they are even more marked when it
comes to Bartels's analysis of Aaron in *Titus Andronicus,* a character often viewed in contrast to Othello. She argues that critics who
read Rome as a "wilderness of Tigers" necessarily "start with the
assumption that Aaron is necessarily out of place in Rome." Instead, she asserts that Rome is a multicultural place which allows
the slave to be "absorbed" into it "to the point that he fathers a
mixed-breed offspring with Rome's new empress" (5). The horror
evoked by this child is also dismissed by her: "Ultimately, we cannot know how the Goths and Romans would react to the 'black'
baby if it were not a sign of the Gothic queen's adultery, or how
Lucius and Marcus would react if they were not staging a precarious and indefensible political coup" (98–99). Of course, we cannot
know, but what we do know is that this play, like so many others,
juxtaposes the horror of blackness with the dangers of female sexuality, emphasizing one through the other.

These plays, including *Titus,* have produced critical disagree-
ments before, and we cannot and should not all read them in identical ways. I am more concerned with the historical and theoretical
assumptions on which the readings here are based. For example,
what does it mean exactly to say that Aaron is "absorbed" into
Rome? Slaves are absorbed into new worlds into which they are
transported, as are colonists and immigrants. But the absorption of
these three groups comes with unequal dangers and rewards and
has differential results. For the modern critic, Bartels argues, "The
danger is . . . that in coming to terms with an overwhelmingly diverse, always changing and expanding set of unfamiliar subjects,
we will either obscure their heterogeneity with homogenizing generalizations or select our differences out, targeting some and not
others as what matters" (7). That is true, but is there not also a problem in making "heterogeneity" a new fixity? If Moors are "not
bounded by any set or single racial, religious or ethnic markers,"
then how can they all tell the same "unique story"? Bartels finds in
virtually all "early modern representations of the Moor . . . their

ability to have it both ways (at least), to distance complex cultural and cross-cultural politics from simplifying moralities, to imagine the embrace and the exclusion of the Moor as constantly competing impulses, and to insist on complicating difference in the face of an ostensibly all consuming difference." Burton rightly warns us that the idea of a "contact zone" should not be romanticized, that both collision and intermingling are not reducible to questions of individual will (22–23). The dangers of using terms like "contact zone," "hybridity," and "absorption" without paying attention to the asymmetries that structure and disaggregate these terms have been debated at length by the debates within and about postcolonial criticism. It is especially unfortunate, then, that "postcolonial studies" is dismissed without engagement here and in the introduction to *Remapping the Mediterranean World,* even as the subjects under discussion, especially the question of "hybridity" and "contact," could have been much more complexly theorized by engaging with it.

In *Speaking of the Moor,* "Moors" not only consistently but *uniquely* represent complexity. Bartels insists that whereas Jews are cast as "others," Moors are allowed to "embed themselves within Venice's political and domestic spheres." Of course, Kim Hall's analysis of a play like *The Merchant of Venice* argues to the contrary that the image of the pregnant Moorish woman functions as a sign of danger against which Jessica's conversion should be read; Burton, Vitkus, and others have also written at length about the similarities between Jewish and Muslim women in many plays of the period. "Moors" were, Bartels argues, the only "African subjects featured on the early modern stage and . . . they were not necessarily connected to Africa, ethnically or geographically" (11–12). This is confusing, because it presupposes a stable definition of the very term Bartels hopes to deconstruct. For example, who are Cleopatra's servants? They are certainly "Africans," although they are not "Moors" and they are not sub-Saharan. Hence, they don't fall into either of the two major blocks into which countless writers of the time, following Leo Africanus, divide the continent: northern from sub-Saharan and southern Africa, Muslims and Turks from Negroes. I agree with Bartels that *Muslim* subjects are too often taken to be Turks, although I disagree that "Moors" and "Turks" are willfully collapsed into one another by all critics. The reason why the figure of Othello is read in the context of Islam is not because critics don't understand the distinction between Moors and Turks (although the two terms *were on occasion* used interchangeably in the period), but because *that particular play* deliberately yokes the question of black Moorishness and Islamic Moorishness, Africa and Turkey. Othello must be read in the context of Islam and Turkey, just as he must also be read in the context of blackness and Africa. Moreover, and this is a point that Stanivukovic also seems to overlook, "Moors" in the period are not confined to the Mediterranean or to Africa—we have plays with "Moors" from other places too, such as the Moluccan islands (Fletcher's *The Island Princess*) and India (Dryden's *Aureng-zebe*). In terms of nonliterary texts, the diverse geographic origins of the historically imprecise term "Moor" are even more evident. Finally, the Mediterranean and Africa are, in these books, in danger of existing only in relation to Europe—what we know is both these regions also had even older and much more extensive ties with Asia and the worlds of the Indian Ocean, and any assessment of global relations of the early modern period cannot afford to neglect this history, even when that history is repressed in English literary representations of cross-cultural contact.

Bartels admits that "I may err on the side of wanting early modern drama and culture to be more open than it really was," and this brings me to a really important point under discussion. Bartels in this book, and Burton in his essay for *Remapping,* both refer to an essay by Myra Jehlen as providing a model for an exemplary critical practice, as opposed to the "postcolonial" flattening of the past. In that essay, Jehlen critiques Peter Hulme's *Colonial Encounters* for emphasizing the colonial construction of cannibalism (and therefore the native agency) to the point where it erases the possibility of its existence apart from that construction: "The trick would be, as everyone in the field understands, to read in a way that uncovers the agency of the colonized even though the texts one is reading are virtually always and only the colonizers' narratives."[1] In the absence of indigenous records, Jehlen suggests, we should read the writings of colonists like John Smith as allowing us to glimpse the voice of the natives. According to her,

> Registering Powhatan's resistance, Smith writes with political intention but also in considerable doubt about his ability to carry out his intention—to make the Indians submit to the rule of the English crown and also to win for himself the rewards of such a victory. Uncertain and needing not only to persuade others but to understand for himself, he

describes more of the elements of the situation than fit into his favored interpretation, including some elements that will turn out, once the incident is closed, to have led toward its outcome, while others will in retrospect appear contrary to historical tendency or just insignificant, ephemeral. . . . Decolonization must begin at home with the recognition that the desire to recuperate the contingency of the European hegemony is not disinterested. We find ourselves, in the millennial twilight of the empire, with the urgent task of establishing that Europe's global dominion was not in the nature of things. (691)

Neither cannibalism nor native agency are the real subjects of this debate, nor is the historian's ability to grasp the open-endedness of history "before the fact." In Jehlen's argument, it is clear that the way to resist present imperial ideologies and practice is to show that in the past colonialism was not inevitable.

A similar impulse informs work in later periods as well. In the writings of William Dalrymple, seventeenth- and eighteenth-century Englishmen in India who went "native," and whom he calls the "White Mughals" with their native *bibis*, hookahs, and turbans, are offered as proof of a more benign phase of the British presence in India.[2] In his foreword to a recent collection of early modern essays entitled *Re-Orienting the Renaissance: Cultural Exchanges with the East,* which rightly seeks to challenge the idea of "an invariable conflict between Islam and Christianity," Dalrymple is frank about his desire to question what he calls the "bleak dualism" of our own time, the ever-hardening contemporary polarization of jihadis and evangelists.[3] But do we have to replace such a narrative with a story of cosmopolitanism that is unable to account for any historical tensions and asymmetry, including that of empire, especially when a spate of other revisionist histories offer supposedly cosmopolitan individuals to argue against the existence of racist or exploitative structures, *even* in the heyday of empire? Thus, Maya Jasanoff's book *Edge of Empire* examines imperial collections of objects and curiosities, claiming that such an approach tracks "real people in the real world," and "counterbalances the tendency in postcolonial scholarship to portray imperial collision with the rest of the world as a fundamentally oppositional, one-sided affair."[4] Similarly, David Cannadine's *Ornamentalism* argues that racial hierarchies and colonial exploitation were undermined by commonalities between the upper classes on both sides of the colonial divide.[5] Individual tastes and desires, as well as "cosmopolitanism" and "hybridity" become arguments against the very existence of colonial structures within which a whole range of attitudes, even contradictory ones, can lodge and even coexist.

If empire can only be established through transparently declared intentions of colonists, we will have to concur with John Seeley's famous remark that the British Empire was acquired in "a fit of absent-mindedness," a view that became peculiarly powerful among apologists of British imperialism. In an analogous vein, a supposed lack of American imperial interests was cited throughout the nineteenth and twentieth centuries to argue that U.S. practices in different parts of the world were not colonial or imperial.[6] Today, it is ironic but instructive to find that advocates of U.S. imperialism, such as Niall Ferguson, exhort the United States to embrace its imperial role openly by arguing that the United States is an empire, whether it says so or not.[7]

Second, imperial and commercial histories are intricately interwoven, as is only too evident today. By oversimplifying and misreading the difference between imperial practices in the "New World" and the "trade of the East," we will end up confusing the very nature of empire. At a time when revisionist scholarship seeks to mystify and defang empire (not to mention openly endorse it), I believe that early modernists have a lot to teach those who do not engage with earlier periods about the processes of globalization. While the early modern world should not be conflated with the later moment of global imperium, I do not believe that the uncertainties of early modern European trade, or the English desire to gain profits and territories from it, are arguments against tracing within these processes the origins of European colonialism on a global scale. Nor should the facts that the English were supplicants in the East, or went "through Africa," not "to" it; or that particular English individuals were relatively open-minded, or even desirous of personal friendships; or that art and objects were exchanged between East and West blind us to the role played by these very interactions in the development of early modern colonialism.

Of course, we must not squeeze the complexity of the past into a narrative of inevitability; radical historiographies, including notable postcolonial ones, have done much to excavate what is occluded by the narratives of historical victors.[8] As I have suggested, however, the methods by which we can do so, are not obvious and require self-reflexivity and debate. In very different ways, both *Remapping the Mediterranean World in Early Modern English Writings* and *Speaking of the Moor* give us the opportunity to grapple with these questions while also allowing us to think in great detail about two crucial areas of the early modern globe. For both these reasons, they should be widely read by early modernists.

Notes

1. Myra Jehlen, "History before the Fact; Or, Captain John Smith's Unfinished Symphony," *Critical Inquiry* 19, no. 4 (Summer 1993): 684. See also Peter Hulme, "Critical Response I: Making No Bones; A Response to Myra Jehlen," *Critical Inquiry* 20, no. 1 (Autumn 1993): 179–86; Jehlen, "Critical Response II: Response to Peter Hulme," *Critical Inquiry* 20, no. 1 (Autumn 1993): 187–91.

2. William Dalrymple, *White Mughals: Love and Betrayal in Eighteenth-Century India* (London: HarperCollins, 2002).

3. William Dalrymple, "The Porous Frontiers of Islam and Christendom: A Clash or Fusion of Civilizations?" in Gerald MacLean, ed., *Reorienting the Renaissance: Cultural Exchanges with the East* (Basingstoke: Palgrave Macmillan, 2005).

4. Maya Jasanoff, *Edge of Empire: Lives, Culture and Conquest in the East, 1750–1850* (New York: Alfred A. Knopf, 2005).

5. David Cannadine, *Ornamentalism: How the British Saw Their Empire* (Oxford: Oxford University Press, 2001).

6. See for example, Herbert Schiller, *Mass Communications and American Empire* (New York: Augustus M Kelley, 1969) 59.

7. See Niall Ferguson, *Colossus: The Price of America's Empire* (New York: Penguin Press, 2004), 294.

8. For example, the subaltern studies historians of colonial India are concerned with excavating the lives and consciousness of native subjects who were marginalized by both colonists and native elites and are thus not to be found in records of both "sides."

A Blessed Shore: England and Bohemia from Chaucer to Shakespeare
By Alfred Thomas
Ithaca: Cornell University Press, 2007

Reviewer: Peter Brown

Alfred Thomas is a leading scholar of the cultural relations between Bohemia and England during the medieval and early modern periods. His expertise in the Czech language and its literature puts him in the enviable position of being able to offer unusually rich and detailed perspectives. An earlier book, *Anne's Bohemia,* focused on the cosmopolitan nature of the Prague court under the Holy Roman emperor Charles IV and its impact on the English court through the marriage of his daughter, Anne, to Richard II in 1382 until her death in 1394. *Blessed Shore* enlarges the scope of the earlier monograph by considering perceptions of Bohemia through English eyes, and of England through Bohemian eyes, from the mid-1300s to the mid-1600s. The spheres covered include diplomacy, the visual arts, travel, literature, politics, and, above all, religion.

Readers of *The Winter's Tale* will be familiar with Shakespeare's solecism, for which Ben Jonson took him to task, when he represents the verdant, landlocked Bohemia as a country with a seacoast and deserts. But he was doing no more than what Robert Greene, his immediate source, and others had previously done: imagined Bohemia as a projection of their needs, desires, and aspirations rather than describing it as it was. For Shakespeare and his contemporaries, Bohemia was a place of religious tolerance that contrasted with the persecution of Catholic recusants in the later years of Elizabeth's reign. The example of Shakespeare's play is emblematic of English responses to Bohemia, and vice versa, in the period covered by Thomas's book. They reveal as much, if not more, of the cultural moment of the perceiver as they do about the place under scrutiny. But Thomas has done much more than orchestrate a series of readings by two countries of each other. He has carefully situated each reading in its own historical context so that we might understand a writer's prejudices and the distortions thereby produced.

While Anne of Bohemia was a real presence as queen of England, interceding on at least two occasions between Richard II and his disaffected subjects, Chaucer responded more to what she represented: patronage, linguistic ability, an international court culture. Her influence is felt in the *Parliament of Fowls* and *Legend of Good Women* (where Chaucer imagines her as his patron). Associated with pearls and other gems linked to the image of her namesake, St. Anne, mother of the Virgin Mary, the *Gawain*-poet's *Pearl* may also be indebted to the presence of a Bohemian queen at the English court. Richard II, for his part, found in the Bohemian court a source of ambition. He planned to succeed his father-in-law as Holy Roman emperor, thereby becoming a rival of Anne's half brother,

Wenceslas IV. The Wilton Diptych, which features the imperial eagle on the king's robes, and other telltale signs, formed part of Richard's campaign. Further evidence of artistic imitation of the imperial style comes from Westminster Hall, modeled on Karlstein Castle in Prague, and the twin tomb of Richard and Anne in Westminster Abbey. Richard's interests as a collector of relics, and as a commissioner of opulent regal images of himself, also link his practices with those in Prague. Praise of Richard's magnificence occurs in Roger Dymmok's refutation of the Twelve Conclusions, fixed by Lollards to the doors of Westminster Hall and St. Paul's in 1395. Dymmok's treatise may have been intended to reassure the imperial electors that Richard was a worthy emperor as well as a stalwart defender of orthodoxy.

In the religious sphere, the traffic was the other way: scholars traveling between Prague and Oxford spread the reformist ideas of John Wycliffe to Jan Hus. When the full impact of his work hit Czech university life, it had a polarizing effect along ethnic and philosophical fault lines: the Czech-speaking scholars were pro-Wycliffe realists; the German-speaking scholars anti-Wycliffe nominalists. As in England, Wycliffe galvanized political differences, too. The archbishop of Prague condemned the English theologian as heretical; the king and queen supported Hus. At the root of their differences was Wycliffe's view that the Church should cede control of its vast wealth. Hus's disciple, Peter Chelčický, was more attracted by Wycliffe's pacifism and his ideas on the separation of church and state, though he drew conclusions more radical than Wycliffe envisaged. Bohemian activists looked to England for support and found it in the person of Sir John Oldcastle, leader of the Lollard uprising of 1414. While Lollardy was suppressed, the Hussite movement flourished as an "imagined community" of the Czechs, with strong support from clerics and gentry alike. The salacious religious parody, "The Wycliffite Woman" (translated in the volume in full), in which a prostitute-heretic seduces a young lad, illustrates orthodox anxiety about heresy and the role of literate laywomen within it. It reflects the Hussites' interest in encouraging women to participate in their program of reform. The success of that program was in part due to the wide availability of a Czech translation of the Bible.

In post-1401 England, the possession of a Wycliffite translation of the Bible was itself an indicator of heresy. Under the Lancastrian regime, Lollards were persecuted and burned, Oldcastle's rebellion put down. Such firmness and success in the face of heresy attracted the interest of the Holy Roman emperor Sigismund of Luxembourg, who visited England in 1414. An architect of the Council of Constance, he was a devout Catholic dedicated to the extirpation of heresy in Bohemia. Henry V accorded him a warm welcome, conferring on him the Order of the Garter, among other honors. From an English angle Bohemia, throughout the fifteenth century, looked dangerously tolerant and seditious, as the writings of Barclay and Skelton testify. Conversely, to strife-ridden Bohemians, England seemed to possess the very qualities they had lost: stability, prosperity, and a unified religion. So much is clear from a mission to England in 1465–67, led by Baron Leo of Rožmitál and chronicled by Václav Šašek. It dwells on England's coastal landscape and seafaring capabilities, the marvels of Canterbury Cathedral and especially the shrine of St. Thomas, and the prosperity of London.

A century later, the shoe was on the other foot. Bohemia had become, as in *The Winter's Tale,* a place of refuge and tolerance to which English Catholics escaped and where they found a utopian, ecumenical society and, under the emperor Rudolph, a place of artistic excellence and intellectual excitement. As special ambassador to Prague in 1575, the Protestant Sir Philip Sidney recognized the city as a site of learning, especially in the arcane science of alchemy. For five years from 1574, the Jesuit scholar Edmund Campion found Prague no less congenial, a "blessed shore." The recusant polyglot Elizabeth Jane Watson made Bohemia her home, as did, for a shorter period, her stepfather, Edward Kelley, and his associate, Dr. John Dee, the queen's astrologer. Both Kelley and Dee found patronage for their angelic séances and alchemical experiments. The marriage of the Protestants Frederick and Elizabeth, daughter of King James and the mother of Prince Rupert of Civil War fame, as king and queen of Bohemia in 1619, was the subject of a laudatory pamphlet by John Harrison, who also wrote the first English history of Bohemia. For Harrison, like Shakespeare, pagan Bohemia was a utopian "desert," a place free of the disfiguring features of religious division and persecution and one synonymous with political liberty. John Taylor, the "Water Poet," also wrote two short accounts about his travels in Bohemia, lauding the country's bounty, freedom, and religious tolerance among Catholics, Protestants, and Jews alike. Similarly, *The Winter's Tale* embodies hopes for an accommodation between rival religions.

The Battle of the White Mountain in 1620, in which the forces of

Frederick and Elizabeth were routed by Catholic troops serving the emperor Ferdinand, brought an end to religious laissez-faire. Protestants were given the option of converting to Catholicism or going into exile. Bohemia's loss was England's gain. In 1636 Lord Arundel brought to England the artist Wenceslas Hollar, who settled in his adoptive country. Hollar's detailed and accurate etchings of London views are still admired for their artistry and documentary value. The Czech thinker Comenius, author of *The Labyrinth* (1631), in which he set out his influential system of universal knowledge, the Pansophia, visited England in 1641, invited by a group of disciples. The likely apocryphal story of his connection with the founding of Harvard College dates from around this time. Before the Protestant diaspora in 1600, Baron Waldstein had kept a diary of his visit to England that is humanist and antiquarian in tone. It sees the country as a "vast library of undiscovered knowledge" in which the monuments and fragments of a vanished religion are part of the appeal.

Thomas's narrative deepens our appreciation of the long-standing reciprocity of English and Czech culture. As an exercise in mapping the presumptions generated by one culture in its interpretation of another, it is fascinating. To those unfamiliar with Czech history in its medieval and early modern phases, it underlines the importance of Bohemia in fomenting the Reformation, and in demonstrating possibilities for religious and ethnic tolerance. Thereby, the country became a powerhouse of creative endeavor in the arts and sciences. But Prague, as we also know from events in the twentieth century, could be the flashpoint of religious and ethnic hatred. The cultural history of Bohemia, real and imagined, has much to teach us, and Thomas is an excellent guide: lively, erudite, and full of thought-provoking insights.

Index